*Colonel Albert Pope and
His American Dream Machines*

Colonel Albert Pope and His American Dream Machines

The Life and Times of a Bicycle Tycoon Turned Automotive Pioneer

by STEPHEN B. GODDARD

To my old friend Dave Harris,
with fond memories and warm wishes!

12/2/00

[signature]

McFarland & Company, Inc., Publishers
Jefferson, North Carolina, and London

Library of Congress Cataloguing-in-Publication Data

Goddard, Stephen B., 1941–
    Colonel Albert Pope and his American dream machines : the life
and times of a bicycle tycoon turned automotive pioneer / by Stephen
B. Goddard.
        p.   cm.
    Includes bibliographical references and index.   ∞
    ISBN 0-7864-0921-5 (illustrated case binding : 50# alkaline paper)
    1. Pope, Albert A. (Albert Augustus), 1843–1909.   2. Automobile
industry and trade—United States—Biography.   3. Industrialists—
United States—Biography.   4. Bicycles—United States—Biography.
5. Highway engineers—United States—Biography.   I. Title.
TL140.P59G66   2000
338.7'6292'092—dc21
[B]   00-58679
                                                       CIP

British Library cataloguing data are available

On the cover (clockwise): The Tribune Blue Streak Chainless bicycle
(Connecticut Historical Society), Colonel Albert Pope, age 50
(Connecticut Historical Society), and Hiram Percy Maxim sitting in
the electric-powered Pope Mark III Stanhope *(courtesy John Lee and
Percy Maxim Lee).*

Manufactured in the United States of America

McFarland & Company, Inc., Publishers
    Box 611, Jefferson, North Carolina 28640
        www.mcfarlandpub.com

To Patty, the love of my life

ACKNOWLEDGMENTS

*T*HIS IS OBVIOUSLY not an authorized biography, which is not to say that it is hostile to its subject. While so many Pope descendants helped me in so many ways, not one ever suggested that I omit or shade material or view their ancestor through rose-colored glasses. As valuable a tool as oral history is, stories handed down through the generations change over time in the re-telling. Rather than viewing themselves as repositories of cast-in-stone history from which I could draw, most of the Popes said they understood the falli-bility or oral history and told me that their information or anecdotes might not be always on the mark. But universally, they urged me eagerly to pursue the truth, wherever it might lie, understanding that Colonel Pope's portrait has warts amid its colorful hues. I commend them for their perspective and courage.

Some delicious anecdotes and recollections came to me through the family. I have tried to confirm the accuracy of such tales where I could. Unfor-tunately, the fact that ten family members relate the same story doesn't mean it wasn't fabricated or embellished by a common ancestor and passed down intact; such is the nature of families. To omit every anecdote whose accu-racy I could not independently confirm would leave this a dull and lifeless book. Yet to pass it on to the reader without attribution would be irre-sponsible, and that's where endnotes come in, as tools that don't restrict the author but rather liberate him to convey what he has heard while offering a caveat as to its provenance.

The memories of working with the Pope family will remain with me for many years: walking with Bill Pope, Sr. to a copy center in a drenching down-pour while he shielded the Colonel's Civil War diary from the rain; sitting at Beth Lum's gracious dining room table and hearing the same sonorous tones of the grandfather's clock that Albert Pope heard on its landing at Cohasset; searching through box after box in a rural New York farmhouse with Albert Pope II, seeking Colonel Pope's personal scrapbook and the Holy Grail—the

Pope Family Book; and riding an early Columbia high-wheeler at the Connecticut Historical Society.

As a long-time library trustee, I appreciate more than I can say the helpful guidance given me by librarians. Among the institutions which have aided me in this endeavor are the Hartford Public Library and especially its Hartford Collection; the Connecticut Historical Society, the Connecticut State Library, the Boston Public Library, the New York Public Library, the National Automotive History Collection of the Detroit Public Library, The Harriet Beecher Stowe Center, the Library of Congress, the Henry Ford Museum, the Automobile History Museum, the Boston Athenaeum, Widener and Baker Libraries at Harvard University and Sterling Library at Yale.

Many people have been helpful in suggesting research topics or leads, reading portions of the manuscript, and offering much-needed moral support. Included among them are Rick Bayna, Elizabeth Bohlen, John Boyer, Kevin Burke, Linda Case, Bob Casey, David Corrigan, Mally Cox-Chapman, Atty. Ken Dusyn, Christine Ermene, Bruce Epperson, Nancy Finlay, Andrew Fleischmann, Linda Fuerst, Tom Grant, Andrea Grimaldi, Katherine Hannan, Susan Hays, Barbara Hellenga, the late Carl Henry, David Herlihy, Mark Jones, Jack Lee, Percy Maxim Lee, David Lewis, Beth Lum, Adrienne Marks, Janice Mathews, Marie-Suzanne Niedzielska, Christine Palm, Mark Patrick, Albert A. Pope II, Leavitt Pope, Thelma Morales Pope, Victoria Pope, William Pope, Sr., William Pope, Jr., Wanda A. Rickerby, Tina Pope Rowley, Howard Sacks, Josephine Sale, Bob Satter, Richard Scarcsburg, Alessandra Schmidt, Ted Terry, the late Frances Walker, Margaret Wise, and Georgette Yaindl.

My wife Patty's mantra, "It's the story, stupid," puts my train back on the track after it meanders onto dead-end sidings, and I greatly appreciate her refraining from rolling her eyes when yet another friend asked me, "How's the book coming?" My children, as usual, have played important roles, each in his or her own ways. Taegan, a fellow author, is an ever-available sounding board and perceptive editor. Chelsey guided me to the gravesite of Colonel Pope in her home neighborhood of Jamaica Plain. And Brad, a chef in Yellowstone Park, helps me regain perspective after days immersed too deeply in the material. Brad and my son-in-law (Chelsey's husband) Patrick served as detectives in helping me track down the Colonel's grave.

TABLE OF CONTENTS

PREFACE

*A*MERICA, 1878. IT WAS the glory days of the railroad. If you owned a railroad, that is. For its riders, the legacy of railways' monopoly control bequeathed high fares, poor service, and a nagging sense that there must be a better way to get around.

So when Albert A. Pope, a 33-year-old Boston industrialist, saw his first high-wheeled bicycle, his gut told him it was the invention Americans had been waiting for. Within a few years, he had established the Columbia bicycle plant in Hartford and made the city the bicycle capital of the world.

By 1895, the bicycle had become a victim of its own success. Market saturation left Colonel Pope casting about for new products, such as an electric or gasoline motor strapped to a bicycle frame, which fledgling manufacturers called the buggyaut, the motorcar or the automobile. Recruiting the young genius Hiram Percy Maxim, Pope launched into production, and soon more than half of all motorized vehicles made in America rolled off assembly lines in Hartford.

Colonel Pope's most lasting contribution was to realize that, unlike Europe, America had no tradition of road-building, so 90 percent of roads outside of big cities were rutted dirt paths. In 1880, Pope founded the Good Roads Movement, which over the next four decades sold the nation on the notion that government, not private interests, should build roads, and saw to it that every county seat in the United States was linked with ribbons of asphalt or concrete. The roads inspired by this movement made possible the American automobile culture we know today.

Pope lived large, with huge appetites for work, play, food, drink and women. His biography attempts to place him in the context of his turbulent times, an era that would change the world forever, a time eerily like our own.

Hartford, Connecticut
June 2000

1

THE WATERSHED

*The bicycle has done more for the emancipation of women
than anything else in the world.*
                                                    Susan B. Anthony[1]

Get a bicycle. You will not regret it, if you live.
                                                    Mark Twain

A S ALBERT AUGUSTUS POPE reflected on his fortunes in 1895, he could
already see the approaching sunset of the American bicycle craze he had
created. And in the eastern sky, far across to Europe, he could make out the
first glimmers of the dawn of a new industry, which would market in one
vehicle the best features of the railroad and the bicycle and in which he would
be a pivotal player.

Life was good for Colonel Pope as the century neared its end. Though
he and Abby had lost two children, they had raised four more to adulthood,
and his oldest and namesake was already involved in the family business,
along with assorted brothers, cousins, and nephews. They shuttled between
their stately brick townhouse on Boston's Commonwealth Avenue and their
50-acre seaside estate in Cohasset on Boston's South Shore. And a million
Americans from Sacramento to Savannah were riding his Columbia bicycles.

Free-trader Grover Cleveland was in the White House, but the fortunes
of Ohio's U.S. Representative, William McKinley, a devout protectionist, looked
promising. If McKinley won the presidency in 1896, he'd help shield Pope
and his fellow American manufacturers against cheap imported products.[2]

While malcontents in the press had begun to assault what they called
corporate greed, Congress's winking attempts to rein in the captains of big
business were popguns aimed at sheets of cast iron. Congress had passed an
income tax in 1895 to siphon off the hard-won gains of entrepreneurs such
as Pope, but the Supreme Court had promptly tossed it out as unconstitu-
tional. In America, business was still king.

So proud was Colonel Pope of his accomplishments that he'd go to great lengths to bring curiosity seekers from home and abroad to study his operations. Were he conducting a tour of his vast domain, he'd be delighted for the reader to eavesdrop on his tumultuous life in the pivotal year of 1895.

No Robber Baron

One would be unwise to group the colonel in with such railroad robber barons as Jay Gould, Henry Clay Frick, and J. P. Morgan, for the days of the iron horse were numbered. Whether bicycles or motorized vehicles would eventually prevail in the twentieth century, Pope knew the future belonged to individual locomotion, marking a radical and welcomed repudiation of the hated railroads and changing forever how people moved about.

Before the railroad age, a farmer on his horse might ride five to ten miles a day on primitive paths, but railroads let a person ride thirty miles in an hour. Yet, as liberating as railways were, riders with lifted horizons were now beginning to chafe at having to travel on fixed tracks and rigid schedules.

So the bicycle did nothing less than transform the way people thought about time, space, and leisure. To be sure, one could ride a horse and wagon where and when one chose, but one didn't have to feed, stable, and clean up after a velocipede. And as bicycle races and tours became commonplace, the notion of riding for fun was born.

Be it steam, electricity, gasoline, or human energy, motive power had captured the country's imagination ever since hulking black locomotives had lumbered into view six decades earlier, awakening ferment not only in the laboratory but on Main Street and in church, where some pastors inveighed against movement by "unnatural means" as immoral.

Just as entrepreneurs a century later would feel their way while exploring the Internet, new modes of power unheard-of even a generation before competed for ascendancy in the market. And, the entrepreneurs realized, new power sources lay still undiscovered.

In this questing climate, front-page headlines in the fall of 1895 heralded the work of John Ernest Worrall Keely, an eccentric 68-year-old inventor from Philadelphia.[3] Keely declared breathlessly that he had succeeded in hitching on to the polar current, and in so sensitizing machinery as to operate from it. His proclamation caused millionaire merchant John Jacob Astor and his entourage to dash to Philadelphia with a man named Samuels, who, with Astor, was laboring to perfect storage batteries.

After seeing Keely's new motor demonstrated, Samuels told his patron it was useless to devote any more time to electricity, that the new method was far better. Astor, grasping immediately the implications of a costless power source, promptly pledged all the money that might be needed to put the gnarled old man's invention into production, only weeks before Keely was shown to be a fraud.

Building a Legend

Albert A. Pope would be on the short list of any knowledgeable observer predicting who would benefit from the power revolution. With thousands of sales agents positioned around the world, his Pope Manufacturing Company was New England's largest employer, and its productive capacity could be placed in the service of whatever new idea had promise.

Taller, heavier, and stronger than most men, with discerning eyes, a salt-and-pepper spaded beard, and big appetites for food, drink, and women, Pope's presence was commanding and embracing. Wrote a contemporary:

> He is alert in movement and resolute and definite in action. His complexion is clear and tinged always with the pink of good blood and fresh life. His rest-less and mysterious brown eyes, in which the boundary between pupil and iris is seldom observable, look out from under prominent brows. His lips are full, his teeth perfect, and his voice deep, strong, modulated and vibrant. He impresses one as being full of life and hope and resolution, made for a mas-ter but benevolent and sympathetic as well as stern and unflinching.[4]

Pope couldn't have written it better himself.

In fact, given his penchant for self-promotion and the insufficient attri-bution of the quote, perhaps he did write it himself. He might have added, "a poor boy who rose to fame and fortune by dint of hard work," a descrip-tion he burnished to a fine sheen throughout his life but which, at best, is overblown.

The truth, by itself, would have been sufficient for legend: father of the American bicycle and the national movement that paved America coast to coast, sagacious mentor to able young men, uncle (if not father) of mass pro-duction, pioneer in labor relations, and the man, who more than any other, ushered in the way his countrymen live at the millennium.

Future in Wheels

The bicycle had burst onto the American scene in 1869, when artist Winslow Homer depicted the New Year riding in on a velocipede, an out-landish steel skeleton with its front wheel nearly as tall as the man who was perched atop it. Seeing one at the 1876 Centennial Exposition in Philadelphia, Pope raced to the first steamboat bound for Britain to inspect them and soon was importing the high-wheelers for sale in the American market.

But Pope's dreams went far beyond collecting a 10 percent agent's fee for some British bicycle maker. He had already made a comfortable living manufacturing small patented items and tools used by shoemakers in Boston's burgeoning footwear industry. Now he bought the American rights to the basic European bicycle patents and went looking for a plant sufficiently sophisticated to mass produce his new obsession.[5]

A likely choice was the Weed Sewing Machine Company in Hartford, a hundred miles to the southwest. In recent years, Isaac Singer's invention of the foot treadle had made home sewing a money-saver for homemakers across America. T. E. Weed's four-story, red brick plant stretched across several blocks along the city's Capitol Avenue, newly named for Connecticut's sparkling, gold-domed state capitol. But so successful had the sales of sewing machines been that the market was now saturated, and whole wings of the Weed plant lay idle and available for new productive use.

Once Weed's owners successfully produced Pope's test order of fifty velocipedes, Pope hired the company to mass produce bicycles. For his trade name, Pope chose "Columbia," a label harking back to Christopher Columbus and redolent of new beginnings. The brand name would resonate for the next century in adults' memories of childhood.

For the next seventeen years, Pope kept a curious schedule. The head of Pope Manufacturing Company stayed at his corporate offices in Boston near his family, while its heart—clanking machinery and several thousand bustling, perspiring workers—lay several hours away in Hartford. Pope shuttled by steam locomotive between the two, spending weekdays in Boston and weekends in Hartford, where he would monitor plant operations and entertain lavishly in a penthouse apartment/office complex punctuated by four fireplaces, several floors above the metallic whir of his factory floor. His growing family remained behind.

One could find the commuting Colonel Pope ensconced in a plush velvet lounge chair in a J. P. Morgan parlor car, watching flakes of black soot from the noisy locomotive float by the window as he plotted the future of an industry that would bring down the robber barons on whose trains he rode.

The Liberating Bicycle

By 1895, 300 companies competed in the frenzied bicycle market, some in huge complexes like Pope's in Boston and Hartford and others in tiny garages, like that of brothers Orville and Wilbur Wright in Dayton.[6] In a day before baseball, basketball, tennis, and golf were mass-market pastimes, bicycling offered exercise and entertainment to those who could scrape together $125, several months' salary for a laborer.

Sales had soared once the industry abandoned "ordinaries," with their five-foot-high front wheels, in favor of "safety bicycles," featuring equal-sized wheels, which set a standard that would continue for more than a century.

The move to safety bicycles appealed especially to women. Feminist leader Susan B. Anthony enthused, "The bicycle has done more for the emancipation of women than anything else in the world," allowing women to throw off their corsets and bustles in favor of "common sense dressing."[7]

Pope had sailed to England to inspect safety bicycles but had come away unimpressed. "One thing I am satisfied of," he declared upon returning, "we in this country have nothing to learn from the Englishmen as to how to build a bicycle."[8] He would back pedal from this view in a few years, and fortunately, the size and scope of his manufacturing and sales operations let him catch up rapidly to the pack. Pope would consolidate the bicycle industry under his control and go on to become America's foremost automobile maker. But other, less easily fixable miscalculations lay around the bend.

Boston in Transition

Albert Pope's Boston in 1895 would have been unrecognizable to one who had lived there a half century earlier. As recently as 1850, fifteen Brahmin families, who called themselves "the Associates," had a lock on nearly half of Boston's banking, more than a third of its insurance capital, and 20 percent of cotton spindleage in the entire country.[9] Investing its profits in arts and culture, the commercial class soon won its city the appellation "the Athens of America."

But while Boston's gentry of mid-century dined contentedly off of Spode china in brownstone Back Bay townhouses, its world was about to change as radically as if an earthquake had hit the city. For millions of Irish people across the ocean were starving as their potato harvests withered on the vine, and Boston's rich could not ignore them for long. Sailing into Boston Harbor in the 1840s and 1850s came ship after ship, disgorging thousands of hungry, semiliterate immigrants from their filthy steerage compartments. By 1860, more than half of the city's population were Irish. As farmers dropped into an urban economy, they sought refuge in whatever manual laboring jobs they could find.[10]

As families found themselves unable to keep bread on the table, fathers often drowned their sorrows on payday at the corner pub, and soon orphans by the thousands roamed Boston's streets, as they did in most major cities on the eastern seaboard. Methodists responded by setting up settlement houses, like the Home for Little Wanderers, and aggressively relocating the waifs to farms throughout New England, even if they sometimes trampled on the rights of the parents in the process.[11]

The Methodists' efforts to divine a purpose in this frighteningly changing world were not lost on Colonel Pope. Industrialists from John D. Rockefeller to Andrew Carnegie had pledged, with much fanfare, to devote their wealth to the commonweal. Pope would help found and later head the Boston Athenaeum, donate to colleges and hospitals, and later, in Hartford, endow a large public park and build employee villages.

Insurance City Beckons

As Colonel Pope rode the train between Boston and Hartford during this banner year, he decided to consolidate his operations in Hartford, a move long championed by George H. Day, his unusually able and deferential right-hand man. Since setting his first machinery in motion in 1878, Pope had gradually enlarged his Hartford plant, which now sprawled through five large brick factory buildings set on seventeen acres.[12]

Hartford was well suited to the task of consolidation. Five rail lines converged there, and *Scribner's* magazine called it the richest city in America relative to its population.[13] A capital city located equidistant from New York City and Boston, it had earned itself already the label of the insurance capital of the world. At first, local financiers had simply pooled risks for trade ships they sponsored, which headed out to sea from Hartford's deep water harbor to bring home wool from Spain, Germany, and Britain, nuts from Brazil, and hides from Buenos Aires. It was a short jump to insuring homeowners against the risk of fire and even gambling against the Grim Reaper, and soon such giants as Travelers Insurance Companies, Aetna Life and Casualty, and The Hartford were born.[14]

More important, Hartford had a skilled work force. Thousands of locals had turned out Civil War weaponry under the blue onion dome of Colt Patent Firearms Manufacturing Company, which snaked along Hartford's Connecticut River. Colt's factory had survived Sam Colt, who never lived to see the denouement of the war whose carnage his armaments had helped make possible. Colt continued to turn out thousands of revolving-breech pistols (fabled in the settlement of the American West) and introduced benefits for its employees that would inspire manufacturers around the country. Sam

Colt's widow, Elizabeth, would later make George Day, Pope's right-hand man, her neighbor by selling him a plot of land next door.

Hartford was a sophisticated city as well, nurturing artists and writers in subsidized lofts, with graceful parks and a literary tradition capstoned by the creation of Nook Farm, a cozy tree-canopied enclave in which Harriet Beecher Stowe, author of *Uncle Tom's Cabin*, spent her dotage. Next door, her neighbors Mark Twain and Charles Dudley Warner wrote *The Gilded Age* about the excesses of the capitalistic heyday, which their neighbor Albert Pope enjoyed in full measure.

Twain Learns to Ride

Twain, whose birth name was Samuel Clemens, wrote his novels on a newfangled machine called a typewriter in the third-floor billiard room of his steamboat-inspired mansion, along a verdant curve of the Park River, a few blocks from Pope's factory complex. "Of all the cities I have visited," the globe-trotting Clemens once remarked, "Hartford is the chief."[15] In this salubrious setting, he worked on *The Adventures of Tom Sawyer*, *The Prince and the Pauper*, and *A Connecticut Yankee in King Arthur's Court*.

A speculator ever intrigued by novelties, Twain had ambled the half mile to Pope's factory in 1886, plunked down the princely sum of $142.50, and bought himself a Columbia Expert bicycle, together with twelve hours of riding lessons. Twain wrote about the harrowing experience of learning to ride on a street near his Hartford home.

"We got up a handsome speed," he wrote of his first lesson, "and presently traversed a brick, and I went out over the top of the tiller and landed, head down, on the instructor's back, and saw the machine fluttering in the air between me and the sun. It was well it came down on us, for that broke the fall, and it was not injured."[16] One can imagine the condition of Twain's trademark white suit.

Twain was learning along with thousands of fellow Americans that the strange metal skeleton seemed to obey its own laws rather than those of nature:

> I perceived how radically and grotesquely wrong had been the lifelong education of my body and members. ... For instance, if I found myself falling to the right, I put the tiller hard down the other way, by a quite natural impulse, and so violated a law, and kept on going down. The law required the opposite thing—the big wheel must be turned in the direction in which you are falling.[17]

Mounting the velocipede proved no easier:

You hop along behind it on your right foot, resting the other on the mounting-peg, and grasping the tiller with your hands. At the word, you rise on the peg, stiffen your left leg, hang your other one around in the air in a general and indefinite way, lean your stomach against the rear of the saddle, and then fall off, maybe on one side, maybe on the other; but you fall off. You get up and do it again; and once more; and then several times.[18]

Finally confident enough to enjoy a solo trip, Mark Twain was wobbling down a wide avenue when a farmer's cabbage-laden wagon approached. "I couldn't shout at him," wrote Twain, "a beginner can't shout; if he opens his mouth he is gone; he must keep all his attention on his business." An onlooking boy saw his predicament and shouted to the farmer: "To the left! Turn to the left, or this jackass'll run over you!" The man started to do it. "No to the right, to the right! Hold on! That won't do!—to the left!—to the right!—to the left!—right! Left—ri—Stay where you are, or you're a goner!"

After colliding with the horse and ending up in the dust beside its hooves, Twain said to the farmer, "Hang it! Couldn't you see I was coming?"

"Yes, I see you was coming, but I couldn't tell which way you was coming. Nobody could—now, *could* they? You couldn't yourself—now, *could* you? So what could I do?"

After taking eight lessons and numerous pratfalls, Twain exhorted his readers: "Get a bicycle. You will not regret it, if you live."

The Age of Magazines

Magazines had entered their golden age in 1895, when *Cosmopolitan* threw down the gauntlet. Starting July 1, the mass-market monthly slashed its price to a dime. The news hit young Sam McClure like a bucket of ice water in the face. Only thirteen years out of college, the lithe young man with dreamy eyes had built *McClure's Magazine* into a national entertainment venue. Readers, yet innocent of twentieth-century distractions, gossiped with focused anticipation about next month's issue, which would serialize the latest work of Robert Louis Stevenson, O. Henry, Thomas Hardy, Rudyard Kipling's *Jungle Books* and Arthur Conan Doyle's *Adventures of Sherlock Holmes*.

But feeding and grooming temperamental writers on a 15-cent newsstand price and $1,500 a month in ad sales was a balancing act at best. A year earlier, McClure had let 23-year-old Stephen Crane slip through his fingers for want of the $75 that a syndicate later paid for his Civil War saga, *The Red Badge of Courage*.

McClure's circulation was 100,000 and holding. But now, John Brisben Walker, *Cosmopolitan*'s aggressive West Point–trained editor, seemed bent on killing off *McClure's* with his predatory price cut. To match his rival, McClure needed money fast.

One might have expected Sam McClure, in times of trouble, to turn to a wealthy publisher, such as William Randolph Hearst or the well-connected dean of American letters, William Dean Howells, bestselling author and mentor to many. But McClure had a patron of a different stripe, a man of industry, who might not know quality fiction from dimestore trash but who understood full well the resonant power of the printed word, a man who had already used it to build an industry.

On an impulse, McClure took the New York, New Haven & Hartford steam train from New York to Boston and caught the trolley to 597 Washington Street, headquarters of the Pope Manufacturing Company, America's largest maker of the nation's favorite new toy. Walking up the front sidewalk, McClure might have reflected on how far he had come since he first passed through Pope's doors thirteen years earlier.

For five years now, a bicycle boom had captivated the nation. Anything a company wanted to market became somehow more salable if a bicycle appeared in its ad. Disguised as a Greek nymph, even a topless model could respectably add her allure to magazines imported from France, as long as she was pedaling feverishly on the latest model. And society was toasting McClure's first boss as "the father of the American bicycle."

McClure had ridden a sooty train all the way from New York only to learn that his mentor had already left for his summer home. The windows of Washington Street's brick facades were thrown open to the fresh air this spring day, as McClure strode purposefully back toward shady Boston Common to the smoky train. Somewhere a scratchy Victrola voice sang, "Casey would waltz with the strawberry blonde, and the band played on." McClure pressed on to "Lyndemere," Pope's waterfront estate.

Pope Bailout

Hours later, Sam McClure showed up at Pope's seaside door, hat in hand. As he gushed in a letter to his wife, Hattie, "The Colonel was hospitable and splendid and took me in and got me supper and listened to our dilemma."[19]

McClure laid out his plight to his mentor, who "instantly offered $5,000.00!" couching it as an advance on future bicycle ads. Pope, McClure told his spouse, "is a great friend." The cash infusion let *McClure's Magazine* match *Cosmopolitan's* price cut and set off a circulation war that would last thirty-four years.

Lowering the price widened circulations of both magazines, attracting working-class readers with an appetite to learn about the lifestyles and male-factions of great wealth, as told in breathless muckraking style by McClure's star reporters, Ida Tarbell, Lincoln Steffens, and Ray Stannard Baker. In a monumental irony, a wealthy capitalist's subsidy had made it possible for S.S. McClure, as he came to call himself, to crusade against the monied interests.

Pope had plucked McClure off the Boston streets right out of college and put the greenhorn in charge of a new magazine, *The Wheelman*. What young English major could have expected such an opportunity! At a time before radio, TV, and the movies were even experimental concepts, magazines were changing with lightning speed. Inky hand typesetting, the standard since Gutenberg, had fallen before the clattering racket of the linotype machine, whose operators typed columnar lines into leaden slugs, which compositors then loaded into metal forms, one for each page.

The linotype and automatic inking produced magazines in a fraction of the time, and the magazines featured handsome pages with halftone photographs and color advertisements. From coast to coast, children of all ages sat on the wraparound front porches of their Victorian houses and awaited the postman's approach. Pope, who was among many using the Civil War honorific of "Colonel," had gone in just a few years from a small-time seller of shoemakers' supplies to, literally, a wheeler dealer, selling 70-pound steel vehicles with huge front wheels.[20]

But the clunky ordinaries were of use only in the cities, the sole places with paved roads in the America of 1880. The Civil War had made Pope keenly aware of how nature slowed even war to a halt by turning dirt paths into troughs. The young lieutenant had slogged in mud up to his knees, as he marched with General Burnside's troops into bloody carnage at Antietam and Fredericksburg.[21] McClure's job, Pope told him, was to so inspire farmers with the possibilities of the bicycle that they'd drive their wooden wagons through the mud to the statehouse to press the case for paving the nation's rutty roads.

His young charge didn't let him down. Within a few years, a "good roads movement" was in full swing. In 1893, Congress put the United States into the road-building business for the first time. And, at the head of the parade was the ramrod-straight Colonel Pope, his beard now turning white.

A Path to His Door

An eager mentor sometimes falls prey to fawning freeloaders, and Abby Pope would shake her head as a stream of callers passed through Lyndemere.

Among them, sycophants eager to touch the hem of greatness, family members down on their luck, and gifted protégés.

As Pope ministered by the sea this spring day to the publisher he had helped create, this Victorian Burl Ives had his eye on still another prospect, a wunderkind who had graduated from the Massachusetts Institute of Technology at age seventeen. Hiram Percy Maxim was the estranged son of Hiram Stevens Maxim, a cruel eccentric who, a decade earlier, had invented the machine gun, a weapon that would remove forever what little romance war had held.

Young Maxim had been toying with hitching up a primitive one-cylinder internal combustion engine to one of Pope's Columbias, although his workshop trials of dropping a lighted match into a cylinder holding gasoline led some to question his sanity.[22] Pope was already up to speed on the idea of motor transport; two years earlier, he had inspected a primitive farm wagon powered by electric batteries at the Chicago World's Fair and understood right away what it portended for twentieth-century recreation and commerce.

But Pope found incredible the notion that people would buy a vehicle with messy, grease-slathered parts and a gasoline engine tucked under its seat. "Who would willingly sit atop an explosion?" he asked.[23] That aside, some of Pope's men were calling Maxim a genius, and he certainly carried an inventor's genes, so Pope hired him to work at his Hartford plant.

Forget this smoky toy of yours, he told the lad. Use your brainpower to perfect the electric motor, because that's where the future market is. Electric cars will be cleaner, safer, quieter than a gas-powered car could ever be. And, oh yes, if you have time left over, I suppose you can tinker with your gasoline contraption.

Dawn of a New Industry

An industry seldom knows when it has reached its apex. Never had bicycle makers turned out more shiny new models than they had in 1895, and, to the public, the future seemed bright. Yet those intent on motorizing America determined to press their advantage.

Early tinkerers had cobbled together enough sputtering workshop models to create America's first automobile race on Thanksgiving Day. The winner accomplished the run from Chicago to Waukegan at the blistering pace of ten miles an hour.

To promote their product, would-be auto manufacturers had to agree on one elementary issue: what to call this machine that looked like a bicycle but took no effort to drive. Names adopted by early magazines in the field reflect the quandary. *Horseless Carriage* published its first issue in 1895, competing with *Motorcycle*, which displayed its first ad for a European vehicle manufactured by Karl Benz. One manufacturer labeled his product a "buggyaut." Another called his the "Electrobat."[24]

By the end of 1895, Benz had sold 271 vehicles in the United States alone. On his heels was French bicycle maker Armand Peugeot, who rang up 170 sales. It would be two years yet before Charles and Frank Duryea would sell America's first domestic automobile.[25]

For his part in the name game, publisher William Randolph Hearst decided to sit on the fence; he named his publication *Motor*, joining cousins labeled *Motor World* and *Motor Age*. A British publication took a more lasting tack, calling its magazine, *Autocar*.[26]

Patents: Protection or Tollgates?

If the industrial age had taught any lasting principles as it neared the end of the century, it was the danger of allowing one company to monopolize an industry. But first Britain and then the United States carved out one key exception. Since inventiveness was essential to stoke the fires of industry, it became sound public policy to vouchsafe the inventor a period of time in which to exploit his brainchild before competitors could horn in.

As capitalists came to realize that a patent really amounted to coinage, the noncreative but monied were allowed to buy patents and then erect their own industry tollgates, exacting a levy each time a product rolled off the shop floor. Rather than spurring industrial production, patent trading actually retarded it by causing product prices to rise and demand, in consequence, to fall.

Nineteenth-century venture capitalists licked their chops as they watched Pierre Lallement, a French carriage maker, migrate to America to patent and then utterly fail in trying to market his "mechanical velocipede." Calvin Witty of Brooklyn bought the disheartened Lallement his steamship fare home by picking up his patent on the cheap; he then exacted a $10 tribute for each bicycle that anyone else made.

The Lallement patent passed from hand to hand, gaining in value as bicycles grew in popularity, until its owners in 1876 called on Colonel Pope, who, they had learned, intended to manufacture high-wheelers. They "pulled out their dusty parchments and promptly made their claims for royalties." Before the session had ended, an annoyed Pope had bought the patent and a dozen relating to its components and learned a lesson he'd not soon forget.[27]

Now, in 1895, as Pope stood at the end of one age and the beginning of another, the U.S. Patent Office issued patent number 549,160. No headlines greeted the event, but George Selden's patent on a crude three-cylinder internal combustion engine mounted on a bicycle frame would help structure the industry that would dominate the twentieth century.

Ironically, Selden, a Rochester attorney, had done everything possible during the previous sixteen years to prevent his patent from being granted. For, after the young graduate of Yale's Sheffield Scientific School had submitted it, he had come to understand that the financial markets were still enamored of the railroads. Investors laughed at Selden's preposterous invention. Had the Patent Office granted Selden his patent in 1879, its protection would have run out in 1896. After each rebuff by investors, however, Selden had filed an amendment to his patent, buying more time for the market to catch up with his technology. By 1895, with Benz and Peugeot shipping cars by the hundreds to eastern ports and mechanics tinkering with their own models from Detroit to Springfield, Selden realized that time was running out. When a young engineer in Pope's employ discovered the Selden patent, Pope dispatched emissaries to check out its claims. And so began a legal battle that would embroil the Colonel for much of his working life.

Positioned for Success

Pope's Hartford bicycle operation positioned him well at the beginning of the automobile age. His manufacturing plant snaked along several city blocks west of downtown and employed some 4,000 workers, making Pope, Hartford's largest employer.

A century later, manufacturers would seek to outsource production of components, for a variety of twentieth-century reasons. But in 1895, Pope's impulse was to buy up and absorb his suppliers.

He knew it was essential to lighten his 70-pound product if he expected women and children to ride bicycles. Borrowing British technology, Pope set up the Hartford Tube Company to turn out hollow but durable steel tubes; these helped bring his bicycle weights down to as low as twenty-two pounds.

Wooden bicycle tires had given way to solid rubber, but when Irishman John Dunlop invented the pneumatic tire in the late 1880s, Pope understood its importance to riders' comfort and soon bought the Hartford Rubber Company to supply his bicycle tires.

Rather than rely on outside technology, Pope created his own metallurgical lab, where his workers developed new methods of pressing metal, ensured quality control, tested parts, and made their own ball bearings.[28]

Most impressive was his network of sales agents, which stretched throughout America, Europe and beyond, including St. Petersburg, Athens, Hamburg, and Holland.[29] Daily, field reps telegraphed or penned progress reports of new agents signed up, urged dismissal of unreliable ones, and reported on customer reactions to new models before they hopped a steam locomotive to their next destination. And if they missed a day, Hartford headquarters, ravenous for sales, would be on their backs seeking news.[30]

Painstakingly, Pope had put all the pieces in place to manufacture, market, advertise, sell, and maintain wheeled vehicles. The unified network that had propelled Pope to control the bicycle industry could be retooled easily to produce motor vehicles. If experts had predicted in 1895 who might eventually dominate the automobile industry, few would have voted against Colonel Albert Augustus Pope.

Efficiency Obsession

Like his contemporaries Carnegie and Rockefeller, Albert Pope exemplified the striving of a largely uneducated man driven by an idea and outsized ambition. In just such rawboned, exuberant fashion were giants like U.S. Steel and Standard Oil created. With little governmental interference and no income tax, impulses toward efficiency fell before ones to maximize production.

The next logical step in the evolution of capitalism was for producers to learn the difference between gross income and net income. As muckrakers emerged in the 1890s to assault monopolistic excesses and Congress grew sufficient backbone to stand up to big business, a new idea called "scientific management" swept through corporate boardrooms. It recognized that, once each industry reached its saturation point, new profits could be realized by streamlining production.

Scientific management's chief proponent was Frederick Winslow Taylor, the son of a wealthy Philadelphia lawyer, who scorned a chance to study at Harvard and chose, instead, to soil himself as a factory laborer. Just as Samuel Gompers was proclaiming that industry was working labor too hard, Taylor began to argue that industry wasn't working labor hard enough.

The father of time-and-motion studies posed as a rank-and-file worker, pitched in on the line, bellied up to the bar after work, and discovered that shocking amounts of time were being wasted in inefficient operations, tarring both labor and management with the same brush. "In the past the man has been first," he declared. "In the future the System will be first."[31]

"He couldn't stand to see an idle lathe," wrote John Dos Passos about Taylor. "Production went to his head and thrilled his sleepless nerves like liquor or women on a Saturday night."[32]

Perhaps because of his privileged background, Taylor's sympathies lay with management. He came to think of labor as little more than cattle being herded from operation to operation. Soon, he became America's first management consultant; he sent in field agents undercover to help plant owners squeeze out more production and fatten their bottom line.

The sub-rosa nature of Taylor's operations soon suggested a sideline for his men as industrial gumshoes, policing, among other things, whether companies were infringing on each other's patents. And so, in 1895, Taylor's operatives infiltrated Pope's Hartford plant.

Taylor was hired by a Fitchburg, Massachusetts, company founded by George Simonds, who had become wealthy from manufacturing ball bearings, which, by reducing friction in moving parts, allowed machinery to work more smoothly. When Simonds fell off a passenger train to his death at age fifty-one, his family feared competitors would steal the patriarch's patent.

Bicycles of the day each employed a hundred or more ball bearings, and since Pope was known for making component parts in-house, his operation was a likely target for Taylor's men. As Pope contentedly enjoyed his business fortunes in 1895, he had fallen, without his knowledge, into the grips of a pincers operation orchestrated by Frederick Winslow Taylor.

While one of Taylor's agents posed as an advance man for unnamed capitalists seeking to purchase prosperous bicycle companies, another gained a job in Pope's plant as a mechanic. From very different perspectives, they took surreptitious notes, drew diagrams, and collected affidavits. Within months, the corporate spies dropped their damning package on Pope's desk as a fait accompli.[33]

Upstart on the Horizon

As Pope prepared to ratchet up his fortunes to a new level through electric vehicles, a 32-year-old mechanic in Detroit labored for $140 a month in the employ of the father of the electric light himself, Thomas Edison. As a reward for diligent work, the young man's supervisor invited him to a Long Island convention of the allied Edison companies and a chance to meet the Wizard of Menlo Park, already an American icon.

Like Hiram Percy Maxim, this young husband and father had tinkered with an automobile that ran on gasoline. After he had sketched his plan on the back of a menu for the developer of electric storage batteries, Edison had said, "Young man, you have the right idea. Keep right at it. This car has an advantage over the electric car because it supplies its own power."[34]

What validation! Edison's words would warm like sunshine in winter during the tough days ahead, for the young inventor faced years of ridicule and rejection. Yet he persevered, reportedly visiting Pope's factory on several occasions to study mass production. In a few years, when Pope and his oligarchy became the gatekeepers for the new industry, many of them muscled him out for not having demonstrated a workable automobile. But they underestimated the man they had spurned. Humiliated as he was, he vowed he'd be back, for no one, not even an entire industry, could humble Henry Ford.

Notes

1. Adams, G. Donald, "Collecting and Restoring Antique Bicycles," p. 6.
2. Kelly, Fred C., "The Great Bicycle Craze," p. 70.
3. Several newspaper articles from November 1895 Maxim, Scrapbook, 1895–1901.
4. Leonard, Irving A., unattributed published article entitled "Colonel Albert Pope and the Bicycle," contained in the papers of Colonel Pope held by his granddaughter Frances Walker.
5. McClure, S.S., *My Autobiography*, p. 34.
6. Kelly, p. 69.
7. Hoehne, M. "Hoehne Pages," p.4.
8. Herlihy, David V., "The Bicycle Story," p. 55.
9. Zinn, Howard, "A People's History of the United States," p. 215.
10. Ibid.
11. Lupiano, Vincent de Paul and Ken W. Sayers, "It Was a Very Good Year: A Cultural History of the United States," p. 122.
12. Connecticut State Register and Manual, p. 897.
13. Courtney, Steve, "Oh Wealth," p. 6.
14. Rybczynski, Witold, "A Clearing in the Distance," p. 30.
15. "Beating the Odds—The People of Hartford," a video for Hartford Public Library, 1996.
16. Twain, "Taming the Bicycle," p. 286; Courtney, p. 6.
17. Ibid., p. 287.
18. Ibid.
19. Lyon, Peter, *Success Story: The Life and Times of S.S. McClure*, p. 131.
20. R.F.S., "The Great Bicycle Delirium," p. 62.
21. Pope, Albert A., "Journal of the Southern Campaign," passim.
22. Kennedy, E.D., *The Automobile Industry*, p. 49.
23. Maxim, Hiram Percy, *Horseless Carriage Days*, p. 48.
24. Haimerl, Duncan, undated column in the *Hartford Courant*.
25. McShane, Clay, *The Automobile: A Chronology of Its Antecedents, Development, and Impact*, p. 23; Flink, James J., *The Automobile Age*, p. 13.
26. Flink, p. 29; McShane, p. 22.
27. Herlihy, p. 52.
28. McShane, p. 23; Williamson, Harold F., et al., *The American Petroleum Industry*, p. 186.
29. "Pope Manufacturing Company Correspondence, 1890–94."
30. "Pope Manufacturing Company Correspondence," box 1.
31. Kanigel, Robert, *The One Best Way*, flyleaf.
32. Dos Passos, John, *U.S.A.: The Big Money*, pp. 21–26.
33. Kanigel, p. 288.
34. Collier, Peter and David Horowitz, *The Fords: An American Epic*, p. 34.

CHAPTER 2

LUMBERING IS WHAT POPES DO

Dorchester is the greatest towne in New England; well wooded and watered; very good arable grounds and Hay ground; faire Cornfields And pleasant Gardens. In this Plantation is a great many Catle, as Kine, Goats and Swine. This Plantation has a reasonable Harbour for ships.

Pope Family Book

SMALL BOYS WATCHED in awe from the Boston docks as three-masted sailing ships and hissing steamboats approached Boston harbor and shopkeepers polished the brass kerosene lamps outside their heavy wooden doors and set out their wares on the brick sidewalk, anticipating another day of bustling commerce. It was the 1840s, and the China trade had boosted the city's growing reputation as the mercantile hub of New England. But of late, Boston's merchandise did not only move along ocean routes, for railroad fever had gripped the nation.

Only two years after the Best Friend of Charleston had become the nation's first rail line in 1832, Boston and Worcester construction crews were snaking rails outward from Boston to the wilderness of Brookline and points west to tap into rival New York's trade with western states. The Boston & Lowell stretched north to service the growing textile industry; and the Boston & Providence siphoned off wagon traffic from a well-established coastal turnpike. During the next decade, seven competing companies would extend lines into Brookline and neighboring towns, luring riders with family fares and weekend round-trip specials, touting the chance to buy suburban land away from the enveloping chaos of the teeming city.[1] Soon, these towns, separated from the downtown core, would become known as *suburbs*.

Settlements lucky enough to have deep water harbors had found that

19

geography is destiny, as waterborne trade built them into teeming cities. But railroads demonstrated that destiny is also manmade, as towns learned quickly that the access that rails gave them clustered prosperity around every railroad station. Overnight, two iron rails four or five feet apart caused land values to jump by a factor of ten, sometimes hundredfold.

If the accelerating disorganization of the central city sent homeowners in search of a more ordered life, suburban land speculators in the 1840s were ready to accommodate them. The basic unit of land development was the orderly subdivision, with lots laid out with geometric precision, standard setback lines behind which houses must be built, and guarantees of municipal services. Planned development around rail connections would, within a generation, cause Brookline to call itself "the richest town in the world."[2] Included among its prestigious gentry were architect Henry Hobson Richardson, municipal park planner Frederick Law Olmsted, financial publisher Henry V. Poor, and poet Amy Lowell. Such a phenomenon was not lost on Charles Pope, the breadwinner for a wife and eight children.

Family Business

Charles Pope belonged to the burgeoning dynasty of Popes, who along with the Pierces, Adams, Shaws, Coles, and Stubbses ruled the Boston roost. It was a 200-year-old dynasty built around wood—lumber, to be exact. For Popes had felled the trees that became the planks that formed the walls and floors of the finest homes in Massachusetts. Now in its seventh generation on American shores, the family tree had branched into an enterprise run by cousins descended from several bloodlines.

Life for a young Pope male involved felling huge trees in Maine, hauling them to the coastal docks for milling into custom-made lumber, and shipping the lumber by boat up and down the eastern seaboard. To ask a young man named Pope what career he intended to set for himself seemed almost superfluous. Lumbering was simply what Popes did.

So, for Charles Pope to break with family tradition was strange to most, heretical to some. Surely, he knew his future was secure in the family enterprise, but Charles had his reasons. And as intriguing as was the lure of an unparalleled fortune in real estate speculation, it was not his main reason for jumping the family ship.

Charles had chosen a strong mate in Elizabeth Bogman, daughter of a seafaring family from Providence. Her father, Captain James Bogman, was one of seven brothers, all but one of whom were shipmasters. Sailing out of Norfolk, Virginia, one day during his daughter's youth, he had encountered a violent storm and was never heard from again. Elizabeth grew up without

Albert Pope's parents, depicted in miniature portraits popular in the mid–nineteenth century, are studies in contrast: open, trusting Charles *(left)*, who would make and then lose a fortune in real estate; and wary, cautious Elizabeth *(right)*, who insisted before marriage that her husband forgo a life on the sea. *(Courtesy Victoria Pope.)*

a father and watched the ocean devour other beloved family members as well. Strong-willed, intelligent, and disciplined, Elizabeth was not about to enter a marriage that the sea, at its whim, could sever.

Early miniature paintings of the couple illustrate how different they were. Charles's reddish-blond hair frames an open, trusting face with deep blue eyes. Elizabeth, with almond-shaped eyes and black hair parted in the middle, has a more guarded aspect and a firm lip line; hers is a face whose life experiences have made sadder but wiser. If Charles was to win Elizabeth's hand, he'd have to agree to stay on land. And so a young man in love chose a marriage that would produce eight children and survive a half century.[3]

Dealing with his family was another matter. The Popes and home building had been synonymous since even before the first Popes arrived in Dorchester in 1634. For Virginia had been part of the Massachusetts Bay Colony in those days, and the family's first years in America were spent in the South.

The Popes' first involvement in the lumber business came in the 1660s, when the family, according to the Colonel's great-grandson and namesake, applied to authorities for stumpage rights, having already acquired rights patent from the British Crown to engage in lumbering. They saw early that a steady stream of immigrants to New England would need homes in which to live.

The notion of the hardy pioneer felling his own trees and erecting his own crude dwelling buttresses the mythic self-sufficiency of early pioneer stock, but it is more fable than fact. Trimming logs into buildable planks is a heavy-duty operation, one requiring special equipment and skill. And so, the Popes harvested lumber in nearby Stoughton and Milton. As their scope widened and the demand for wood increased, they headed to the wilds of Maine, where in the seaside village of East Machias, they found a port from which they could export timber on ships and deliver it to major cities all along the eastern seaboard.

Over the years, the Popes built a prosperous business, selling "dimensioned" lumber to prosperous merchants and dairy farmers, who in the first burst of an American trait which much later would be labeled conspicuous consumption, built sprawling federal-style mansions along such streets as Canton Avenue in Dorchester. They did business with and later intermarried with New England's "best" families, such as the Pierces of S. S. Pierce fame and the Adamses, who produced two American presidents.

Rift in the Family

By the account of Colonel Pope's great-grandson, Albert A. Pope II, when Charles eschewed the family enterprise to make quick money in real estate, his father's family was disappointed.[4] The abundant profits from the Boston real estate boom of the 1840s—when neighborhoods of homes hard by railroad depots in such towns as Newton were built—were soothing balm for his wound. When Albert was only three, Charles moved his growing family to the burgeoning suburb of Brookline, where new investments would presumably provide wealth beyond measure. By early 1852, however, the bottom fell out of Charles Pope's promising real estate empire.

How much money his family had was of small moment to Charles's fourth child. What was much more difficult for young Albert to swallow was being suddenly written off as one of the poor relations. Whereas up until now, the Popes had still been included in family gatherings, Albert playing with his cousins and being admired by his uncles and aunts, at this time a curtain fell over the Brookline Popes. If you had agreed to stay in the family business, the family seemed to be saying, none of this would have happened. Don't expect our help now.[5]

And so, at age nine, according to Albert Pope II, his great-grandfather felt the sting of rebuke from his own family as well as a loss of wealth. Although he would never forget the sting, Albert would recover from the relative poverty soon enough, although the business collapse took the starch forever out of Charles. The former man of zeal and ambition became an empty husk, still beloved by his wife and brood of children but no longer the breadwinner. Young Albert applied himself mightily to supplement the family income and eventually became the sole support of his mother, father, and seven siblings. If some in the wider family spurned Charles, they remained supportive of Albert.

Decades later, Colonel Pope would tell the story in what he evidently hoped would be the version that history accepted: that when his father ran into trouble when Albert was nine, the young lad hired out to plow for a neighboring farmer in Brookline during the afternoons after attending school in the mornings. Three years later, he began buying fruit and vegetables to sell to neighbors, netting himself in one season the tidy sum of $100. At age fifteen, he took a job at the bustling Quincy Market, then a stew of raw sights amid the smells of fresh beef and salt spray.[6]

Beginnings in a New Land

Mattapan: The name that the Algonquians used for the chocolate-colored flats nestled at the headwaters of the Neponset River, far down the south shore from a deep blue-water harbor nestled against the peninsula that the earliest inhabitants called Shawmut and the English settlers would rename Boston. In May 1630, after a 71-day passage by sail from Plymouth, England, a shipful of farmers, fishermen, and merchants from southwestern Britain landed on a slim neck of land adjacent to Mattapan under a charter granted by King Charles. In so doing, they created the third colony, after Plymouth and Salem, in the Massachusetts Bay Colony. Records of how many came are vague, although their numbers forced them to abandon a smaller craft in favor of a 400-ton vessel sailed by one Captain Squeb. Their stated aim, as that of their predecessors, was to flee harassment by the Church of England and to "worship God according to the light of their own conscience."

It is a grave business to create a settlement in a new, unforgiving, and sometimes hostile land, particularly for those not used to being in charge of creating and maintaining a workable society. Clearing land, building houses, a school, and church, and protecting against predators were obvious chores. But in the more subtle tasks resided the glue of the community: writing and enforcing laws and crafting the underpinnings of an economy. First, the settlers needed to create an identity for the community that would resonate with its residents. And so, because a number of the earliest colonists hailed from the town of Dorchester in England, this name supplanted the Indians' Mattapan, although its river continued to be called Neponset.

Unlike the rock-encrusted coast north of Boston, the south shore offered wide bays and rivers in which boats could be beached at low tide and their cargo unloaded. High tide would carry them back to sea. As early as 1631, a chronicler of New England settlements sang the area's praises, as the quotation that opened this chapter has shown.

By 1634, the town of Dorchester felt the need to declare fifty-four people as freemen, designating men of good standing and repute, erecting them as pillars of the growing community. Among this group was a man named John Pope. While it is uncertain whether he was among the original group of settlers, he evidently arrived early enough to be included among the nascent gentry. The freemen took oaths to submit to and enforce the laws established for the plantation, thereby becoming the backbone of the community, agreeing to the social compact necessary for any such settlement to survive.

Popes had been recorded in England since the Domesday Book, a census of sorts, which had been ordered by William the Conqueror in 1086. Like tentacles, their lines suffused the country and may have included the poet Alexander Pope. And while no record exists to show John Pope to be a man of means when he emigrated to the New World, upon his death in 1649, he left a considerable estate, for the times, worth £184, consisting of a dwelling house, seventy acres of farms, pastures, and orchards, and scores of items of apparel, kitchen implements, and livestock.

Hauled on the Carpet

As was common in those days, John made his oldest son his namesake. Younger John's son Ralph followed suit as did the younger Ralph's son Frederick. As the family grew, scores of cousins greeted each new addition, cousins who would soon be joined not only by blood but by occupation. Although steeped in the culture of his growing community and the son of a freeman, John the younger was chastised by the town fathers in 1674, along with "such of his chilldren as are of Capaccetie for learning," for John had failed to send his children to the town schools, thus undermining the goal of an educated populace, which freemen swore to uphold.

Whether or not John's eldest daughter, Margaret, ever received an education, she attracted while still in her teens the attentions of a young man named Peirce (also spelled Pierce), a bloodline that would intertwine with the Popes over the next centuries like two hardy vines. John the younger enhanced his father's modest fortune, with its homestead and seventy acres of land. A century before Webster's dictionary was published, John's estate inventory reported among his property "on house and barn with fower acers land Joyning to the hous." He left this world in 1686 with an estate totaling £238, including more than 200 acres, various musketry, butter churns, and spinning wheels.

By that time, the Massachusetts Bay Colony had created a General Assembly, which drew on English common law to set up a formula to dole out the assets of those, such as John, who died without a will. With one son having predeceased his father, leaving no heirs, a second son having sold his interest for cash early on, and a third son having been probably lost at sea years earlier, John's modest fortune passed to his fourth son, Ralph. Ralph instantly became, at age twenty-four, one of the more comfortable of Dorchester's townspeople, moving into what his father had come to call the "Squantum" farm and leaving his new wife, Rachel Neale, one of twenty-one children, to negotiate control of the household with her mother-in-law, who she called "mother Margaret." Rachel and Ralph raised a brood of nine, of whom seven survived to adulthood, and Ralph prided himself at his success as a "yeoman," a term borrowed from the English for an owner and cultivator of soil.

Ralph used the head start his inheritance gave him to build an impressive estate stretching through Dorchester, Braintree, and Milton. In 1750, at age seventy-one, "being weak in body but perfect in mind and memory," Ralph penned a last will and testament, which makes clear that the Popes had diversified far beyond farming. Among other things, he left to his namesake and to another son, Lazarus, his interest in a sawmill in nearby Stoughton, where already Popes were carving up dimensioned lumber to be used for fine mansions for the agricultural elite and merchant traders, who had reaped their profits from overseas investments.

Ralph saw to it that his widow would have sufficient cut firewood carried to her house and enough bread corn milled "so long as she shall remain my Widow and no longer." In spite of his voluminous properties, two family members chose to challenge, unsuccessfully, his gift of £20 for the communion table of the Church of Christ in Dorchester when "Father Pope" died.

Perhaps most notable among Ralph's progeny was his son Ralph, a kindly, open-faced man, whose life ushered in the eighteenth century for American Popes. Lovingly known as "Dr. Ralph," he was a physician who trained at nearby Harvard University and received the balance of his training from the Reverend Richard Billings in a day when credentialing was more informal than it would come to be. Dr. Ralph also farmed and, with Lazarus, managed the lumber business their father had left them.

Benevolent Slaveholder

New Englanders in the eighteenth century had developed a schizophrenic attitude toward slavery. Dr. Ralph, for example, owned a "negro" slave named Scipio, yet had him baptized at his church on the same day as his firstborn. Dr. Ralph's carved smiling visage shines down from his granite tombstone in Stoughton Village cemetery, where he was laid to rest at age forty-four of "nervous fever." His grave marker's inscription offers a cosmic warning to passersby:

> You Reader stay & lend a Tear
> Think on the Dust that slumbers here
> & when you thus my silence see
> Think on the glass that runs for thee.

Dr. Ralph's will called upon Frederick and Samuel Ward Pope to carry on the family's lumber business, and, for their trouble, Dr. Ralph bequeathed to them "Pine Timber enough To make Three Thousand feet of Boards apiece, to build their Houses with."

By now, the Pope family had begun its fifth generation on American soil and was multiplying at such a rate that the cousins could not have all known each other. Rebecca, Dr. Ralph's eldest daughter, for example, gave birth to eleven children and left, at her death, seventy-five grandchildren.

At the time of Dr. Ralph's untimely death, Frederick had not yet turned seventeen. At first, he turned to Uncle Lazarus for help with the sawmill, but in short order, Lazarus succumbed as well, leaving the tall, well-muscled lad in full charge. With diverse holdings to manage, it was essential that Frederick marry a strong woman, and Molly Cole proved, according to contemporaries, to be "wide-awake, capable ... and a worthy companion." She would need all her diverse skills for in 1775, Captain Frederick Pope enlisted in the colonial forces to fight in the Revolution, mustered out as a colonel, and went on to represent Stoughton for seven terms in the Massachusetts House of Representatives.

Frederick was the fifth of Colonel Frederick's children, born in 1772. He advanced the family's lumber interests a notch by adding to the Popes' holdings wharves and a lumberyard at Boston's Commercial Point; he also constructed ships to be used in coastal trade. With his brother William, Frederick carried on the business for three decades under the name F. and W. Pope.

Adopting the name of Dorchester for their new settlement was crucial to the feeling of solidarity necessary for community building in an unknown environment. But a century and a half had passed, and town fathers now decided to rename the town Milton, a name that would also attach to a select public school they founded in 1789, Milton Academy. Here, children of mercantile wealth would prepare for careers in medicine and law or, as in the case of the Popes, a livelihood in lumbering and trade. Unfortunately for Albert Pope, his family had relocated to Brookline by the time he entered school. In a day of rutted dirt roads, the distance to Milton would have been insurmountable for a commuting student.

By the nineteenth century, the need for lumber had outstripped the supply in towns surrounding Boston. A burgeoning population pressed the city outward, and work crews cleared maple, elm, birch, and oak trees in the wilderness to build federal-style homes and more rustic saltboxes. Needing new forest land to harvest, Frederick sailed to the village of East Machias, Maine, first buying shiploads of lumber from local sawmills and then establishing a store, with Pope relatives as clerks. The robust Frederick, who stood above six feet in height, would regularly commute from Dorchester to East Machias for years thereafter.

Economic obstacles and the War of 1812 hindered the firm's progress, but Frederick stayed with it and branched out into the wholesaling of wines and spirits as well. Peripatetic and questing until age fifty, Frederick thereafter reached what a family chronicler calls "premature old age, exchanging the fire and vigor which had thrilled his majestic form so many years for the good-natured, bland, easy-going spirit which delighted all who met him, but brought a paralysis upon his business." His unexpected decline would parallel eerily that of his son Charles, the father of Colonel Pope. At age fifty-four, friends at the house where he was boarding in Maine went to his chamber to find Frederick "sitting upright in his chair, fully dressed; peace was written on his face, and his eyes were closed in the sleep that knows no waking."

Cashing in on the Gold Rush

As the Machias operation prospered, Pope cousins entered the firm. Then, in 1849, gold was discovered clear across the continent in California. Eager to cash in on the gold rush, even from afar, the Pope firm sent out a large quantity of lumber and goods to San Francisco, presumably overland through Panama in Central America, a route heavily favored by traders in the years before construction of the Panama Canal in the early twentieth century.[7] At the time, the business was operating in Boston under the name William Pope & Sons, in East Machias as S. W. Pope & Co., and on the Pacific coast by Andrew J. Pope, a cousin of the Milton Popes. The family enterprise now stretched its tentacles throughout the civilized world, with

Pope-made vessels sailing the Pacific Ocean, to the East Indies, Australia, and the Sandwich Islands.

William Pope, who had conducted the lumber business for nearly thirty years, retired in 1861, having also served as a compassionate representative in the Massachusetts legislature, where he voted to abolish capital punishment, "exposing himself to the censure of many of his Friends." In so doing, he exhibited a fiercely independent streak that would show itself later in the lives of Albert Augustus Pope and his father, Charles. Liberal in religious views, William supported the church, where he found himself "with the belief that it was better to educate a family under almost any religious society, than without the restraints of any."

Over the years, the Popes' affection for America's and Massachusetts's leading families showed in the names they gave their children, such as John Adams Pope, George Washington Pope, Andrew Jackson Pope, Benjamin Franklin Pope, and John Quincy Pope.

Only twelve at the time of his father, Frederick's, untimely passing, Charles grew up in a family steeped in lumbering and trading. His fateful decision to forsake it all for the love of a strong woman may have stemmed less from Charles's own backbone than from the strength of Elizabeth Bogman, a woman of whom it was said, "She infused great ambition and energy for all good into her children, and was a most sagacious and loving counsellor." Charles, with the backing of independent family wealth, tried his hand at furniture making and the feather trade before settling on real estate as the means to his fortune.

The Bubble Bursts

Indeed, buying and selling land was the choice of many men of ambition in the 1840s, for the access that numerous rail lines and horse-drawn streetcar lines from Boston gave to the verdant farmland on the city's outskirts meant people could escape the immigrant hordes at the end of a day's work and retire to a quiet, bucolic haven, quite within commuting distance. In response to the cacophony of jumbled land uses which overpopulation had forced on Boston proper, planners of Brookline set about to create order. In 1843, the Linden Place subdivision required buildings to be set back thirty feet from the street and to be limited to dwellings. Later, in a xenophobic reaction to the heterogeneity they had lately left, the subdivision's owners forbade sales to "any Negro or native of Ireland."[8]

Two years later, 32-year-old Charles bought his first building lot in Brookline, on Vernon Place.[9] In February 1846, Elizabeth delivered twin daughters, Emily Frances and Caroline Augusta, the couple's fifth and sixth children, who joined Charles Allen, eleven; Adelaide Leonora, nine; Mary Elizabeth, six; and Albert Augustus, three. Later that year, Charles transplanted his family from Milton to a sprawling house on Harvard Street in Brookline. Here he would pursue the monumental profits available in trading on inside information. He learned the location of future streetcar lines, bought nearby land on the cheap from unsuspecting owners, and resold it for a killing once the horsecars began to plod along broad, tree-lined Beacon Street and its tributaries.

Charles soon found himself drawn into the classic pattern of real estate speculation. He would buy a lot for cash on the cheap and put a mortgage on it to free up money to buy another lot. Word that a new streetcar line would pass by the first lot would inflate its value, letting Charles sell it for enough money to buy two new lots, which he would mortgage to generate still more cash to buy more lots. Charles enhanced his earnings by giving mortgages to the buyers of his lots, thus becoming a banker as well. The cycle works fine as long as land can be bought for a reasonable price and demand for new lots holds. Yet, the nature of a capitalistic market is that it cannot limit the number of speculators engaged in buying and selling. Since the amount of land remains constant, every new speculator entering the fray requires the pie to be sliced thinner and thinner, leaving a declining stream of income for each remaining speculator to pay his increasing burden of debt.

Charles bought lots on Summer Street, Vernon Street, Washington Street, and Harvard Place, including one from his brother-in-law, George Bogman, and quickly resold them at a profit. The lifestyle of the streetcar suburb had caught the public imagination, and soon notables began to appear, such as famed historian Francis Parkman, who perhaps used some of the profits from his recent book, *The Oregon Trail,* to buy lot 24 on Vernon Place.

Charles was making a killing. He bought and sold more lots in 1848 than 1847 and more in 1849 than in 1848. The center continued to hold in 1850, by which time he was expanding to Davis Place, Catlin Street, and Boylston Street. While the Boston immigrants packed into tenements bore such names as Egan, O'Connor, and Lafferty, the buyers of Pope's Brookline lots were named Stearns, Plummer, Mellen, Warren, and Leeds, old names symbolizing the Yankee flight from downtown.

In 1851, Charles's purchases began to slow. He bought five properties in May and June, but then the record is silent. In November of that year, his real estate tower came tumbling down as notes came due with no money to pay them. By now, Arthur Wallace had joined the family, and soon Elizabeth would be pregnant with her eighth, Louis Atherton. Just after Thanksgiving, Charles signed an Assignment for Creditors, in effect giving up all his property to a trustee to sell and repay those he owed. In five years, his

Albert Pope at age 7, the fourth of nine children raised in a rambling house in the Brookline suburb of Boston. *(Courtesy Albert A. Pope II.)*

empire had begun, crested, and fallen. Penniless at age thirty-seven, Charles was forced to begin a new life. A year later, family lore has it, nine-year-old Albert would hire himself out to a neighboring farmer to till fields after school to help put bread on the table.

In the years following, in spite of his relative youth, Charles failed to rebound, seeming to be permanently uprooted and lacking the resilience and resourcefulness that successful entrepreneurs use to recoup after a fall, a fact that has puzzled those who have studied the Pope family. Given the "premature old age" experienced by his father, however, one wonders whether a hereditary illness was also at work.[10] Charles fell back on the largesse of friends and family and managed to do some work in settling the estates of people who had died.

William, Charles's twin brother, had accompanied him in the move to Brookline, and their children grew up not only as cousins but as playmates. William's son George, a year younger than Albert, bonded early with his cousin and, in spite of a detour into the family lumber business, later joined Albert as a trusted high-level associate in the Pope enterprises for many years. Bald as a cue ball in his middle years, his appearance marked a stark contrast with the hirsute Albert.

The 1850 U.S. Census shows Charles, thirty-seven, as a "merchant," which reflects his activity in furniture and feathers but not his escapades into real estate, which by then were well underway. Next to his name is the notation "$27,000." If this represented assets, Charles would appear to have been quite comfortable in the days prior to his fall, since that figure would represent several hundreds of thousands in year 2000 dollars, most of it real estate profits. Also listed in Brookline were brother William and his wife, Mary Bogman Pope, sister of Elizabeth. William, listed as a crockery merchant, was doing well enough at age thirty-seven to employ two Irish house servants, a luxury Charles and Elizabeth evidently lacked.[11]

Albert and George attended the Brookline grammar school which, if not offering the superior education that earlier and later generations of Popes would enjoy at Milton Academy, at least, in Pope's later estimation, furnished "a moderate schooling." A natural leader at schoolyard games, Albert would soon have little time for play. But in the carefree days before his father's business reverses, Albert was the garrulous, fun-loving child in the middle of a pack of eight siblings, five girls and three boys.

While the *History of the Dorchester Pope Family* dwells in detail on the disastrous effect Charles's father's illness had on his business fortunes, virtually nothing is written about Charles's parallel experience. Instead, it rather blandly observes that Charles and Elizabeth lived to celebrate their fiftieth anniversary, surrounded by loving family. The answer may lie in the fact that Albert A. Pope financed the *History of the Dorchester Pope Family* and, as an unusually devoted son, may have wished to spare any pain to his father, who was still alive at its writing in 1888. Indeed, if Colonel Pope ever felt any resentment toward his father, whose failures forced him to support his parents and educate his siblings, it is not found among his voluminous writings.

Throughout history, the salubrious effect of a focused, nurturing mother on her progeny has been duplicated time and time again. Strong, loving, and ambitious for her children, Elizabeth raised and nurtured two female physicians, one of the century's leading industrialists, a minister, a schoolteacher, and a company president. Albert was the fourth-born, and his closest relationships were with the twin sisters three years his junior, who he supported through the New England Female Medical College in Boston. They graduated in 1870 before studying further in Paris and London and then at the New England Hospital for Women and Children, on whose staff they remained for many years while maintaining a practice on Newbury Street in Boston.

Albert's was the eighth generation of Popes in America, and a hall would be needed to accommodate a family reunion of the hundreds of far-flung cousins. His first cousin Andrew united with his wife's brother, Captain William C. Talbot, to form Pope & Talbot Mills, which ratcheted the family lumbering business to a new level. Had Albert chosen not to duplicate his father's heresy of eschewing the lumber trade, such an enterprise could undoubtedly have used a young man of Albert's unusual promise and ambition. The record is silent on whether the family's reaction to his father's misfortune had soured him against rejoining the Pope business. Nevertheless, lumbering never seemed to have factored in Albert's thinking. From his teens, Pope found the need to make the most money the quickest way. For before he could grow a mature beard, Albert had a family to support.

Notes

1. Jackson, Kenneth, *Crabgrass Frontiers: The Suburbanization of the United States*, p. 37; Martin, Albro, *Railroads Triumphant*, p. 15.

2. Jackson, p. 100.

3. Interviews with Albert Augustus Pope II on May 8, 1999 and on various other dates. Albert Pope II has become somewhat of a family historian, not surprisingly, since he is the only Pope to bear the same exact name as the Colonel. The facts gleaned on this interview were learned on a day-long tour of the Colonel's Boston neighborhoods and his seaside estate in Cohasset, together with Albert's sister, Tina Pope Rowley. Much of Albert's knowledge, he says, comes from an extensive autobiography by his great-grandfather, the only known copy of which he reports to be lost. The story of his ancestor's break from the family business Albert draws from this volume. See also Pope, Charles Henry, *A History of the Dorchester Pope Family, 1634–1888*. Much of the material in this chapter is drawn from that book, which was written by the Colonel's cousin and underwritten by Albert Pope. Since the book was self-published and his not in general circulation, page numbers of citations are not supplied.

4. Interview on May 8, 1999, with Albert A. Pope II. That Charles Pope's family was disappointed in him is not elsewhere corroborated, either in documentary sources or in the memories of Pope family members. *A History of the Dorchester Pope Family*, chronicling the family's rise through 1888, does not touch on it, although the book is largely an upbeat account of the family's heritage and characteristically avoids intra-family unpleasantness.

5. Again, this is the interpretation of Albert A. Pope II. While it is uncorroborated, it should be said that no contrary account exists either.

6. Pope, Charles Henry, p. 130.

7. Kinder, Gary, *Ship of Gold in the Deep Blue Sea,* p. 156.

8. Pope, Charles Henry, p. 158.

9. Information on Charles Pope's real estate purchasing, selling, and mortgaging during the 1840s and the 1850s is drawn from the records of the Norfolk County Courthouse Registry of Deeds in Dedham, Massachusetts, and the Suffolk County Courthouse Registry of Deeds in Boston.

10. Albert Pope II told the author during his May 8, 1999, interview that his grandfather and his father (who would have been the Colonel's son and grandson, respectively) both suffered from Parkinson's Disease, which slowed them down considerably during their fifties. As the reader will discover later in this book, Colonel Pope was afflicted with a wasting disease in his mid-fifties, diagnosed at the time as locomotor ataxia. Whether any essential medical tie among the generations exists is not certain.

11. U.S. Census, 1850, Brookline, Massachusetts, per U.S. Census Bureau.

CHAPTER 3

A BLOODY CRUCIBLE

You cannot transform the negro into anything one-tenth
as useful or as good as what slavery enables them to be.
Jefferson Davis

VEN AS A TEENAGER, an inner need drove Albert Pope to make his world
your world. Only seventeen and a $4-a-week store clerk when the Civil
War broke out, Albert felt himself drawn inextricably into its vortex. But it
was not enough for Pope to pore over tomes of army tactics and regulations.
He bought a musket, brought it to Brooks & M'Cuen's store on Boston's
Milk Street, and eagerly engaged his fellow clerks, customers, and even his
bosses in military drill.[1]

What the lanky youngster lacked in experience, he made up in motiva-
tion: he joined the 1st Company, 35th Massachusetts Volunteer Regiment
on August 27, 1862, as a second lieutenant, a commission one family member says may have been purchased for him.[2] When Albert returned to civilian life just short of three years later, he had endured extreme hardship and
hunger, led thousands of men into battle, escaped death in desperate circumstances when his close friends were meeting theirs, fought within yards of
such legendary generals as Ulysses Grant and Ambrose Burnside, sat on
courts-martial, which sentenced others to die, and returned to a nation deeply
grateful for his service.

A young man coming of age in the Boston of the 1850s could scarcely
avoid being touched by the passions generated by the proposition that no
man should own another. The logical conclusion, that American slaves
should be freed, might not have won the day at a local referendum, but few
cities were greater hotbeds of abolitionist sentiment than Boston.

Smith Court on Beacon Hill, the site of the oldest surviving black church
in America, served fittingly as the local headquarters for abolitionists of both
races. Many passing through its doors, with their top hats, capes, and walking sticks, were figures of national repute.

William Lloyd Garrison, editor of a Boston newspaper called the *Liberator*, was perhaps the shrillest of a cadre of local essayists and poets, which included James Greenleaf Whittier and James Russell Lowell.[3] While they excoriated the moral blight of slavery on the printed page and at the podium, theologians, such as the fiery congregational preacher Theodore Parker, took the cause into the pulpit. Orator and writer Frederick Douglass, son of a slave, began his abolitionist efforts in Massachusetts and organized the state's 54th and 55th regiments, comprised of black soldiers commanded by whites. Pope's cousin and boyhood friend George Pope would join and rise to lieutenant colonel in the 54th, which was commanded by Boston abolitionist Robert Gould Shaw.[4]

The debate over slavery swirled around Pope during his formative years, and while little in Pope's own writings suggests a deep idealistic commitment to abolition per se, he was drawn to the war effort with the undiluted fervor that young men feel to right wrongs.

Confederate troops had fired on Fort Sumter in April 1861, providing the spark that ignited the conflict. Yet Pope did not enlist until more than a year later. Albert's family had come to depend on his income, once his father's fortunes and spirit had declined, and the lad evidently sensed a need to hone his skills until he felt confident to step onto a field of battle. He joined the Home Guards in his home town of Brookline and an artillery company, with which he drilled regularly. Barely nineteen, Pope entered the Union Army, considerably more than a greenhorn, with the war well underway.[5]

Pope family lore has it that Albert's first commanding officer, aware of his young charge's sensitivity about his lack of education, prevailed upon him to keep a daily diary as a tool to hone his writing skills. Whatever the initial inspiration, Pope kept a meticulously detailed account of his experiences in the South for thirty-four months, including service in such key battles as Antietam, Fredericksburg, and Vicksburg. Later in life, Colonel Pope had it published, in handsome leather binding, as a family monument.

Bound for Battle

The 35th Massachusetts embarked from Boston in late August on a steamer bound for Washington, D.C. There, while waiting for orders to move south, they stopped near the train station at a large armory, which Pope estimated held about 2,000 injured soldiers. On the first page of his 276-page diary, the untested soldier wrote of first witnessing the fruits of battle: "Some were lying out doors on the cold damp ground. It was a sad sight to look at the poor fellows who had hardly strength enough left to move."[6] Within three weeks, Pope would write similar words as a participant, no longer a mere observer.

After several days of toughening, the 35th was ready to cross the Potomac on September 7 and march south, in late summer heat, along dusty Virginia roads. Pope's immediate commanding officer, whom he identifies only as Captain Lathrop, quickly gained enough confidence in his young lieutenant that he placed Pope in charge when he was unavailable. The company of volunteers trudged on toward Leesboro, Virginia, setting up camp along a country road, where they picked wild grapes and slept beside a denuded cornfield and potato patch, where soldiers before them had foraged for food.

"It is one of the hottest days I ever saw," recorded the Bostonian. While an army travels on its stomach, it doesn't have space to carry its pantry along, so Pope watched his men bag a farmer's forty hens and a pig to eat along the way. Any thought that the conflict would be over quickly had been quelled on August 30, when the Confederates had defeated the Union forces for the second time at Bull Run.

As they marched south, Pope notes, the raw recruits watched in awe as General George McClellan, commander of the northern forces, passed by on horseback, his mount kicking up clouds of dust. The sight of the charismatic West Point graduate commanded respect: finely chiseled features, a thick mane of dark hair swept back at the sides, riveting eyes, and a drooping mustache above a closely trimmed goatee. At age thirty-six, McClellan had already served as president of the Illinois Central Railroad, a key player in the nation's most dynamic industry.

Ambrose Burnside, one of McClellan's key executives at the railroad, followed his boss into the war, again as his subordinate, commanding the division in which Pope served. Burnside was unforgettable in appearance, too, with eyes set deep in his huge, round, bald head; a rim of grey hair led downward to bushy white muttonchop whiskers, which swept upward over his shaved chin and met above his upper lip.

Bloody Antietam

Adoring soldiers inverted the syllables of their commander's surname to call such facial foliage "sideburns," and contemporary photographs show that Albert joined them in imitating the new tonsorial style. On September 17, Burnside would lead the 35th into one of the bloodiest battles of the Civil War: Antietam, named for the Maryland creek that separated the combatants.

On the way to Antietam, Burnside's troops had to traverse South Mountain, a ridge running northeast as an extension of the Blue Ridge. Robert E.

Lee's army lay in wait on its western side and held the mountain passes that the Union troops would have to negotiate.[7] The event gave Pope his first taste of combat:

> As we advanced up the hill, we met ambulances full of wounded and men on stretchers being borne off the field.... The cannonading was awful; the rattle of musketry very sharp. We halted behind a fence, the men threw forward their pieces, the long line projecting over the fence.... The rebels were piled up in the woods pretty thick. We had to step over them and walk through rebel blood.

They soon found themselves behind rebel lines.

Confederate shelling continued without respite for the next two days. On September 17, Pope entitles his entry "The Battle of Antietam," a headline evidently added in later life, since battles are rarely named until their conclusion or by historians thereafter. Antietam would match McClellan's Union forces against the army of white-haired General Lee and would claim 23,110 dead, wounded, or missing: the bloodiest day of the entire war.

To gain an overall perspective necessary to give orders, General Burnside sat on horseback atop a hill facing Antietam Creek. Fatefully, by not realizing that the creek was fordable (his men could have crossed along its length), Burnside instead ordered his troops to cross a small, triple-arched stone bridge. It was a narrow gauntlet, making Pope's men sitting ducks for rebels on the far side, who trained their rifles on the bridge from behind trees, delivering to the enemy soldier, in the words of historian Shelby Foote, "a faceful of bullets."[8]

Amid ferocious fire, those who survived charged up a steep hill beyond the river until repulsed at its brow. After an hour of digging in and ducking enemy fire, reinforcements joined the 35th, and they advanced over the hill into a valley, where it appeared in hindsight, though not to Pope at the time, that the Union forces would win the day.

"Our men were supplied with sixty rounds of ammunition," Pope wrote. "The rebels were posted in a corn-field behind a stone wall. They were about four to one of our men, besides having a battery of artillery, with which they kept up a steady fire all the time." As outnumbered as the Union forces appeared to Pope, Lee, in reality, was down to a skeleton force and was waging a ferocious battle to prevent being overtaken before reinforcements arrived. Soon thereafter, rebel troops charged the Union's left flank, Pope wrote, "and got us under a cross-fire, which mowed our men down at a fearful rate." Reinforcements had arrived just in time to save Lee from what would have been a pivotal defeat.[9]

Pope's troops were exhausting ammunition at an alarming rate, and three regiments reportedly coming to their relief failed to show. Soon his men had used up all their cartridges, including what they had pilfered from the wounded and from corpses of the dead. "We were at last obliged to fall back and the order was given to retreat, and the regiment fell back over the hill." The 35th sustained 79 dead and 189 wounded.

While North and South had suffered approximately equal losses at Antietam, McClellan had blunted Lee's attempt at a general invasion of the North. For Lee to retreat south, his troops would have to cross the broad Potomac River, and there McClellan would have a chance to finish him off. But McClellan believed reports which greatly inflated the actual size of Lee's army and so disregarded orders from President Abraham Lincoln, his commander in chief, to engage Lee or, at least, to drive him south across the Potomac. Playing it safe, McClellan made a fateful decision to let Lee escape across the river back into Virginia. When Lincoln found out, he was enraged.[10]

Duality of War

Pope was beginning to learn the duality of war, in which armed conflict coexists with workaday life. While antagonists are using their last breaths to snuff out the lives of their enemies, civilian quotidian life goes on as before, each person simply trying to muddle through the daily cycle of work and rest.

It was natural, therefore, that while marching through hostile Confederate territory, Pope often found himself befriended by southern homeowners, simple folk who saw before them not the representative of an ideology but only a hungry soldier. Rarely, Pope reported, would such country people accept money for food, a simple charity that made a deep impression on the young soldier.

As the fall deepened, combat conditions began to wear on Pope and his comrades. On October 8, he wrote, "I washed my underclothes, which had not been washed for more than five weeks" at a brook near Harpers Ferry. There, the fanatic abolitionist John Brown had seized an arsenal in a bloody shootout in 1859; he later was hanged for his trouble.

Pope reported on October 9, "I have got the Cholera Morbus," a disease marked by diarrhea and vomiting, for which a doctor prescribed laudanum (an opium derivative), cayenne pepper, and brandy. Feeling better six days later, Pope received a pass from the general of his brigade to walk to Harpers Ferry to visit the siege site which had done so much to make the Civil War inevitable. "A good many of the buildings showed marks of shot and shell," Pope reported, "and some were completely riddled."

By October 18, the war and the weather had taken their toll on Pope's regiment; its ranks had dwindled from more than 1,000 to 300. The stark reality of this loss of life may have prompted a sober Pope to note, "I have been converted into a Christian, and trust with the help of God, to hold fast to my faith."

A week later, having spent two hours packing his company's mess chest, Pope sat up in bed and leaned against his valise while he wrote in his journal, as had become his daily custom. He notes without comment that his captain, dozing on his bed, had just stolen a bottle of wine in a package mailed to one of his men and used it to fill his canteen. Pope's canteen, he observed pointedly, was filled with cider.

Pope may have been young and unschooled, but his writings show an unquenchable thirst for improvement. He often vividly described a moment, as if to sharpen his powers of observation: "The clouds are so low down that in some places we cannot see the top of the mountain. The men are all huddled up in their shelter tents, and you may look all along the line and yet hardly see a man."

As November approached, Pope began to reckon with the oncoming winter: "It looks as though this was the beginning of the rainy season. If it is we may as well 'hang up our fiddles' ... and go into winter quarters at once, for after the rainy season once sets in, all operations cease until Spring."

An Objective Diary

Pope's diary is especially notable for his objective reportage, remarkable because even news columns of the day rarely separated news from opinion. Yet what he chose to write about often revealed a somewhat straightlaced moral philosophy. For example, leaders of the competing forces were sensitive, in varying degrees, not to pillage civilian homesteads needlessly as they made their way. But orders come from on high, and on the ground, men do what they must to survive. "The orders are not to take any rail fences for fires," Pope pointed out, "but the men take all the rails they want, notwithstanding the orders to the contrary." Typically, even to his diary, Pope withholds his opinion on the practice, but one can sense an element being added to his developing wisdom.

In America's only war on native soil, President Lincoln felt it important to be close to his troops. On one occasion, Pope witnessed the commander in chief along with General McClellan, Secretary of the Treasury Salmon Chase, and Vice President Hannibal Hamlin riding in an ambulance drawn by four horses. Pope watched in evident awe as the lanky, bearded president waved his hat to a wounded soldier.

Lincoln had been repeatedly frustrated by McClellan's failure to seize the advantage, as the temporizing general failed to obey Lincoln's order to cross the Potomac. When McClellan complained about fatigued horses, Lincoln replied, "Will you pardon me for asking what the horses of your army have done since the Battle of Antietam that fatigues anything?"[11]

On November 5, Lincoln relieved McClellan of his command of the Army of the Potomac and bestowed it on Pope's commander, General Burnside, allowing him to succeed the man who, in civilian life, had been his boss. Lincoln had twice tried to prevail upon a reluctant Burnside to accept the commission, to which Burnside felt he was not equal. Events would soon prove Burnside right.[12]

On November 9, Pope attended a church service in a country meeting house for the first time in three months, but it soon became a custom he'd follow for the rest of the war. Pope wrote that the Union soldiers seemed well received in southern churches and suggested the irony of northern soldiers fighting rebels to the death one day and joining their southern families in worship the next.

The teenager who had dined only at his mother's table was now getting a sense of how troops on the move gained their bread and butter and of his own responsibility for seeing that the men in his charge didn't go hungry:

> I went out foraging this morning, and got some milk and a chicken.... I got some butter besides, and bought some honey (of a fellow who brought it into camp) for two dollars.... The Adjutant has killed half a dozen cattle, and half a dozen pigs, besides one half. The men have got all they can eat now.

A Different Pope

As Burnside's division crossed the Rappahannock River on tree trunks laid across it, Pope was reminded that the bridges over which they ordinarily would have crossed were destroyed during the retreat of General John Pope during the second battle of Bull Run. Nowhere in Pope's diary does an entry appear confirming or denying a blood relationship with the controversial leader, and no reference to him is found in *A History of the Dorchester Pope Family* either.

Were there, in fact, a blood link, it is not one that the young lieutenant may have wanted to admit. For the general had alienated both friend and foe, not only for his ineffective leadership and blustering pronouncements, which made him a laughingstock for his troops, but for his orders to plunder southern farms and terrorize civilians. It would have made Albert Pope wince to hear the general's father, a federal judge from Illinois, described as "a flatterer, a deceiver, a liar and a trickster; all the Popes are so."[13]

Pope, hardened at nineteen in some of the most brutal battles in the Civil

War, viewed war's rigors stoically, or at least that's what he told his diary. After a forced march on November 16, he said, "Taking all things together, it was pretty hard on our regiment, fighting one day, on picket the same night, making a forced march of twelve miles the next day, and all without anything to eat for the whole day. It is what very few regiments do, but such is the fate of war."

Following McClellan's ouster, Burnside moved his dispirited troops down the Rappahannock River toward the sleepy small city of Fredericksburg. By November 18, Pope's troops were camped in an open field about seven miles outside the city. There, they would dig in for four weeks, waiting for engagement. Burnside had divided his army into three divisions, with Pope's division under the command of General Edwin Sumner.[14]

Pope was determined to make the best of things. For Thanksgiving dinner on November 27, he wrote that they ate beefsteak, hardtack (a flour and water biscuit), and cold water, "out of which we made a very hearty dinner, although I do not think we shall be troubled with indigestion, as we might have been, if we had eaten dinner at home." What pangs went unspoken as the young man missed New England's celebrated turkey, stuffing, and cranberries for the first time.

In the calm before the storm, Pope reported that the city of Fredericksburg had been "nearly deserted" by the rebels, but some of the people were left "for we can hear the church bells strike the hours…. The drums can be heard very plainly, beating in the rebel camps."

Imminent Conflict

By December 11, conflict was at hand. Pope reported:

> The cannonading was terrific all day. It was the heaviest I have ever heard, and I think beat the Antietam firing. We had a pontoon bridge nearly across this morning, when the rebels opened upon it with artillery, throwing grape, canister, shot and shell. The houses in the vicinity were filled with rebel musketeers, who poured volleys into our men, causing them to fall back with a loss of fifteen or twenty.

Some of the men received whiskey rations on December 12, and it would be the last drink of their lives. Because of troop attrition, Pope had advanced to company commander when Captain Lathrop was appointed acting major. During the day, Pope wandered through abandoned houses in Fredericksburg, finding, "Everything was ransacked, there were books in any quantity laying around. Some of the houses were furnished splendidly, having nice pianofortes and splendid paintings, and engravings, equal to some of our own houses in Boston."

Pope's next entry, with a label added later, is entitled "The Battle of Fredericksburg." By midmorning of December 13, Burnside's troops had begun firing at rebel encampments. After moving a mile along the river, rebels opened fire, and Pope's company hid behind a one-story house. At one point, he writes, "One six pound round shot struck in a beam close behind my back, and another passed through the roof, knocking down the boards, bricks and shingles on our heads.... Grape and canister shots flew around striking just at our feet, and plowing up the ground all around."

A little past noon, Pope's company began its advance up a street that led out of the city and toward temporary fortifications. At an open plain a half mile across, his troops formed a line of battle, under heavy artillery fire from the enemy. Upon order, they charged across the plain "under a galling fire from the rebel artillery. Our Major was leading us gallantly on, when he was seen to fall."

Moving into position, Pope's men "opened on the rebels, although we had no orders of any kind, and poured the bullets into them, though we could see very few, they keeping behind their breastworks, and in the woods." The company remained in place, receiving reinforcement after reinforcement, with little artillery support until nightfall, by which time, "I should think we were eighteen or twenty deep." Burnside would later be roundly castigated for "sending wave after wave to the slaughter," when he ought to have known the Confederate troops held a practically unassailable position.[15]

"The firing was deafening," Pope wrote, "and the shells burst right in my face. I was covered with dirt no less than twenty times by the bursting of shells and by shots striking the ground, and throwing the dirt up on me." They continued lying in the field until after dark, in mud three to four inches deep. Finally, he received orders to drop back. Pope reported, "I had but three men left in my company, the rest having got straggled, or killed or wounded."

Fiercest Battle Ever Fought

"This was the fiercest battle ever fought on this continent," Pope concluded. "Our men fought like tigers and the rebels the same, but they had an almost impregnable position, and kept close behind their fortifications. Our men fought all day, but could not drive them an inch." Pope criticized the lack of artillery support as "the greatest fault of the battle." In the end, the Confederates sustained 5,000 to the Union's 12,700 casualties, more than 6,000 of them dead.

Lincoln shortly before had chosen Burnside to replace McClellan, who had not been aggressive enough against Lee. Now, he despaired because

McClellan's successor was too aggressive, almost foolhardy, having ignored Lincoln's warning not to attack the heavily fortified positions of the rebel troops.[16]

Pope's immediate commanding major fell during the heat of battle on December 13 and died the next day at noon, a parting that shook the spirit of his men. His death hit particularly close to home for Pope, who revealed the depth of his fear as he wrote, "My trust is in God, and if I fall, I trust and pray, that he will take me home to heaven, where there will be no more sorrow, no more parting."

For the next two days, firing continued, albeit from more protected positions. "Our dead are laying thickly around, our men having not yet had a chance to bury them," Pope wrote, amid the stench of rotting flesh. On December 15, accepting defeat after three days of continuous shelling, Pope's troops crossed the pontoon bridge back over the Rappahannock to their old camp and a dispiriting winter.

The remnants of Pope's company ate a Christmas dinner of canned turkey, potatoes, onions, apple sauce, and mince pie. In spite of the physically grueling few months he had passed through, Pope weighed himself and found he had gained twenty pounds, having added muscle to his teenaged frame. By December 30, Pope allowed himself a rare self-congratulation. As his troops marched out of camp, Pope took command of five companies, which "is quite a command for a Second Lieut."

Bad News from the Frontlines

Pope's family back in Brookline, anxious for news of their neophyte soldier, could hardly take comfort from war correspondent Charles Coffin's dispatches in their hometown *Boston Journal*: "The winter was severe, the snow deep. The soldiers were discouraged. They knew that they had fought bravely but there had been mismanagement and inefficient generalship. Homesickness set in and became a disease."[17]

Troops in the field, however, aren't privy to the success or failure of grand strategies, only to what they can witness with their own eyes. So when the commander of the Army of the Potomac came through to review the regiment on January 6, Pope wrote, "Gen. Burnside was cheered with great spirit by the soldiers, as he rode down the line."

January offered a surreal tableau of warring troops, arms laid down in winter quarters but within shouting distance of each other and reveling to pass the time. Pope reported hearing the rebel band playing across the Rappahannock.

Albert Pope soon learned that not all casualties of war come from fighting. On January 20, a man in Company A shot off a part of his hand. "He died a short time after from the effects of chloroform, which the doctor gave him," marking the third death that week in the regiment.

Also on January 20 came word that Pope's men were to put three days' cooked rations in their haversacks and sixty rounds of ammunition in their cartridge boxes and be ready to march before dawn. Burnside, stung from the ignominious defeat at Fredericksburg, for which he admitted sole responsibility, was determined to try again. This time, he vowed to cross the Rappahannock.[18]

Fording the river proved problematic. Pope recorded:

> Major Hawks, thinking he had found a place he could ford, plunged into the stream, and called upon his boys to follow, but he soon found himself up to the armpits, and the next moment, the force of the stream took him off his feet, and he was completely submerged. Finally we succeeded in getting a log and a plank across, over which a good many crossed, myself among the number. We arrived on the picket ground at about ten o'clock, cold, hungry, wet and tired.

Burnside's plans for revenge ran up against a torrential rainstorm, which drowned his men in mud and would be known in Civil War history as "the mud march." To rub it in, rebel troops mocked the Union soldiers with signs on their side of the river reading, "Burnside Stuck in the Mud." Pope wrote, "The great movement that would have taken place if it had not been for the weather, is, I think, all a fizzle."

Burnside Falls

President Lincoln was no more impressed, as he recalled Burnside to Washington on January 26, naming Massachusetts native and West Pointer Joseph Hooker in his place. The weather underscored Hooker's clean slate by replacing soaking rain with a foot-deep blanket of snow.

On February 9, Pope's troops found war profiteering rampant, as they embarked on schooners, which had been called into action as troop transports. Pope wrote:

> I got such a supper aboard the boat, for fifty cents, as could be got in Boston for ninepence.... My boy bought me a half bushel of oysters this afternoon, for which he paid but twenty-five cents. Oysters are the only thing that can be bought here at a reasonable price.... The officers occupied the staterooms of the boat. I had one for myself and servant.

Even junior officers such as Pope regularly had servants assigned to them and, not infrequently, they were black.

Morale in the wake of one disastrous defeat after another troubled Pope and tested his resilience. His instinct, as expressed in his diary, was to counter defeatism and bolster his superiors. "I had a long argument with three or four of my men down in the cook tent about the way the war is conducted. The men were demoralized and running down the government.... I finally came off conqueror," he observed, in an interesting choice of words. "I frequently go among the men in the company and talk with them." Albert Pope was honing his powers of persuasion, which he would need later in life to persuade his countrymen to change their way of life.

Pope seems to have been shrewd enough to know which side his bread was buttered on and often reports doing favors for superiors, which would surely have ingratiated himself with them, with what meager raw materials were at hand. He made an easy chair for Captain Lathrop, for instance, out of a barrel and a shelter tent and stuffed it with hay. When the time came for promotion, such good deeds couldn't hurt.

Revelations of Himself

Pope's journals reveal him as a somewhat rigid fellow, who abjured drinking, carousing, and disrespect of authority, although he evidently could enjoy a good joke or pun. "I have stopped nearly the swearing, profane language etc. in the company, since I have been in command, about two weeks," he wrote.

Yet Pope had an acute eye for the ladies, and his diary is filled with dozens of visits to parlors of young women, who he typically described not as blondes or brunettes but as rebels or Unionists. His diary suggests that females of both sides welcomed his overnight attentions. He reported, "I met a young rebel lady at the house and went home with her to her own house." Five days later, he reports spending the evening at the home of another.

In Paris, Kentucky, Pope wrote, "I spent the evening with a rebel lady at the house of some Union people." The rebel woman must have enjoyed Pope for the next day she came down to see him off on a 22-mile march to Mount Sterling. At the end, "I was so tired that I could hardly draw one foot after the other."

On March 26, Pope's men took a steamer to Baltimore, where they boarded a train; the men were loaded into a baggage car, while the officers occupied a passenger car. They arrived the next morning at Pittsburgh, where city fathers threw a reception for the soldiers at city hall.

For reasons of security, troops seldom know the ultimate destination of their unit. "Charge the next hill" is often the limit of their orders. So, Pope's troops pressed on through Kentucky, Columbus and Cincinnati, Ohio, and then Covington, Kentucky, not realizing that they were bound for a fateful engagement in Mississippi.

Segregated in a War to End Segregation

In a war to end slavery, blacks were still kept in segregated fighting units, except when they were servants to officers such as Pope. Even then, they had to cope with the fact that the federal Fugitive Slave Act, making it a crime to harbor slaves, was still on the books.

Pope wrote:

> My negro has been very much frightened lately. His master has been after him twice. Today he saw his master in camp, and was frightened so much that he came rushing into the tent, knocked over two officers that happened to be in his way, tumbled over a valise, and made a dive under the bed, striking his head against one of the posts, but I guess that it made more impression on the post than it did on his head.... I went out tonight to see the negros dance. It is very amusing to see them. They had a fiddle and were dancing in big style. One negro keeps time with one foot and pats with his hands while another dances his jig.

In border states such as Kentucky, Union and Confederate sympathies divided communities, even families. Pope left for Lexington and stayed overnight with "my friend, Miss Ingalls," whose parents "are strong Unionists, while the daughter is as strong a Secessionist." Pope's amorous attentions would do little to change her.

On May 22, Pope reported: "I went over to a neighboring house this morning, got some milk, biscuits, etc., and sent them back by my darkey, while I stayed to see the old lady's daughter." In Covington, Pope wrote that many of his men "got drunk, thereby causing a number of rows, that had of course to be stilled by somebody. I stilled about a dozen fights, and came near getting my head broke."

Wars are not infrequently won by strategies quite apart from hand-to-hand combat, such as starving out the enemy. In this way, the Mississippi River played a strategic role in the Union Army's calculations. Although he had captured or held key cities along the Mississippi, General Ulysses Grant, by the summer of 1863, seemed unable to capture Vicksburg, Mississippi, the last major Confederate stronghold on the river.

If Union forces could accomplish this and thus control the length and breadth of the river, sympathetic states west of the Mississippi, such as Texas, Arkansas, and western Louisiana, would no longer be able to supply Confederate allies east of the river with such basic needs as cattle and grain. But when General Grant attacked Vicksburg on May 23, he sustained heavy losses while failing to capture the city.

On June 14, having moved steadily south during the spring, Pope's company encamped four miles outside of Vicksburg; its mission was to try again. While there, Pope wrote, "We passed the first negro regiment I ever saw. The place is full of contraband negros who live in little huts built of bushes. Some of the contrabands are nearly white. There are hundreds of them on the peninsula." On July 4, the city surrendered to General Grant.

Competing with Cousin George

As Albert wrote, George Pope, his cousin and, later, his business partner, was working his way up in his unit of all-black enlisted men, the Massachusetts 54th, winning promotions that would allow him to muster out at a higher grade than Albert, whose competitive nature would doubtless chafe under that reality.

Pope found the flat Mississippi country "full of snakes, bugs, ants, mosquitoes, spiders, and all kinds of insects, which crawl over you in your sleep, making it very unpleasant to go to sleep, but I suppose we shall soon get used to these things."

While war histories condense hostilities to convey the drama of its high points, soldiers living through it know that most field duty is spent in boredom and homesickness. As things turned out, Pope's troops didn't get to play a major role in Vicksburg. As they were bivouacked at roadside, other Union forces took Vicksburg with 27,000 men and 280 guns. Mississippi was sealed off from the rebels.

July in Mississippi was an experience the New Englander would not soon forget: "The heat was intense, the sun pouring down its scalding rays upon us. The heat could only be compared to a fiery furnace…. Many [men] fell down exhausted from the heat."

On July 9, Pope's troops came upon a planter's house, abandoned during the conflict:

> There was nobody living in the house, but all the furniture and household goods were left, and it looked as though the people had just left it. The men were allowed to ransack the house, and take anything they wished, among which were quite a number of barrels of molasses, pork, meal, etc. After the house was upset from top to bottom, it was set fire and burned to the ground, and all the out buildings with it.

On July 12, a mix-up at daylight caused Pope's troops to be besieged by friendly fire, until Pope was able to send word to regiment headquarters. Rebels posted themselves in trees, sniping down at Pope's troops, causing Pope to station five men in a log house to pick them off. By now, sickness and battle had caused Pope's company to dwindle to twenty-six men, of whom five had to be detailed "to guard the Lunatic Asylum."

By mid–July, Pope's troops reached Jackson, the state capital, and on July 17, the 35th Massachusetts Regiment entered the town, becoming the first northern troops to reach the state capitol building; the Confederate troops had abandoned it. One of Pope's leaders "tore down the rebel flag, and planted the stars and stripes of our regiment in its place." Northern guards were posted outside occupied houses but the men were permitted to take anything they wanted from abandoned houses, including sizable quantities of sugar, whiskey, and ammunition.

Broadening Influence

Pope, who had done little traveling before his wartime service, was experiencing and carefully chronicling differences in customs, culture, and climate from what he was used to. He gained from the South as well an appreciation of its natural bounties. "The trees that grow here are splendid. Among them are the magnolia, birch and gum trees."

Pope's narrative seems surprisingly free of either opinion or bias. In the clash of ideologies and cultures that the Civil War represented, one would have forgiven Pope for yielding to regional assumptions and biases of his youth. And yet a camera's eye view prevails. While a desire to free slaves animated the North's mission, Pope comments neither for nor against the institution of slavery; neither does he exhibit any racial bias of his own. He describes blacks as "negroes," a respectful term in a day when "nigger" was frequently employed (only once in 276 pages did Pope use the word). He did, however accept "darkies" as his personal servants.

On downtime, Pope and two other junior officers went to Vicksburg and "took a little stroll around it." "Some of the buildings were completely riddled with shot, and I saw one building where a large shot had passed through, making a hole three or four feet square."

Much of Pope's time in Mississippi was spent aboard riverboats, fighting mosquitoes and close quarters. Gambling was long a tradition on the Mississippi, and the northern soldiers, including officers, rushed to the poker tables. And here, in a rare passage, Pope does wax judgmental:

> It is a shame that the officers should set such an example to their men. I have endeavored to stop it in my company but cannot entirely while other officers allow both their men to practice it, and themselves also.... One old gambler told me that he had been gambling for fifteen years, had lost and won thousands of dollars, but had made up his mind to stop now, for he was no farther ahead than when he first began.

Replaced by Hooker, Burnside's division headed back north. In Tennessee, troops crammed into railcars so crowded that even officers had to stand:

> The engine was short of wood, and what we did have being very poor, we went very slow, until we got to Concord, which is about half way. Then Gen. Burnside got on the engine himself, gave the engineer and fireman a good blowing up, and then told them how to keep up a good fire and run the engine. The General had run an engine himself when he was a young man, and had afterwards been Supt. and Prest. of a railroad [the Illinois Central, under George McClellan's presidency].[19]

Welcome Reunion

A stop in Lexington, Kentucky, allowed Pope to reunite with the Ingalls and their rebel-sympathizer daughter, with whom he had become so smitten. In Cincinnati, Pope, who had sat on court-martial panels, experienced the other side of martial law on November 12, when he went to the front to reconnoiter a position and stopped to have breakfast with an old man who had served Pope's men well but would accept no pay. Upon returning, Lieutenant Pope was charged with leaving his post. The next day, charges were withdrawn and his sword returned. This would be the only recorded black mark on his military record, at least the only one he would report for posterity.

On November 14, the soldiers boarded trains for Knoxville. Pope's troops camped just inside the town "on a commanding hill affording a strong position." Five days later, while Pope's men were awaiting battle, Lincoln delivered the Gettysburg Address.[20]

Pope wrote on November 24:

> The troops on our left formed in line of battle this morning and advanced to charge on the rebel rifle pits. At the same time I advanced my men as skirmishers, and in about ten minutes we had cleared the rifle pits of rebels. We had a very severe skirmish for about two hours. Private Henry of my company was killed, being shot through the head.

Yet Union forces prevailed. When the Confederates abandoned Knoxville, Tennessee came under Union control.[21]

Victory must have been sweet to Pope's men as rebels put up the white flag about 2 P.M. on November 29 "to ask permission to bury the dead lost in assaulting Benjamin's Battery." And, after trying to kill one another, "the men yelling like fiends," they reverted to normal young men in the aftermath. "There were about one hundred and fifty rebels and fifty of our men talking together, and shaking hands in a very friendly manner."

The prolonged battle had left the men and their usual supply sources exhausted:

> Our breakfast this morning consisted of wheat coffee, and flour and water mixed together, and poorly baked. It turns a man's stomach to look at the bread, to say nothing of eating it. The men are still on half-rations, and so are the officers.... We have tried to forage some along the road, but the people have been cleaned out by the rebels, so there is nothing left for us.

At age twenty, Pope was developing the backbone of leadership that would serve him well as a captain of industry. "One of my guards disobeyed orders and was saucy to me," Pope wrote, "so I put him under arrest, delivered him over to the division provost and preferred charges against him."

Supplies Dwindle

Supplies and even bedding had grown scarce as the grueling war ground on. On December 15, Pope wrote, "I lay down on three rails and slept about an hour and a half, but it was too cold to sleep, for I had no blankets, as they were on the wagons which were far away on the road to Knoxville." As wearying as that was, duty beckoned; Pope reports, "We were very busy all day making out my returns and squaring up my books."

Ordered to Knoxville on regimental business, Pope found time on the day after Christmas to spend the evening "with my friends, the Misses Boyd. They are very strong Union young ladies, although cousins of the notorious rebel spy, Belle Boyd."

Pope passed the time by reading a popular book called *Hospital Sketches,* the first published work by a 31-year-old author named Louisa May Alcott, who had signed up as a Civil War nurse after reading Florence Nightingale's *Notes on Nursing,* chronicling her adventures in the Crimean War. Alcott would later win fame for writing *Little Women,* a book about her childhood.[22]

In the Tennessee hills, Pope witnessed poverty whose images would haunt him later:

> Every family in this country (no matter how large the family is) all live in one room. They have fire places large enough to take in half a cord of wood at a time, and no matter how cold it is, always keep the doors wide open, for they have no windows.... The children call their father "Pap" and their mother "mammy," they call corn cakes corn doggers.

Even a stoic such as Albert Pope, in the midst of a dreary winter, made a rare confession on January 7: "I feel blue tonight, and have been feeling so nearly all day; I suppose it is somewhat on account of the trouble I am having in making out my ordinance [sic] returns; and another reason may be, that I have received no letters from home for over a week, the mails being very irregular."

As 1863 yielded to 1864, regimental supplies dwindled. "We have commenced having only two meals per day, breakfast at ten o'clock and dinner and supper at half past four." Ever curious, Pope wrote on January 13, "I spent the forenoon in learning how to spin, having a pretty girl and her aunt for my instructors."

Much of the winter, Pope's troops spent around Knoxville, having little knowledge of what was going on in the war during that time. On January 23:

> The men drew rations this afternoon, which they were very glad to get. They have only had a pint of flour, and a small quantity of pork for five days, and the officers have not been much better provided for. I think these are the shortest rations that any army ever lived on.

To lighten its wagon loads, the regiment discarded all kettles and mess pans. On February 7: "The scurvy is beginning to show itself among our troops, and I think they are all more or less affected with it."

Short Trip Home

In mid–March, Burnside's troops moved farther north, from Tennessee to Cleveland, then to Buffalo, Albany, and Boston. On March 23, Pope stopped at Worcester to see his teenaged brother, Allen, and found his mother at the house, the first time he had seen her in nearly two years. Elizabeth beheld a heavier, more self-confident Albert than the one who had left her home to go to war. The next day, he took the train to Boston with his mother. "Went home to Brookline in the afternoon, where I surprised them all. Of course, they were all overjoyed at seeing me."

The next three weeks marked Pope's first extended leave in nearly two years. On April 13, he received orders to take a detachment of 240 recruits to Baltimore and other points. Soon after, Pope left Philadelphia for New York. The next day, a Sunday, he traveled to Brooklyn to hear a sermon by Henry Ward Beecher. In a pre-mass media age, in which Victorian scruples frowned on public entertainment, lecturers—many of them preachers—were the closest thing the times offered as celebrities.

Beecher was, by all accounts, a mesmerizing speaker, with wavy white hair that touched his shoulders and large, protruding eyes. His passionate sermons on the biological theory of evolution and on the abolition of slavery drew visitors from hundreds of miles around to his Plymouth Church of the Pilgrims in the isolated borough of Brooklyn, a generation before a graceful bridge would link it to Manhattan.

In a few years, Beecher would be embroiled in one of the most controversial trials of the nineteenth century, in which journalist Theodore Tilton alleged that Beecher had bedded his wife. One of her brother's staunchest defenders would be writer Harriet Beecher Stowe, who would be a neighbor of Pope's Hartford plant in the 1870s.

Visit to a Showman

Enjoying more downtime than he had in nearly two years, Pope also visited P. T. Barnum's New York Museum. The self-promoting Barnum had in recent years exhibited the midget Tom Thumb and the original Siamese twins, Chang and Eng. A year later, as the war neared its end, Confederate President Jefferson Davis would be captured, reportedly disguised in women's clothing, and Barnum would put on display for eager throngs the dress that he claimed Davis had been wearing.

Still in New York on Independence Day, Pope recounted a typical day of revelry: "We had a mock dress parade this morning, which was a very good thing. Then followed the foot race, sack race, greased pole, and greased pig, winding up with a dress parade, with non-commissioned officers in command."

In mid–July, Pope's men moved on to Washington, D.C., and Alexandria, Virginia, turning over 145 men to the provost marshal at Fortress Monroe. On July 19, Pope "went before Casey's board and passed the examination. I should have obtained a Colonelcy if I had been seven or eight years older; as it was I passed the examination." Pope doesn't say what rank the achievement gained him, although he mustered out a year later as a captain.

However, Captain Pope would carry a considerably higher rank into civilian life. For, after the battle of Petersburg, "an innovation was introduced which we, at first, thought must be a joke," according to a historian of the 35th Regiment, upon word that the higher-ups sought a regimental officer who had particularly distinguished himself. "The notion that meritorious conduct in battle was to receive immediate recognition from headquarters struck us as a new rule in the management of our army."[23]

Actually, five regimental officers, including Albert Pope, received honorary commissions through breveting. Pope was first promoted to major, for "gallant conduct at the Battle of Fredericksburg, Virginia," then to lieutenant colonel, for his service at Knoxville, Poplar Springs Church, and Petersburg.

While those commissions would carry no more authority or compensation, they were a mark of distinction by which many fortunate soldiers

Brevetted a colonel at the end of the Civil War, 22-year-old Albert sports sideburns—the facial hair craze of the age—named after his wartime commander, General Ambrose Burnside. *(Courtesy Albert A. Pope II.)*

would be known until they died. Albert Pope would be among many who affixed "Colonel" to his name in civilian life and expected to be so addressed. His cousin George, who had earned the actual rank of lieutenant colonel but spurned the honorific, must have been amused in later life as their coworkers referred to his cousin as "the Colonel."

On August 17, Pope reported, "The photographist stationed there took a picture of a portion of the battalion." The photographer likely was one of many assistants who, in the employ of Mathew Brady, built photographic studios into wagons and traveled with the troops, amassing some 3,500 images of the war, which comprise the great bulk of Civil War photographs and which popularized the medium.[24]

"The officers in my quarters had a regular drunken row last night, and two of them were put under arrest. I am disgusted with the crowd, and have therefore moved my quarters, and now quarter with the Adjutant, next to HQ." Nowhere in his diary does Pope suggest that he ever drank alcohol. Of course, he also was writing recollections he knew might be read by others, including his dear mother.

Lincoln's Uncertain Reelection

Lincoln's uncompromising stand in favor of abolition made his reelection in 1864 far from sure. Democrats in August nominated the 38-year-old George McClellan, who Lincoln had fired and replaced with Burnside after Fredericksburg, to face the commander in chief. As fall approached, Atlanta fell to the forces of Union General William Tecumseh Sherman, and much of the city burned.[25]

Embarking from Washington by steamer, Pope's troops engaged in heated debate over Lincoln's campaign and finally decided to take a vote. "The cabin passengers, composed mostly of officers, gave a large majority for Lincoln. But the steerage and deck passengers, composed of soldiers of the rank and file gave a majority in favor of McClellan, carried the majority, much to my regret," Pope recalled.

"We have some splendid singers among the Germans of our regiment," Pope observed in one entry, written against a background of Bavarian music. "There are about a dozen of them singing together now. It sounds beautifully in the woods especially at night.... I spend a good portion of my time in studying Rhetoric [public speaking] and like it very much."

Caught up in personal recollections, Pope's diary sometimes fails to mention where his company was located during a given conflict. Yet he was motivated by the season and the desire to refine his writing technique as he observed, "Men fell on all sides like autumn leaves, and Officers were killed in endeavoring to rally their men." Pope wrote of the fear that gripped him: "The rebel cavalry came down on one flank, and there was a fire on us from the other side. I expected nothing less than that we all should be taken prisoners."

Maturing Perspective

In hindsight, Pope demonstrated an increasing grasp of the overview required by successful military as well as business leaders, as he reflected that the nearly disastrous battle of the day before was "a poorly managed affair on our part.... we advanced right into the jaws of the rebel works. The works are in the form of a horse shoe, and we advanced in the center, so that the rebels were on either flank."

In a reflective mood on October 4, Pope admitted, "I do not like fighting. I dread going into a fight, but when I am there no one can accuse me of not doing my duty." The next day came a report from a knowledgeable local in Petersburg, Virginia, that "the confederacy is about played out." Rampant inflation had hit the region, with a barrel of flour selling for $350 and a cord of wood for $100.

Pope noted, "Ferraro's Division of colored troops have done good service, and distinguished themselves remarkably in several charges upon the enemy." "Gen. Grant is here superintending the movements in person. He rode by us with a private's overcoat on, and altogether is the plainest looking General on the field."

On Tuesday, November 8, Pope wrote ominously: "Today is the eventful day, big with the fate of America. Nations tremble at the issue. Lincoln or McClellan." Three days later, the word of Lincoln's victory reached them, "and our soldiers are jubilant over the victory."

As Thanksgiving neared, it fell to Pope to disinter all the dead that were buried within the limits of his regiment and deposit their remains in the 9th Corps burying grounds. "There were in all eleven bodies, and they had been dead nearly two months," a suggestion of the repellent task that their survivors faced. "It took us until late in the night to finish the work."

Thanksgiving came late for Pope's troops that year. Not until the Saturday after did "a large quantity of turkeys, pies, apples, etc." come to the regiment. "At night the pickets keep up a steady firing. The lines are very close, and in the daytime, our men exchange codfish for tobacco with the Johnnies [the rebels]."

Witnessing a Hanging

Desertion is always a risk in wartime, and Pope reported somberly on December 10 that "at twelve o'clock today, at the Div. Headquarters, two men were hung for desertion. Nearly a whole division was formed in a square around the gallows to witness the execution. It was a sad affair."

So short of ammunition were the Confederates that Pope reported:

> The rebels spend a good part of their time in searching after lead bullets (that we fire into their lines) for every man that collects two pounds of bullets, gets a furlough of forty-eight hours to Petersburg; and the man that gets fifteen pounds of lead, gets a furlough home of fifteen days.

Pope wrote:

> Capt. Myrick and I have a man who does all our work and small jobs. He belongs to my company, and lost one of his fingers at Antietam, so it is difficult for him to carry a gun. His name is Cleveland, but we call him Friday. He keeps at work on our cabin continually, so that now it looks quite comfortable. Capt. Myrick and I spend our evening's [sic] studying Rhetoric and playing checkers. Then I read a sermon, after which we turn in.

On December 23, 1864, came an early Christmas present: word "through rebel source" of the capture of Savannah. Two weeks later:

> There was a flag of truce this morning, and during its continuance, one of the rebs jumped over their works and ran into our lines. The rebels did not fire at him, but when he had reached our lines, waved their hats in approbation. No doubt some were wishing he were they.

Thirst for Knowledge

Whether honing his skills as a diarist, learning how to manage men, or poring over books sent from home, young Albert was to knowledge as a sponge is to water. At twenty-one, he had reached the age at which he would have graduated from college had he attended after high school. A reader of his diary senses that, as an autodidact, he had kept pace with collegians of his age while gaining a layer of practical wisdom they lacked. If his family could not afford to send him to college, Pope would send himself.

In January, Pope received the *Cyclopedia of Biography* he had sent for, a useful choice for an ambitious young man seeking role models for success in life. The next day came a dictionary and "an algebra" from home. Two years prior to the publication of Horatio Alger's first book, *Ragged Dick,* biographies were the major source of inspiration for young men on the rise. "I am getting quite a collection of books here."

Later that month, Pope matter-of-factly reports that a panel on which he sat court-martialed a man for desertion, and the execution took place that day. On February 20, by telegram, General George Meade, who had succeeded Hooker as commander of the Army of the Potomac, announced the evacuation of Charlestown, South Carolina, by the rebels and the capture of Columbia, South Carolina, and Waynesboro, North Carolina, by Union troops. "The Confederacy is doomed," Pope concluded.

On March 19, "Nearly all the line officers came down to my tent this P.M. and I read them a sermon. Then Lieut. White and I argued religion for about two hours. I was the only officer present that was evangelical, and the only professed Christian officer in the regiment."

Sensing the End

With the Confederacy's increasingly porous intelligence, Union forces sensed their battlefield lives would soon end. "A rebel deserter came in tonight and I talked to him in my Sergeant's tent. He expressed his opinion that the rebel cause was about 'gone up.'" On March 2l, indicating the confidence a study of rhetoric had given him, Pope wrote, "I made an extempore speech on 'The Crisis of the Rebellion,' and had nearly all the line officers for auditors."

On April 3, Pope's troops found the city of Petersburg evacuated and occupied it that morning. While they were there, President Lincoln, Secretary of State William Seward, and Admiral David Porter rode by on their way to the city. "They were rec'd by the soldiers with rounds of applause." Soon, the soldiers received official notice of the capture of Richmond, capital of the Confederacy.

On April 10 came word that "Gen. Lee had surrendered at two o'clock P.M. of the 9th of April at Appomatox [*sic*] Court House. Cheer upon cheer rent the air, and both officers and men were almost wild with enthusiasm." On April 12, "Three or four of our officers went out beyond the picket line, to visit half a dozen young ladies of strong rebel proclivities. We stayed an hour or two, and kept up quite an interesting conversation."

On Sunday, April 16, came the word that President Lincoln had been assassinated. Pope wrote:

> The news filled the whole army with profound grief at the dire calamity, for never was a president so beloved by the army as he. The soldiers are full of rage at the disgraceful affair, and if they could lay hold of the assassin, would tear him to pieces. The country could not suffer a greater loss at this time."

May 20 was Pope's twenty-second birthday. He marked it by traveling north through the nation's capital, where he dined with a friend from Boston at Willard's, then and, as of this writing, now a fashionable hotel. With the war effectively over, Pope's troops headed home to Massachusetts: "Arrived at Providence at seven A.M. Was received with the 7th R.I. by the State Authorities and partook of a collation."

Pope spares any ceremony in ending his diary:

> Started for Readville on the half past ten train, and arrived at noon; drew tents from the Quartermaster for the men, and a wall tent for the Officers, and soon had the camp pitched. Rode over to Brookline in the afternoon and got home at about four P.M.

Less than three years after he had left, Albert Augustus Pope returned to Boston, with a massive catalog of life's lessons he'd now seek to employ in the wider world. Not the least of the assets he'd brought home was the battlefield commission of "Colonel," a mantle which may have hung a bit heavily over the shoulders of the 22-year-old but into which he'd grow quickly during the next decade.

Notes

1. *Boston of Today*, p. 351.
2. Interview with William Pope, Sr., September 15, 1998.
3. *Encyclopedia Brittanica*, vol. 1, p. 29.
4. *Columbia Encyclopedia*, p. 2497.
5. *Boston of Today*, p. 351.
6. Most of what follows is excerpted from Pope's "Journal of the Southern Rebellion." Since it was privately printed and is not otherwise available, no page designations are supplied.

7. Catton, Bruce, *This Hallowed Ground,* p. 162.

8. Foote, Shelby, *The Civil War*, vol. 50, p. 696.

9. Catton, p. 168.

10. Foote, p. 749; Davis, Kenneth C., *Don't Know Much about the Civil War,* p. 261.

11. Davis, p. 262.

12. Ibid.

13. Foote, p. 527.

14. Davis, p. 262.

15. Ibid., p. 267.

16. Ibid.

17. Ibid., p. 270.

18. Ibid., p. 278.

19. Ibid., pp. 278–79, 149.

20. Ibid., p. 313.

21. Ibid.

22. Ibid., p. 250.

23. Committee of the Regimental Association, *History of the Thirty-Fifth Regiment Massachusetts Volunteers, 1862–65,* p. 394.

24. *Columbia Encyclopedia,* p. 352.

25. Davis, p. 391.

CHAPTER 4

HE CASTS HIS LOT

*A lady of rare discernment and quiet decision of charac-
ter, who taught her son the habits of economy, order and
method.*[1]
Biographer's description of Elizabeth Bogman Pope

$\mathcal{A}$s ALBERT POPE SLOGGED through the final days of the southern campaign, a new graduate of Harvard Divinity School basked in the glow of rave reviews for his first novel. The positive response encouraged him to move to Manhattan, where in 1867, he created a genre so powerful that it would bear his name, Horatio Alger. *Ragged Dick or Street Life in New York* was the first in a series of Alger's formula novels, in which a young man born to poverty perseveres cheerfully against overwhelming odds to gain riches and fame.

In publishing, then and now, timing is everything. Colonists had, during their first two centuries in the New World, sifted into a social stratification hard for a newcomer to penetrate, in spite of the sweeping egalitarian principles set forth earlier in the U.S. Constitution. Since the 1840s, a steady stream of immigrants from Ireland and Western Europe had settled in coastal cities but found the doors to their advancement locked. But now, through Alger's rags-to-riches tales, the newly arrived who had learned to read English found role models, who demonstrated that anything was possible. Alger, an outspoken social reformer, had created a path of righteous behavior which would, if followed, land a little ragamuffin in clover rather than in jail.

Alger, by then an ordained minister, addressed a need that others of the cloth approached by transplanting urban street orphans from broken homes to stable families on American farms. "Orphan trains" moved 150,000 urchins from eastern tenement districts to the opening American West in the half century following the Civil War.

The Horatio Alger novels were wildly popular from the late 1860s through the end of the century, and the way in which young Albert Pope carved out his post–Civil War career suggests that their message was not lost on him—not as an exemplar for his own behavior necessarily but as a model he could create for those who followed him. The 22-year-old colonel showed a public-spiritedness that would carry on through his life; in later years, he claimed, notwithstanding evidence to the contrary, that public benefactors begin their giving early or not at all. But one suspects that Pope was motivated by a good deal of self-interest as he burnished an image of himself as a rags-to-riches success story. The daily press and the popular magazines gushed praise for Horatio Alger models as America's new heroes, equal to those who had recently risked their lives to save the Union.

Useful Title

Albert had already begun to use his Civil War honorific of "Colonel," understanding, as generations of war heroes before and since have, that a grateful populace is eager to elect to office or to give their business to a man who fought for their freedom. A generation or more before the field of public relations evolved, Colonel Pope would create in his management offices a publicity department, which churned out reams of press releases not only about his products but about the virtues of the man who made them.

The official Pope line claimed that an eager nine-year-old hired himself out to till fields after school to help support his father, mother, and seven siblings, who had been devastated by Charles's "financial reverses." Nowhere did he spell out just what the nature of those setbacks were. However, they had continued, and the able lad was forced to quit high school altogether at age fifteen to help put bread on the table. After serving gallantly in the Civil War, publicists wrote, Colonel Pope built a small fortune in the shoe-finding industry before becoming the world's largest bicycle manufacturer and making Hartford, for a time, the automobile capital of the world. And all this from a high school dropout. Could Horatio Alger have written a better script?

So goes the Pope myth. And while it is undeniably true that Albert quit school at fifteen to work at bustling Quincy Market, a study of his life suggests that his well-connected wider family helped him get ahead and that his leaving school had less to do with providing for his needy family than with perceiving that he could go further, faster on his own. For when the returning soldier climbed the steps to his Brookline home in 1865, he was preparing himself to embark on a career that would not only provide for his family but bathe him in luxury. Erect, fit, and handsome, with bushy sideburns caressing his long cheeks, Pope was without question one of Boston's most eligible bachelors. Croquet was sweeping the nation, and young women who had read its lengthy set of rules in the *Nation,* would have loved the chance to play a match in their backyards with the young colonel.[2]

But marriage and diversion would have to wait. Albert's first responsibility was to his parents, long diminished in substance as well as stature, and for his siblings, many of whom showed promise under Elizabeth's doting attention and encouraging hand.

Albert had saved $900 from his Civil War earnings, a goodly sum for a young man in that era. Were education so important for this ambitious lad, one would have expected him to finish his high school education and go on to college, as scores of Popes before him had done. Instead, he invested the money in his first business, located on Boston's Dock Square, making slipper decorations and artisans' tools for the shoe industry, which had become one of Boston's larger employers. On his own for the first time, Pope boasted proudly that his initial $900 by year's end had become $9,600. Pope adopted his regiment's motto, "Promptly," as the watchword for his new enterprise. Within five years of its creation, the business would be the largest of its kind in America.[3]

Pope now had a grubstake worth more than $100,000 in year 2000 currency, which would allow him to attend school full time, to become an engineer, a physician, or an attorney. Yet not only did Albert choose no further schooling, he began to make his resources available to educate his siblings.

Doctors in Skirts

For a family to produce a daughter who aspired to become a physician in the male-dominated 1860s was unusual to say the least. For a family to raise two may have been without precedent. Albert, who lacked even a high school education, took it upon himself to put his twin sisters through college, a gesture whose generosity neither would ever forget. He would also support his youngest brother, Louis, through Brown University and Newton Theological Seminary.[4]

In the 1860s, when most young men still did not attend college, women undergraduates were few and far between. Yet Elizabeth Bogman Pope was not one to sit by quietly while her children, whatever their gender, were denied access to their dreams, suggesting a turn of mind one would have to call radical for the times. Indeed, Albert Pope talked of himself proudly as "an independent of the most radical type" and attributed much of his success in life to his mother. It may have been she who decided to invoke the name of the first Roman emperor by giving the middle names of Augustus to Albert and Augusta to one of her twins, who eschewed her first name, Caroline, and became known as C. Augusta.

The siblings who flocked to greet Albert adoringly upon his return from the war included 30-year-old Charles, who had already married and entered the hardware business; 28-year-old Adelaide, who taught in the Brookline public schools; 19-year-old twins Emily and Augusta, brimming with intelligence and ambition; 15-year-old Arthur, whose visits to Albert during the war lifted his spirits and who would join him in the shoe supply business; and 13-year-old Louis. A sister, Mary Elizabeth, had died as a teenager.

One sign of the possible estrangement of Charles Pope's family from the lumbering Popes is that none of his seven surviving children would choose as their livelihood the industry that had made the family wealthy and prosperous. Cousin George, Albert's childhood playmate, hadn't grown up in the same climate of alienation and would follow the many other Popes into lumbering before finally joining Albert in Hartford, working many years at his side in the bicycle and automobile industries.

Albert, the young entrepreneur who shunned formal education for himself, apparently venerated it for others. Institutions of higher learning, such as Boston's prestigious Massachusetts Institute of Technology, would be among his beneficiaries, during life and after. Perhaps he had come to realize that his business instincts themselves were enough to propel him high in life and that several years in a classroom would only delay his quest to make his fortune. After all, Albert's Civil War service was a college education of its own. Not only did he learn firsthand how to motivate, control, and reprove men under pressure, but he had honed his skills by writing a book-length diary and maintaining the records for his regiment.

Sisters on the Cutting Edge

Emily and Augusta were, in fact, triply blessed. Not only did they have a "radical" mother and a brother with the resources to send them both through medical school, but their training culminated just as a highly unusual institution was born. Far from the norm, the New England Hospital welcomed women doctors with open arms. Founded in the 1860s by the legendary Marie Elizabeth Zakrewska, the single-minded daughter of a Prussian officer and the descendant of Polish aristocrats and agitators, the New England Hospital was staffed largely by female physicians. Having been brought up as a radical freethinker, Zakrewska welcomed young women such as Augusta and Emily Pope, whose upbringing had taught them they could move mountains and whose ambitions cut against the grain.

"The teachers disliked me," Zakrewska wrote later, "because I would not obey arbitrary demands without being given some reason ... and because I insisted on following my own will when I knew I was right."[5] In New

England, she won the admiration of other windmill-tilters, such as abolitionist William Lloyd Garrison, who described Zakrewska as a woman of "decided opinions and the frankest speech."

To say Zakrewska was difficult to work with would be an understatement. However, none of her colleagues could doubt the sincerity of her passion. Of her first mentor, Emily Pope would write fondly, "It [New England Hospital] was the Object of her most intense affection, the child of her prime and of her old age. Through every Vicissitude, from the poverty of its beginning to the time in 1900 when she rejoiced with us at the opening of our beautiful new surgical building, it was her pride and joy."[6] Emily and Augusta were part of the original cadre of physicians with whom Zakrewska worked, after they had returned from Europe, where they had gained clinical experience at hospitals in Paris, London, and Zurich, no doubt at Albert's expense.

Rather than feeling jealousy at his sisters' accomplishments, academic attainments this high-school dropout would never savor, Colonel Pope seems instead to have burst his buttons with pride. He became a benefactor of their hospital and, in at least once instance, helped select applicants.[7] In gratitude to the hospital's absolutely essential role in their professional development, the Pope sisters and their pioneering colleagues devoted their entire careers to its mission. By 1876, only thirty-three years old, they had risen to leadership positions within the hospital and would serve on its Board of Physicians for more than twenty years.[8]

Being admitted as equals into the male medical fraternity was quite another matter, and so they established their own society for women doctors, the New England Hospital Medical Society, whose meetings were a far cry from those of their male counterparts. "There was a feeling of home-iness about the meetings," Emily would recall later, "as most of the members saw each other frequently. ... Hands used to being employed often busied themselves making tampons."[9] Their persistence to win acceptance into the profession paid off in 1886, when Emily and Augusta were among the first handful of female physicians accepted into the Massachusetts Medical Society. They opened the floodgates, and by 1903, their number had risen to seventy.

Painful Ties

Charles had been a favored Pope name since the 1700s. Albert's father was named Charles and, according to custom, he bestowed it on his firstborn, whose younger brother, Albert, affixed it to his fifth child.[10] Yet only one of Albert's six children chose it for his own progeny. Perhaps the name was unfortunately tied to Albert's father's inexplicable fall from wealth and from family grace. In 1868, Albert Augustus's oldest sibling, Charles, a world adventurer and gold hunter, watched his wife die shortly after childbirth, only to expire himself during Thanksgiving week a year later, at age thirty-three. Family lore has it that the Prince Albert tails that Charles was wearing became caught under the wheels of a train, dragging him under and severing a leg. Rushed to Massachusetts General Hospital, he developed an infection and died, leaving orphans aged seven and four.[11]

Albert shared the devastation of the family at the loss of his brother. Yet, as became typical of his reaction to need, he took the unusual step of adopting seven-year-old Harry Melville Pope, raising him, sending him through the Massachusetts Institute of Technology, and gathering him into the Pope industrial flock, where Harry spent many years as a mechanical draftsman.

Albert had long had a wanderlust, which made it impossible for him to content himself with being simply a prosperous local merchant and small-parts manufacturer. Perhaps the breadth of his Civil War experience had whetted an appetite which he moved to satisfy as the 1860s drew to a close. As developers of Boston's Commercial Wharf, the extended Pope family traveled far and wide in pursuit of trade. Now, Albert relied on those traveling family members with whom he was on good terms to aid him in importing articles from far corners of the globe to supplement his sales of shoe supplies. Operating under the name of the Pope Manufacturing Company, Albert also began to develop and sell small patented articles, such as an air pistol and a cigarette-rolling machine.

Strong-Willed Bride

Albert's twin sisters graduated from medical school in 1870, and although he still had his youngest brother, Louis, to look after, the successful merchant decided it was time to seek a life partner. The words "strong-willed" and "capable," which were used so often to describe Albert, could be applied in equal measure to Abigail Linder, daughter of George and Matilda Smallwood Linder, who lived in the increasingly prestigious Boston suburb of Newton. George Linder had emigrated to America from Britain as a young man and had done well as an importer. A contemporary source described him as "a well-known and much respected merchant."[12]

As the New England maple leaves burnished from green to gold and russet in the fall of 1871, Albert took his bride. Abby gave support to the notion that men look for a wife who emulates the best virtues of their mothers. She was a supporter of the Boston Symphony, was an ardent believer in

Abby Linder Pope, with whom the Colonel had six children, shuttled her family between the townhouse on Boston's Commonwealth Avenue and their 50-acre seaside estate in Cohasset, on the city's south shore. Rarely, if ever, did she travel to Hartford. *(Courtesy Albert A. Pope II.)*

women's rights, and belonged to the Women's Industrial Union, a challenging affiliation for a wife of the captain of industry. Yet indications are that the Colonel greatly admired his wife and her accomplishments. Also bear in mind that this is the capitalist who backed Sam McClure, the founder of muckraking journalism, either a sign of foolhardiness or of great self-assurance.

Children came soon to the Pope household. In an indication of either Albert's fondness or of Abby's assertiveness, all children but one would bear Linder as their middle name. Albert Linder made his appearance in 1872, followed by Margaret Roberts in 1874, Harold Linder in 1879, Charles Linder in 1881 and Ralph Linder in 1887. Mary Linder died in infancy.

The growing family filled a sprawling Victorian house in Brookline, with plenty of nooks and crannies for the children to play in. There, Abby nurtured her brood, including one who, she feared, would never grow up. When her back was turned, the Colonel would encourage young Albert to climb onto the dining room table and run the gauntlet through the family's fine china and crystal glassware, as his father laughed uproariously.[13]

The Colonel loved the bustle of family life and of entertaining, often adopting—literally and figuratively—additions to his family. In addition to legally adopting Charles's son Harry, he would from time to time take in young charges to care for, according to his great-grandson and namesake. His extended family was always welcome in Boston or Cohasset, where later the Popes would summer, a circumstance which drew the consternation of Abby when guests overstayed their welcome.[14]

One indication of the health of the enterprise created by the 29-year-old businessman came in 1872, when a massive fire swept through Boston's downtown. While structural steel had only recently made its appearance, most downtown buildings were still constructed of wood and highly vulnerable to windswept flames. Fire insurance, an innovation introduced earlier in Hartford, wasn't yet widely used. Pope's uninsured loss amounted to $60,000; he reportedly was able to pay it off within two weeks of the fire.[15]

By Pope's thirtieth birthday, he was not only financially self-sufficient but an employer of family members as well, including cousins George and Edward and brother Arthur, his junior by seven years. By age thirty-two, he called himself a millionaire, no small feat in a day when a working man earned less than a dollar a day.[16] When the Colonel decided to leave Boston in later years, it was Arthur he would tap to assume the presidency of his shoe supply firm.

But shoe findings, air pistols, and cigarette rollers, as lucrative as their trade might be, would never make Albert a world-class manufacturer. Entering his fourth decade, Albert plainly felt a need for something more in life. As the mid–1870s approached, that something would fall, quite without warning, into his lap.

Notes

1. Powell, William H., Ed., biographer's description of Elizabeth Bogman Pope, in *Officers of the Army and Navy Who Served in the Civil War*, p. 103.

2. Lupiano, Vincent de Paul and Ken W. Sayers, *It Was a Very Good Year: A Cultural History of the United States*, p. 130.

3. "Colonel Albert Pope Dies of Pneumonia," *Hartford Courant*, August 11, 1909, p. 1.

4. Interview May 8, 1999, with Albert Pope II.

5. Drachman, Virginia G., *Hospital with a Heart: Women Doctors and the Paradox of Separatism at the New England Hospital, 1862–69,* p. 23.

6. Ibid., p. 41.

7. Ibid., p. 150.

8. Ibid., p. 107.

9. Ibid., p. 126.

10. *A History of the Dorchester Pope Family* lists ten Charles Popes within the family line.

11. Interview September 28, 1999, with Elizabeth Bohlen.

12. Selected Book Master, p. 75.

13. Interview September 9, 1999, with William Pope, Sr.

14. May 8, 1999, interview with Albert A. Pope II.

15. Obituary, *Boston Post*, August 10, 1909, p. 1.

16. Interview May 8, 1999, with Tina Pope Rowley.

CHAPTER 5

WHEELS FOR ALL

*We expect no contradiction from any except those who
do not know, when we say that for dispelling dullness,
nervous depression, and sluggish circulation, for restoring a happy glow to the body and freshness to the mind,
the bicycle surpasses any devices of man, or any creature,
except a horse of at least sixfold its cost.*
                                        Seminarian Louis Pope

FOR THE BRAWNY, can-do nation into which the thirteen American colonies
had evolved, 1876 offered a rare interval of introspection, as Philadelphia, the cradle of liberty, hosted the Centennial Exposition, which showed
off to enthralled consumers the wares of the Industrial Age and those that
lay around imagination's corner.

That America's centennial called for the largest exposition in world history was a foregone conclusion. With a main structure costing $4.5 million,
the big show sprawled over 236 acres and had an electric railway circling
the grounds, dropping off and picking up passengers.

To mark the occasion, the exposition's organizers had commissioned the
celebrated German composer Richard Wagner, fresh from completion of the
Ring cycle, to write a "Fest Marsch," which would open the exposition on
July 4 and mark the celebratory arrival of President Ulysses Grant. The work
was a grave disappointment to everyone, including the composer, who com-
mented, "The best thing about that composition was the money I got for
it." Just as well that President Grant canceled at the last moment.

The attendees salved their wounds by listening to tenors croon the new
Irish song, "I'll Take You Home Again, Kathleen," a tip of the hat to the
proliferating immigrants from the Old Sod. Strains from rousing popular
concerts filled the fairgrounds, as France's comic-opera composer Jacques
Offenbach led an orchestra that included a 22-year-old musician named John
Philip Sousa.[1]

Not only did the inventors of machines that would shape the coming age strut their peacock plumage for the admiring throngs but so did their describers, as if the press needed to reach new heights of eloquence to match the unparalleled accomplishments of the inventions they profiled. In the cavernous Machinery Hall, which stretched over thirteen acres, were displayed a telephone, a typewriter, a mimeograph, and a huge, 2,500-horsepower Corliss engine that George Pullman would later purchase for his sleeping-car factory.

Dean of American letters William Dean Howells wrote of it:

> The Corliss engine does not lend itself to description. ... It rises loftily in the center of the huge structure, an athlete of steel and iron with not a superfluous ounce of metal on it; the mighty walking beams plunge their pistons downward, the enormous flywheel revolves with hoarded power that makes all tremble, the hundred life-like details do their office with unerring intelligence."[2]

Speed and Verticality Prevail

Henry Bessemer's blast furnace had shown the world in recent years how to convert molten pig iron into steel, and Elisha Otis had cooked up a contraption called an elevator to lift passengers into the sky. The two inventions together created critical mass, enabling the skyscraper and the vertical city of the twentieth century, in whose aeries businesspeople would soon communicate with each other by another invention of 1876, the telephone.[3]

And on the ground, the railroads in the forty years previous had transformed the notion of travel, letting people take a one-day round trip to a distant city that used to take days to reach by horseback. America was drunk on the ale of Manifest Destiny, which proclaimed the country's God-given right to claim the continent, from sea to shining sea; its restless people would soon find confining the idea of fixed tracks and schedules.

It wasn't surprising then that the hit of the Centennial Exposition was the velocipede, an ungainly metal skeleton with a solid rubber front wheel as tall as a short man and a back wheel as small as a basketball. Ironically, it was imported for the occasion from the country the colonists had vanquished a century earlier, a nation which called the contraption a penny-farthing.[4]

Ten million citizens swarmed through the exposition grounds that hot summer, many with copies of a popular new novel titled *Tom Sawyer* tucked under their arms. Industrial leaders came as well, seeking ever-new practical applications of the new technologies. Among them was Boston businessman Albert A. Pope, 33-year-old owner of a modest plant in Boston, manufacturing shoemakers' tools and supplies. Tall and full-bearded, Pope had not yet attained the girth that businessmen of the age emulated as a sign of prosperity.

If the Carnegies and Rockefellers were called captains of industry, Pope would rank at best as a second lieutenant, although he would have been pleased to have you call him an industrialist. He would have been even happier if you addressed him as "Colonel."

Not Yet a Household Name

Pope would pass through the grounds largely unnoticed in July 1876, yet within a decade his name would be on the lips of common folk from coast to coast. For the Civil War veteran, whose import business had already taken him to the far reaches of the world, was on a quest to redeem his family name.

If perchance he had bumped against a lanky attorney and engineer from Rochester in the crowd, Albert would have been hard pressed to identify George Selden, even though Selden was on the same quest for cutting-edge ideas as Pope. Yet, within a generation, the fortunes of the two men would intersect in a way that would change their lives forever.

The Colonel had taken the train from Boston for the occasion. Baseball's new National League had just inaugurated play that spring, and if Pope had wanted to live dangerously, he might have ribbed Philadelphians that his team beat the City of Brotherly Love six to five in its celebrated first contest the month before.[5]

Pope swung through the exhibits, was fascinated by the velocipede, then visited the others. But he found himself drawn back time after time to the strange contraption, unable for the life of him to figure out how one would ride the thing.[6] Yet, while some visitors saw bicycling as an offbeat pastime, Pope's vision went far beyond, to a day when travelers could burst the strictures of the railroad and journey when and where they chose.

So taken was Pope by the velocipede that he embarked soon thereafter for England to visit the British factories that made them. Rightfully suspicious of would-be competitors seeking trade secrets, the first factory turned Pope away. Exhibiting what successful nineteenth-century capitalists liked to call derring-do, he and his party disguised themselves as workmen and slipped through the gates.[7]

Pope's English friend, cycle maker John Harrington, visited the United States the next year and taught his American cousin to maneuver the high-wheeler, no small feat for the uninitiated, and manufactured for him an experimental model. Pope was so impressed that he ordered eight Duplex Excelsiors for study and sale in his Boston factory, at a price of $313 for the 70-pound vehicle, not much less than a buyer would pay for a Model T automobile a generation later.[8]

Pope Captures the Patent

Sold on the concept, the Colonel set about in 1877 to obtain the basic bicycle patent, so he could produce them himself without shelling out royalties to the patent holder. Pierre Lallement, who had invented the basic concept in 1865, had been frustrated in his attempts to market them in America and had sold out his rights to Calvin Witty for the price of a steamship ticket back to France. Witty set his royalty claims so high that he made it impossible for anyone to manufacture velocipedes at a profit. By the mid–1870s, half the patent rights had ended up in the hands of Richardson and McKee Company of Boston with a Vermont carriage maker owning the other half.[9] To control patent rights, Pope knew he'd have to acquire at least a majority interest.[10]

And here Pope demonstrated the cunning that he'd need to succeed in the laissez-faire economy of the late nineteenth century. He knew Richardson and McKee intended to actively use the patent, so he offered them a sum beyond their wildest dreams to buy half of their one-half interest, representing a one-quarter interest in the patent itself.

Richardson and McKee may have taken Pope for a rube, as they knew that the one-quarter interest they and Pope now each held was worthless without adding to it the half-interest the Vermont firm owned. Pope knew full well that Richardson and McKee would attempt to use the proceeds from his purchase to buy out the Vermonters.

So, completing the transaction at the end of the workday, Pope dashed to the train station and climbed aboard the night train to Montpelier. First thing the next morning, he burst into the offices of Montpelier Manufacturing Company with an offer it couldn't refuse for its one-half interest. No sooner had the parties inked the purchase agreement than a letter arrived, containing the anticipated offer from Richardson and McKee. But it was too late; Albert Pope owned a three-quarter interest in the basic bicycle patent.[11]

Within a year, eager to test the American market for the new toy, Pope shrewdly set about to find a company that could turn out a test order of fifty velocipedes, rather than risk his own modest fortune on retooling his shop for a venture that might fail. In Hartford, a hundred miles to the south, he found his opportunity.

Sewing Machines to Bicycles

Few industries at the close of the Civil War were healthier than the manufacturers of the sewing machine. From the 1840s to the 1860s, inventors had captured a series of patents for such innovations as the stationary bobbin, automatic feed, and foot treadle, each improvement making it easier for home-makers to use. Just as Elias Howe and Allen B. Wilson seemed set to exploit their contributions to the field, they were beset by Isaac Merritt Singer, whom one historian has called "a hot-tempered, arrogant and profane Lothario, who sired twenty-four children by five different women, only two of whom he ever married."[12]

Singer was more eclectic than inventive, but he had combined the most advanced features of the day into a machine destined to dominate the market. Yet Howe, driven to penury by patent wars, still held the basic patent, and he forced Singer to pay him $28,000 as well as $10 for every machine he sold.[13]

Into this world of cutthroat competition and overproduction strode T. E. Weed in 1865, clutching a patent all his own. Weed had supplied the Colt Armory as an outside contractor, and several of his key lieutenants had worked there.[14] He leased a sprawling complex of four-story, red brick factories, formerly the home of the Sharps Rifle Manufacturing Company, at 436 Capitol Avenue in uptown Hartford. Within a few years, Weed became a regional player in a city already leading in firearms, leather belting, silk textiles, and machine tools. Yet by 1878, overproduction and competition had so enervated Weed Sewing Machine Company that whole wings of its noisy production floor had fallen silent.

One spring day in 1878, Albert Pope packed his velocipede onto a railcar and rode from Boston to Hartford's brownstone Union Station. He jumped astride the high-wheeled contraption and pedaled uphill along Hartford's bumpy earthen streets to Weed's plant, as gleeful boys and girls raced to keep up with the machine, so strange it might have come from Mars. Pope had come to Hartford to meet George Fairfield, president of Weed, a company which had gained a reputation for skilled machinists and efficient production in a day when the routinized production line was yet a dream.[15]

Fairfield convinced his recalcitrant board of directors to let him sign a contract to manufacture fifty bicycles, which Pope would sell at September's Framingham (Massachusetts) fair.[16] In the weeks ahead, Fairfield might have asked himself, "What have I done?"

"Weed encountered one difficulty after another," recalls historian Ellsworth Grant, "learning to forge the head, shaping the rims of the wheels properly so as to hold the tires, finding a cement to bind the latter to the flat sides of the rims, fabricating the handlebars and cranks without brittleness (by using Norwegian iron)." The finished product, which became the first commercially self-propelled vehicle in America, Pope called the Columbia, a name whose mention would trigger grandfathers' memories of childhood for generations to come.

Sales at the fair went so successfully that Pope decided to order more

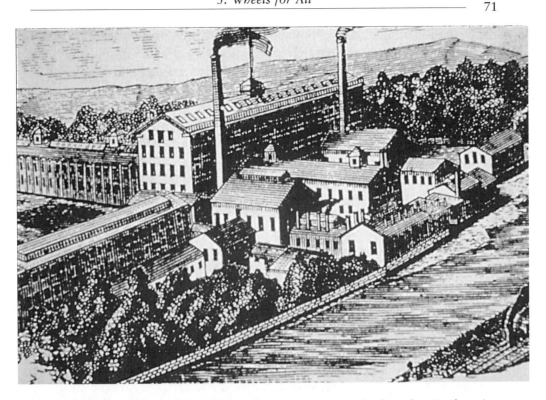

During the late 1870s, sewing machine industry declined, leading the Weed sewing machine plant on Hartford's Capitol Avenue to devote its excess capacity to manufacturing Columbia bicycles for Pope. By 1890, the Colonel would buy the plant outright. *(The Connecticut Historical Society, Hartford, Connecticut.)*

from Weed. As the decade wore on, the Weed Sewing Machine Company would make fewer and fewer sewing machines and more and more bicycles. In 1878, Pope imported nearly half of the ninety-two bicycles he sold. But by 1880, he had turned out 12,000, with back orders of 2,500, and his workforce had grown to 350.[17] He added to his operations in Boston as well, expanding his sales showrooms, hiring cousin Edward Pope as a bookkeeper, and establishing a riding school at 87 Summer Street, headed by Will R. Pitman.[18]

By 1881, as the ascending trend lines of the bicycle intersected the sewing machine's descent, Colonel Pope gained corporate control of the Weed Sewing Machine Company, although a formal merger of the Pope and Weed companies lay far in the future. The news of the take-over caused Weed stock to soar from $5 to $75 a share.[19] In the reorganization, urbane 30-year-old George H. Day, a Connecticut Yankee who prided himself on being a direct descendant of revolutionary war general Israel Putnam, became Weed's president.[20]

A biographer of Colonel Pope must linger over the name George Day, for as mild-mannered and self-effacing as he was, Day would become a key to the Colonel's rise as the moving force in the bicycle and automobile industries. Born in eastern Connecticut two years after Pope, he dropped out of college at age twenty-five and took a job with the Charter Oak Life Insurance Company. Polished and engaging, Day was at the top of dinner party invitation lists of the best homes of Hartford. Day's marriage to Katherine Beach, daughter of one of the pillars of the Hartford community, only enhanced his social standing.

Day endeared himself to his patron by not only proving a loyal and resourceful administrator but by developing a zeal for the bicycle itself, as founder of the Connecticut Bicycle Club. "He is never too busy to greet a visitor," associates said of Day. Soon he was implored to run for mayor and then lieutenant governor, petitions he politely but firmly rejected. Day, it was said, "is one of the most extremely modest men in the trade."[21]

Change Overwhelms Beantown

The Boston that Pope had left in 1876 on his fateful journey to Philadelphia had changed beyond recognition from the city that had hosted a Tea Party 103 years earlier. Horse carts jammed the streets, "giving the air a rich equine flavor," especially on days when stablemen pitched manure into gardeners' trucks to take it away.[22] Immigrant throngs from Ireland and Europe had overwhelmed the town, with orphans begging by the thousands on the streets as the gentry hid fearfully behind lace curtains on Beacon Hill.

In a wonderful example of New England ingenuity, Boston's State Street entrepreneurs devised a way, in one stroke, to clear their streets, find the orphans homes, and further their own economic interests. Many had invested in the same railroads to which Congress had granted charters in the 1860s to settle the West. Sustaining settlements in the "great desert" would be difficult, they realized, without a burgeoning population to create a market for goods that the railroads could then supply. And so, in 1876, the Unitarian community of Boston sponsored the first of 3,800 children who Boston would send west as "orphan train riders" to live with farm families west of the Mississippi.[23] They were among the first of 150,000 such urchins "placed out" in the West during the next half century. Pope watched the process and internalized the lesson that one could do well by doing good.

Bicycle's Roots

The strange contraption on display in Philadelphia traced its origins back to 1817 and the invention of a wooden walking machine, which had wheels front and back, wooden spokes and rims held together with steel bands, and a crossbar over which the rider would hover, using his feet to propel the thing along the ground. Known as a "dandy horse" or "draisine," it was introduced by Baron Karl Drais von Sauerbronn, chief forester of the Duchy of Baden, to speed his inspection tours. With a solid steel body and ivory handgrips, it became a favorite toy of the rich but didn't do much to propel a man any faster than he could stride.[24]

The Hanlon brothers from New York introduced a front fork which allowed the axle and pedal crank to be easily lubricated, with a slot in the arm so the length could be adjusted to the length of the rider's legs. The firm of Pickering and Davis in New York lightened the frame by using hollow tubes instead of solid steel bars and introduced the "self-acting brake," whereby a rider could push against the handlebars to compress the seat spring, causing the brake shoe to engage against the rear wheel.[25]

Still, by the 1870s, only the British were producing bicycles. James Starley introduced his "ordinary," characterized by the size of its huge front wheel with a rear wheel just large enough to maintain balance. By 1878, 50,000 ordinaries were in use in Great Britain.[26]

Henry Bessemer's blast furnace, which could convert pig iron to steel, had enabled metal to replace wood in bicycles by 1870, but the product still lacked a way to allow the wheel to turn without pedaling. The velocipede was a precarious ride at best for its pilot, perched above the high front wheel and vulnerable to "take a header" if he sat too far forward on his seat or if the front wheel collided with an uneven surface. Not for nothing were the early velocipedes called "boneshakers."[27]

The Threatening Bicycle

Nineteenth-century America assimilated change no better than any other age has. As ungainly conveyances entered public thoroughfares, a public outcry arose from those who feared being run over, as their horses reared up in fright when these skeletons on wheels sped by. Attacks by dogs led cyclists to carry small syringes that squirted diluted ammonia, to discourage canine predators.[28] Soon, local governments responded to public pressure and banned velocipedes from city streets and parks.

But if cities could ban bicycles in public parks and streets, then the national fad that Pope foresaw would die aborning. The Colonel, therefore, spent $8,000 defending his industry against attacks by local governments, including an injunction that had been filed against three cyclists who challenged New York City's 1880 ban against bicycle riding in Central Park.[29] Actually, Pope had staged the infraction, knowing an arrest would move the

A riot of Pope's high-wheelers converge at the busy corner of Main and Pearl streets in Hartford during the 1880s. *(Courtesy Dr. Tracey Wilson.)*

dispute into court, where rationality, not political passion, should hold sway. Unfortunately, he lost the case and subsequent appeals. Finally, Pope turned to Albany, where the state legislature in 1887 passed a law giving bicycles the same rights accorded to carriages.[30]

Recognizing that the best defense is a good offense, Colonel Pope decided to fight fire with fire and set up the Boston Bicycle Club; one of its goals was to challenge restrictive ordinances. Clubs, such as the Knights of Columbus, the Elks, the Moose, and the Masons, were the current rage. Henry James had written in 1879, that the best things come, generally, from the talents of members of a group, so Pope was tapping into a vein of contemporary sentiment.

Creating for the sport a positive identity, with mottoes, chants, and characteristic clothing, gave the bicycle clubs an investment in fighting those who would challenge their right to be on the road. The movement spread, and by 1880, forty bicycle clubs had organized in New England, New York, and Pennsylvania.[31] Clubs sponsored bicycle parades in Hartford and 75-mile tours, such as the Wheel Around the Hub Tour in 1879, in which cousin George, brother Louis, and Weed's George Fairfield joined to prove their mettle. After cycling over rutted dirt roads for a few miles, they stopped and took

Colonel Pope happily subsidized bicycle rinks and velodromes, where weekends featured popular races by celebrity bikers, events that stimulated spectators to buy Pope bicycles. *(The Connecticut Historical Society, Hartford, Connecticut.)*

a group picture in which the Colonel stands, arm outstretched commandingly on the frame of a high-wheeler, wearing a riding cap, his tie tucked into his shirt, and long trousers.

Mad about Bikes

Since bicycles cost several months' pay for a worker, the sport at first was limited to the elite. New York's Michaux Cycle Club, named for the French bicycle inventor, included the Vanderbilts and Goulds among its members. With American roads so bumpy and velocipedes so sensitive, bicycling initially was forced indoors, and the club named for Pierre Michaux leased a former armory on upper Broadway. While newcomers repaired to dressing rooms to outfit themselves in the latest bicycling attire, other members rode to the accompaniment of a brass band.

Some cycling clubs rode at night and used Japanese lanterns to light their way and adopted their own distinctive yells of warning. One stunt exhibition featured Annie Oakley from Buffalo Bill's Wild West Show, who traded in her horse for a high-wheeler and, dressed in buckskin and a cowgirl hat, shot at glass balls with her rifle.[32]

Pope's horizons, even in the early days, went far beyond Boston. He already had set up agencies in Buffalo, Philadelphia, Chicago, Louisville, and San Francisco,[33] and in 1880, he went national. In May of that year, Newport, Rhode Island, hosted a grand parade of a hundred cyclists as part of its Decoration Day ceremonies, and Pope seized the moment of festive hoopla to announce the formation of the National League of American Wheelmen. No mere sportsmen these, for Pope proclaimed a loftier goal.

The Wheelmen, he declared, would create the symbolic infrastructure for a sea change in American life, as they lobbied for a lifestyle in which roads, not rails, became the primary arteries of American recreation and commerce. Not only would they press their state legislatures to improve roads, but they would serve as the point men of a new culture by publishing maps and endorsing hotels and taverns along the road. They would shine a spotlight on road dangers that needed correcting and fight tolls on bicycles. In short, they would be the first to assert and defend the freedom of the American road, a mantra that would be echoed fervently by the automobile industry, not yet even in existence.

Obstacles to Overcome

When Pope's people in the 1880s asked themselves just how far the bicycle would go, they spoke not of a vehicle's range but of an industry's future. Would the market be limited to a few thousand well-to-do sportsmen, riding highly calibrated, expensive machines? That might offer the Pope companies a comfortable success, but might the bicycle have the potential to become a pastime for the masses? In that case, wealth beyond measure would be theirs for the taking.

Four major obstacles stood in the way of Pope's dream of a bicycle in every garage: price, weight, flexibility, and road quality.

By 1880, the Weed factory had already succeeded in shaving the price of a bicycle dramatically. While the imported Duplex Excelsior from Britain sold for $112.50, Pope's version of the same model sold for $90.[34] And yet, in an age when a family man earned $1,000 a year or less as a factory hand, bringing home a new bicycle would certainly land him in the doghouse. Pope knew from experience that producing larger lots would inevitably reduce unit costs, and as demand grew, more people might be willing to pay for the new luxury. By the turn of the century, increased competition, mass production, and new technologies would cut the price of a bicycle in half.[35]

Pope knew that a bicycle weighing seventy pounds, practically speaking, would limit his market to sturdy men. But experiments with tubular steel in Britain had discovered that heavy-gauge metal was needed only at the stress points and not throughout the vehicle, a development that eventually lowered the weight of British racing bicycles to twenty-two pounds.

If weight meant only the strong could ride, so did the fact that the pedals of the early ordinary connected directly to the wheel axle. The larger the front wheel, the faster it could go, but working up momentum required good quadriceps. By the 1880s, geared bicycles were developed, in which pedals were connected to the wheel by chains. This made a high front wheel irrelevant, since chain-driven bicycles could attain the same speed with smaller wheels. And so was born the "safety" bicycle, its very name expanding the market beyond daredevils.[36]

Out of Pope's instinct to absorb the companies that made bicycle components and to gather his research and development forces around him, Pope set up his own metallurgical lab on Capitol Avenue, hard by his Bicycle Riding School, where the in-crowd happily paid fifty cents admission to learn how to ride the latest thing.[37] Harold Hayden Eames, a former naval engineer who would manage Pope's Tube Department, suggested incorporating nickel into a steel alloy for bicycle frames, an innovation that contributed to the industry's weight-loss program by helping to trim a bicycle's weight by 40 percent.[38]

Even with gearing and lightweight metals, the bicycle continued its war against metal's natural enemy, friction. Pope directed his engineers to find new ways to limit the places that metal surfaces touched, for by reducing friction and thus resistance, wheels could turn more easily, widening the bicycle market to women and children. By the late 1880s, manufacturers were experimenting with ball bearings, caging tiny steel balls in an angular grooved track; their rolling action reduced friction. A fellow Massachusetts Civil War veteran, George Simonds, had perfected a method to mill the smooth, hard spheres of steel down to within a few ten-thousandths of an inch of one another. Until Simonds, ball bearings had to be cut one by one on a lathe or screw machine, an unrealistic process for a bicycle, each of which required a hundred or more to operate smoothly.[39]

The Weed factory now turned out 5,000 bicycles a year, requiring a half million ball bearings. It went against Pope's nature to buy these components from others, so he began to manufacture them in-house. In a few years, industrial spies would infiltrate the Pope empire, and the Colonel would find himself again embroiled in patent wars.

No Place to Ride

Perhaps even more important than price, weight, or flexibility was the abysmal quality of American roads compared to those in Europe, which had enjoyed a history of road building dating back to the Roman Empire, which had used road building as a tool of military conquest.[40] While Romans had used stone to pave the 350-mile Appian Way three centuries before the birth of Christ, American roads outside cities were largely muddy, rutted troughs.

"American roads are among the worst in the civilized world, and always have been," fulminated Colonel Pope in a pamphlet he published, entitled "Highway Improvement." "I hope to see the time when all over our land, our cities, towns and villages shall be connected by as good roads as can be found." To illustrate his point, Pope paved a short stretch of macadam road along Columbus Avenue in Boston "to show people how wonderful a smooth pavement could be."[41]

Understanding that his fortune depended upon changing the fundamental mindset of Americans, the high school dropout financed courses at Boston's Massachusetts Institute of Technology to develop road engineers, and he persuaded the Commonwealth of Massachusetts to set up a highway commission to improve the roads. In addition, Pope's League of American Wheelmen published *Good Roads*, a periodical that spread Pope's gospel and served as a clearinghouse for efforts to lobby state legislatures and Congress for good roads.[42] By the 1890s, Pope's efforts resulted in most states and the federal government creating road-building programs.

Raw Recruit

Into this industry, striding rapidly but clumsily to invent itself, Sam McClure walked in 1882. Fresh out of college, the young writer arrived in Boston to look for work with only $6 in his pocket. "Every boy in the West knew the Pope Manufacturing Company and the Columbia bicycle. The Pope advertisements were everywhere," he later wrote.[43] When he had landed nothing after several days of pounding the pavement, McClure took the trolley to Scollay Square and walked to Pope's brick offices at 597 Washington Street. Romanticizing the moment in later years, McClure recalled it was a clear fresh day, "where even in summer the air often has a peculiar flavor of the sea."

In spite of the faddish popularity of bicycles in 1882, only 20,000 had been sold in the United States.[44] Within a dozen years, however, the number would rise to a million. As he walked through the office doors, McClure could sense the energy of a new industry. Expecting to deal with a clerk at Pope's office, McClure found himself ushered into the suite of Colonel Pope himself.

The interview got off to a rocky start, as McClure told Pope he was here because of an ad. Pope brushed him aside, saying he was buying no more ad space that season and returned to reading the papers on his desk. McClure pleaded that he had nowhere to go and no job. Pope looked up and appraised the young man, perhaps reflecting on the financial insecurity of his own early days. "Willing to wash windows and scrub floors?" he asked the young college graduate. McClure, without hesitation, said yes. But Pope had only been testing the new recruit; he had better things in mind for Sam McClure.

"Has Wilmot got anybody yet to help him in the downtown rink?" Pope called to an associate. "Very well," Pope said, telling McClure he could work at the bicycle rink the Colonel had built to increase interest in the sport. What Pope didn't tell the youth, who had never been astride a high-wheeler, was that his job would be to teach riding.

McClure later described his plight as "the predicament of the dog that had to climb a tree." Somehow, in two hours, he taught himself to stay atop the ungainly conveyance and received $1 for his first day's work. Because no one said, "don't come back tomorrow," he showed up again, and by the end of the week he had so impressed his supervisors that Pope put him in charge of the uptown rink.[45]

McClure might have carved out a permanent career as a bicycle instructor were it not for his boss's anger at the media. When the League of American Wheelmen decided to import bicycles for their own use, Pope, who until then they had revered as an icon, told them they'd need a license from him. The magazine *Bicycle World* lashed out at this arrogant demand, causing the Colonel to yank his ads.[46]

A Better Job

Teaching bicycling wasn't exactly what the young collegiate editor had had in mind, but it was a job. So he was thrilled when Pope, recalling Sam's college training, summoned him to the office and asked if he could edit a magazine. "I could edit a monthly," said the young greenhorn, adding with candor, "I hardly think I could manage a weekly."[47]

The 35-cent newsstand price of most magazines of the day had placed them out of McClure's reach, but now he took as his model the *Century*, an established publication that ran such writers as William Dean Howells, then working on *The Rise of Silas Lapham,* his novel of class conflict in Boston.

Authorized to hire his brother, John McClure, and John Phillips, Sam set up shop at 608 Washington Street, a block from Boston Common and hard by the Pope headquarters, while the three men shared a garret apartment for $4 a week. While the two Johns laid out the magazine and sold ads, Sam rode trains to New York, Philadelphia, Baltimore, and Washington, searching out writers who could attract readers to the fledgling publication.[48]

Enthusiastic buyers of high-wheelers, Mark Twain among them, either took riding lessons or bought instructional manuals on the proper ways to mount, ride and dismount a Columbia bicycle. Here is an illustration from one such manual. *(The Connecticut Historical Society, Hartford, Connecticut.)*

Pope was not content to simply print articles about the sport but determined instead to integrate bicycling into the zeitgeist of the 1880s. The Colonel wanted "an interesting, valuable and profitable magazine," McClure later recalled, that would "weave the bicycle into the best in literature and art."

McClure called to his boss's attention the fact that the *Century* had run an illustrated article on bicycling entitled "A Wheel around the Hub." Pope sent him to Manhattan to buy plates of the article and the rights to republish it, which McClure bought for $300. He then proceeded to crib the magazine's format and fonts for the rest of his magazine's first issue, to the consternation of the pirated magazine.[49]

Only two months out of college, Sam published volume l, number l of the *Wheelman*, with eighty pages of text and wood engravings in an era before halftone photographs emerged. It carried a newsstand price of twenty cents.

The *Wheelman* was an instant success, capitalizing on the dual popularity of bicycles and magazines. Bicycling was one of America's first outdoor pastimes, and magazines published in America had grown fivefold since the Civil War; by 1885, 3,300 periodicals would be in print.

Sisters to the Rescue

McClure had only been at work a few months when he fell seriously ill. Pope's twin sisters, fledgling physicians Emily and Augusta, heeded their brother's call to look in on his stricken employee. Together they swished up the stairs in the floor-length skirts of the day, to Sam McClure's tiny apartment, found their brother's young charge "well advanced in typhoid," and sent him to the hospital.

Although McClure's compensation would become a rankling issue between him and his mentor before Sam's departure a year later, Pope ordered a private hospital room for him and, McClure recalled, "paid all my hospital expenses as well as my salary during the time I was ill."[50]

In 1883, the busy young editor met a girl he wished to marry. Before taking his vows, he shared the news with his mentor, who had become somewhat of a surrogate father to him. "Marry!?" Pope exclaimed, in mock horror. "When you're so young? You'd better wait a while." Sensing his young charge was unconvinced, he added, "Remember your Bible. Remember Jacob and Rachel."

"I've already waited seven years," protested McClure.

"But Jacob saved for fourteen years," Pope said in triumph. "You see? You don't know your Bible."

Not to be outdone, McClure shot back, "Jacob married two sisters. I'm marrying only one." "Routed on exegetical grounds," noted McClure's biographer.

Pope raised his salary to $15 a week on the spot. Yet McClure was already earning $35 a week as a freelancer for such publications as *Harper's Weekly* and *Modern Age,* and the lure of a larger city had entered his blood.[51] Though he earned only $2,000 a year at the time, McClure remarked to an associate, "I shall be married next month and able to keep my wife nicely in Cambridge in a beautiful home."[52]

McClure Settles Down

Sam McClure married Hattie in 1883 and moved with his new bride to a frame starter house at 22 Wendell Street in Cambridge, where the sight of grapes ripening on the vines covering their back verandah aided McClure's recovery. It was a glorious chapter in their lives, with Sam challenged by his work and Hattie stimulated by Shakespearean plays starring Edwin Booth and lectures by Matthew Arnold at Harvard.

In 1883, Pope bought another magazine, *Outing,* and combined it with the *Wheelman.* S. S. McClure, as he had taken to calling himself, was still in his early twenties, but he had known heady experiences, which confirmed his own worth. His work attracted job offers from *Scribner's* and the *Century,* which at first he turned down. But when Pope told McClure that he would have to share editorial control of the merged magazine with W. B.

Howland, the former publisher of *Outing,* Sam balked and left Pope's employ to work for his model of perfection, the *Century,* in Manhattan. Roswell Smith, its publisher and "a very solemn, severe old man," told McClure, "I shouldn't think it any robbery to steal you away from Colonel Pope at your present salary."[53] Yet the paths of McClure and his early mentor would cross often again in the years ahead, to their mutual benefit, as McClure became one of America's leading publishers.

Pope not only spawned his own magazines, but he bankrolled other writers of like mind, such as attorney Charles Pratt, who wrote the popular book *The American Bicycler,* which would excite laypeople's imaginations in much the same way as *The Joy of Running* would a century later. Intense, with wireless glasses, a bushy dark mustache, and a receding hairline, Pratt was a morose man who could speak ten languages and "desperately needed exercise." He would become one of the Colonel's key aides-de-camp while continuing his law practice. He moved into Pope's Boston headquarters and remained there until ill health forced him to curtail his schedule in the 1890s.[54]

By the early 1880s, Albert Pope was the acknowledged leader of the bicycle industry, but 300 other companies were nipping at his heels. In a move to stay ahead of the competition, Pope introduced in 1881 the Columbia Warrant, its name trumpeting the product guarantee it offered against defects in use.

Seeking to stay on top, Pope set up a "branch house" in New York City, seeking to capture the business of the swells as well as the attention of the New York press. And, to demonstrate the durability of the Expert Columbia, Pope hired Thomas Stevens in 1884 to ride it from Oakland, California, to Boston, 3,700 miles in 103 days.

Technologically, Britain was still superior to America and turned out a better product, but a protectionist Congress had succeeded in subjecting foreign bicycles to a 35 percent tariff, allowing domestic models to flourish. By 1884, the year Pope established a branch office in Chicago, the bustling plant on Capitol Avenue was turning out 5,000 bicycles a year and creating the "second era of American cycling."[55]

The "In" Thing

Pope instinctively understood people's need to be identified with the "in" thing, and his League of American Wheelmen catered to that need, sponsoring parades and bicycle tours. To be seen on a bicycle was to be au courant, following the lead of such notables as Diamond Jim Brady, House Speaker Thomas B. Reed, and U.S. Supreme Court Justice Edward D. White.

The Chinese ambassador to the United States fell in love with the bicycle and could be seen pedaling down Washington streets, his flowing silken robes trailing behind him.[56]

Just as the running boom a century later set off pitched debates about the medical benefits and hazards of the sport, so too did some doctors declare that bicycling offered excellent conditioning while other colleagues warned it would cause permanent nerve damage to hands and feet. Bending over the handlebars while riding, one doctor counseled gravely, would produce "a nation of humpbacks."[57]

Pope saw in the medical pronouncements a way to persuade the yet unconvinced that bicycling was indeed good for you, so he offered cash prizes to doctors who wrote the best essays about the benefits of cycling. In so doing, Pope proved himself unusually astute in gauging the public pulse and learning what motivates people, paving the way for fellow Bostonian Edward Bernays, who a half century later would elevate such insights into the science of public relations, relying not a little on the teachings of his uncle, Sigmund Freud.

By the mid–1880s, Britain's Queen Victoria had been on the throne for a half century, and her strict moralisms had permeated her own people and Americans as well. So the need to adopt more informal dress while riding a bicycle offered a welcome change from a more formal way of life.[58]

Indeed, the bicycle changed fashion trends. By the 1890s, the Sears catalog featured ladies' "bicycling suits" with skirts at midcalf.[59] "Voluminous petticoats gave way to the divided skirt or bloomers topped by colorful jackets with leg o'mutton sleeves. Men appeared at their offices in knickerbockers, knee-length stockings, gay sweaters and peaked caps."[60]

By 1885, demand for the bicycle had reached an all-time high, and innovators on both sides of the Atlantic raced to develop refinements that would give them a competitive edge. New Jersey inventor George Pressey sought to reduce "headers" by reversing bicycle wheels so that the small wheel was in front, and he used a pair of independent treadles that drove a ratchet mechanism.[61]

In 1885, an American bicycle was patented, using a beveled shaft rather than a chain to power the rear wheel. To promote it, bicycle racer Marshall "Major" Taylor, America's first nationally recognized black athlete, used the model to set a number of records.[62]

Such innovations suggested America might be ready to overtake the British in technological supremacy. But then the British unveiled a new product, the Rover, which featured a triangular frame and a rear wheel driven by a chain and sprocket. By removing the pedal from the axle, the British determined to make the chain drive the industry standard. By 1886, they were exporting the Rover to America.

Once more, Pope scoffed at the coming thing only to embrace it later, as he had once declared the high-wheeler would remain the industry's big seller.[63] Having dismissed the safety bicycle a few years earlier, Pope now raced to the head of the parade, introducing his Veloce in 1888 and, two years later, shutting down production of the high-wheeler.[64]

Bicyling World reported in 1887, "The rear-driving safety has come to stay, and while it is bound to run the old timer [high-wheeler] for honors on the road, it can never hope to crowd it entirely out."[65] But crowd it out is exactly what it did—and fast.

Family lore has it that the Colonel became a millionaire at age thirty.[66] If so, in the twelve years after that, it appears that he multiplied that figure several times over. Ironically, he dabbled early with real estate speculation, which had been his father's ruination, buying his first lot in Brookline several months before mustering out of the Civil War. He bought several more in the next few years in Brookline and Needham.[67]

By 1885, Pope was in his early forties. As his family expanded, he and Abby outgrew their home in Brookline and moved to Newton, where Pope served one term on the town council, the only elected office he would ever enjoy. Now, with four children (Mary Linder had died in childbirth in 1874) and planning more, it was time for another relocation.

Move into Town

While the in thing for prosperous businessmen in the 1850s had been to move to the new streetcar suburbs, for those who wished to float to the top of Boston society, "the way to get in was to buy a town house on Commonwealth Avenue," which sported a treed center esplanade based on the Paris model.[68] The move made sense; it would be a ten-minute carriage ride from the Washington Street corporate headquarters.

As blooms erupted on the first azaleas in the spring of 1885, the six Popes moved into a four-story, red brick townhouse at 378 Commonwealth Avenue, a short walk from Kenmore Square and the Algonquin Club, in which Pope would become an active member. With a broad center entrance and multi-floor bay windows on either side, the move signaled the Colonel's arrival in the top ranks of the industrial elite. The Popes purchased the home from a trust headed by Henry M. Whitney, who years later would be the Colonel's next-door neighbor in Cohasset and would introduce him, fatefully, to his brother William Whitney.[69]

Thomas Edison had electrified lower Manhattan three years earlier, but residential electric lighting wouldn't come to Boston until 1910. At dusk, the Pope's household servants would turn on the keys to gas chandeliers and wall brackets. They might wave through the massive front windows to the public lamplighter, who arrived on their corner as darkness set in, with a long pole capped by a spark at its tip, which would ignite the streetlights.[70] A dense network of streetcars comprised the horse-drawn trolley system, whose operators used one bell to signal horses to stop and two bells to start. Streetcars' colors signaled their destination, with Brookline cars painted pale blue, for instance, and Dorchester's a royal purple.[71]

A brisk, 20-minute walk from the plant to the Commonwealth Avenue townhouse might well have proved irresistible to the Colonel on a mild, sunny day. Yet, given his disinclination to exercise, it is likely that he rode in his carriage far more often, perhaps perusing papers or drinking in the rich scenery.

Soon after clip-clopping down Washington Street, his carriage would reach Boston Common, with its cornucopias of plantings tended by armies of gardeners. A right turn and a quick left would put them onto Commonwealth Avenue,

Double bow-fronted brick townhouse at 378 Commonwealth Avenue, Boston, would house the growing Pope family during their formative years. Years after Pope's death, the Harvard Club next door would annex the building. *(Photograph by Stephen B. Goddard.)*

where a riot of variegated lintels, arches, and colonnades vied for attention with the profusion of mountain laurel, rhododendron, and forsythia.

Bending Metal to Their Will

Since the dawn of time, people had teased metallic ores from the earth's crust, with only modest success in putting them to practical use. But metallurgy had taken a quantum leap in 1856, when Britain's Henry Bessemer discovered that blowing cold air through a huge tub of molten iron caused the impurities in the ore to separate out, leaving steel as the residue. So it followed that the next generation of inventors would labor hard to work this malleable metal into products that commerce had begun to convince the consumer were needed.[72]

One of the great hotbeds of American metalworking proved to be on Hartford's Capitol Avenue, where the Sharps Rifle Company yielded to the Weed Sewing Machine Company, which, as sewing machines peaked, gave way to the Pope Manufacturing Company, which, in turn, would sell out to Pratt & Whitney Machine Tools. Sharps, having supplied Civil War weaponry, pioneered in developing metal parts that could be used in more than one tool or product, and the blue-domed Colt Armory a mile away further refined the idea of interchangeable parts to its own profit.[73]

Pope's metallurgical lab, for its part, developed frames and hydraulic pumps useful for mass production, improved automatic screw machines and the turret lathe, "while single-purpose machine tools for making pedals, hubs, spokes and so forth became common."[74] Pope's lab succeeded in achieving tolerances machined to two-thousandths of an inch—"hitherto undreamed of fineness."[75]

Inventors on both sides of the ocean endeavored to make a lighter, safer, more comfortable product. Overman's Victor line built on Irishman John Dunlop's pneumatic tire by marketing "cushion tires," which were lighter and more yielding than solid rubber. Another American innovation was the coaster brake, which one activated by pedaling backward.

But even Pope had to concede in 1886 that the English were unlikely to surrender their edge in bicycle production any time soon. "As yet," he noted, "labor and material are cheaper with them though we have the advantage of using machinery more generally."[76]

Lawyer's Bonanza

Pope actually had more to worry about in his own backyard than from across the Atlantic. Patents for American manufacturers had become dual-purpose instruments, which served both as shields and bludgeons. Pope's purchase of the Lallement patent gave him the right to charge a $10 tax on every bicycle manufactured. But in the rough-and-tumble world of laissez-faire commerce, his competitors continually contested his right to charge it, keeping Pope's stable of patent attorneys working long hours.[77]

Pope turned to attorney/engineer Hermann Cuntz whenever he had a knotty patent problem. A fierce supporter of Pope, Cuntz defended his boss's need for aggressive patent protection:

> The Pope company had a rapidly mounting investment in development with a profitable market in some years to come, the public to be educated and many uncertain factors. Protection for that "in the red" period with the hazard of successful models being copied, lay in patent protection, insurance for the costly pioneering.[78]

For example, no sooner did the firm of Jeffrey and Gormully introduce their Rambler model than a sheriff sent by Colonel Pope swooped down with a lawsuit, alleging they had infringed on Pope's patent for the crank and pedal. After several years of pitched battle, however, Jeffrey and Gormully prevailed.[79]

As every litigant knows, letting a case go to trial is an admission of failure by the parties to settle their dispute and move on. A steely-eyed pragmatist, Pope kept his lawyers constantly at his elbow and was not averse to using the courts. But the record shows he nearly always managed to settle a case before putting it into the hands of a judge or jury and, thereby, losing control of its outcome.

One notable exception concerned the Overman Wheel Company. Pope prided himself on the quality of his Columbia bicycles, but with twenty-five inspectors conducting 500 inspections on each product, he needed to charge the $125 each bicycle sold for. Inevitably, a competitor would try to shave its price to garner the purchases of working people, who earned an average of $1 a day. That is what Albert Overman, a local manufacturer, set out to do in the early 1890s.

Pope must have known such a challenge was coming, but what was he to do? Ignore the threat and tout his product's quality? That was simply unacceptable for the largest bicycle maker in America, but he'd be damned if he'd stint on Columbia quality either.

A third choice occurred to him. Soon, a new corporation, the Hartford Cycle Company, began operations, with the goal of going head-to-head with Overman by selling lower-quality products. If you asked the Colonel who was behind Hartford Cycle, he'd shrug his shoulders. But if you read his mail, you'd soon learn the truth.

Pope had dispatched trusted aide D. J. Post to cozy up to Overman employees, to learn how many bicycles the company turned out. Post reported back to the Colonel that he might convince some Overman employees to work for Pope, workers who would bring with them inside information on Overman's cost-cutting methods.

"We should not think it is advisable for us to do it," Pope wrote Post in 1891, "but the Hartford Cycle Company is another organization, of which the public are in the dark as to the ownership." Transferring his chief operatives to the new enterprise would be risky, since they were already well known in Hartford circles. So Pope lured his cousin George back from Montreal, where he had been working in the family's lumbering business, and dispatched nephew Harry Pope, an MIT graduate, to become plant superintendent.[80]

Damaging price wars among competitors, fought with Darwinian ruthlessness, had left the carcasses of steamboats, railroads, and manufacturers strewn by the wayside earlier in the century. Now the parties feared that another fight to the death was likely to ensue. Mobilizing their lawyers, Pope and Overman grappled for three years, each side spending more than $10,000 a year. No subject was too trifling to litigate, as the parties circled each other like lions, grappling over seventeen separate patents, before attorneys for both sides counseled their clients to sign what David Herlihy calls the "Treaty of Springfield."[81]

The ascent of the American bicycle from the workshop into American garages came during two periods of popularity a decade apart. In the first, well-to-do sportsmen strove to be seen astride their pleasure craft, while their wives and children looked on. In the second, with the advent of safety bicycles, rubber tires, and headlamps, Mom, Jack, and Jill jumped onto their gleaming, less pricey new models and created the second, vastly more profitable bicycle age.

Notes

1. Lupiano, Vincent de Paul and Ken W. Sayers, *It Was a Very Good Year: A Cultural History of the United States,* pp. 153–55.

2. Schlesinger, Authur M., *The Almanac of American History,* p. 331; Lupiano and Sayers, p. 153.

3. Lupiano and Sayers, pp. 153–55.

4. Grant, Ellsworth, *The Miracle of Connecticut,* p. 212; Norcliffe, Glen, *Popeism and Fordism: Examining the Roots of Mass Production,* p. 268.

5. Lupiano and Sayers, pp. 153–55.

6. Grant, p. 212.

7. Courtney, Steve, "Oh, Wealth," p. 15.

8. Adams, G. Donald, *Collecting and Restoring Antique Bicycles* p. 6; R.F.S., "The Great Bicycle Delirium," p. 62; Grant, p. 212.

9. Grant, p. 51.

10. Courtney, p. 15.

11. Ibid.; Epperson, Bruce, "A Model of Technological Dissonance," p. 4.

12. Grant, p. 195.

13. Ibid., p. 196.

14. Epperson, p. 12.

15. Grant, p. 196.

16. Ibid.

17. Epperson, p. 4.

18. Untitled paper by Albert A. Pope II, delivered at Cambridge University, September 3, 1994.

19. Burpee, C.W., *History of Hartford County, Connecticut, 1633–1928*, p. 527.

20. Ibid., p. 528.

21. *American Wheelman* profile of Day, April 8, 1897.

22. Morison, Samuel Eliot, *One Boy's Boston*, p. 23.

23. Holloran, Peter C., *Boston's Wayward Children: Social Services for Homeless Children, 1830–1930*, pp. 45–47.

24. Herlihy, David V., "The Bicycle Story," p. 50.

25. Ibid., p. 51.

26. Ibid., p. 52.

27. Hoehne, M., "Hoehne Papers," p. 1.

28. Kelly, Fred C., "The Great Bicycle Craze," p. 72.

29. Herlihy, p. 52; DePew, Chauncey M., *One Hundred Years of American Commerce*, p. 551.

30. Norcliffe, p. 269.

31. Depew, p. 551.

32. Kelly, p. 71; Herlihy, p. 51.

33. *Bicycling World*, May 1880.

34. Kelly, p. 72.

35. Herlihy, p. 59.

36. Ibid., p. 53.

37. Ermenc, Christine, talk on bicycle history, Connecticut Historical Society, August 29, 1999.

38. Nevins, Allan, *Ford: The Times, the Man, the Company*, p. 187; also comments from civil engineer Theodore Terry in October 1999.

39. Kanigel, Robert, *The One Best Way*, p. 265.

40. Goddard, Stephen B., *Getting There: The Epic Struggle between Road and Rail in the American Century*, p. 44.

41. Lewis, Tom, *Divided Highways: Building the Interstate Highways, Transforming American Life*, p. 7.

42. Ibid., p. 8.

43. Epperson, p. 6.

44. Lyon, Peter, *Success Story—The Life and Time of S.S. McClure*, p. 34.

45. Ibid., p. 35.

46. Epperson, p. 6.

47. McClure, S.S., *My Autobiography*, p. 148.

48. Lyon, p. 40.

49. Ibid., p. 36.

50. McClure, p. 156.

51. Lyon, p. 47.

52. McClure, p. 43.

53. Ibid., p. 47.

54. Epperson, p. 6.

55. Herlihy, p. 52.

56. Kelly, p. 71.

57. Ibid., pp. 71–72.

58. Ibid., p. 72.

59. Brown, Carrie, *Pedal Power*, p. 15.

60. Kanigel, p. 265.

61. Herlihy, p. 55.

62. Ibid., p. 59.

63. Ibid., p. 55.

64. Norcliffe, p. 269.

65. Ibid., p. 56.

66. May 8, 1999, interview with Tina Pope Rowley.

67. Norfolk County Courthouse Registry of Deeds, Dedham, MA.

68. Morison, p. 63.

69. Suffolk County Courthouse records, Boston, MA.

70. Morison, p. 19.

71. Ibid., p. 27.

72. *Columbia Encyclopedia*, p. 284.

73. Grant, p. 196.

74. Nevins, p. 187.

75. Ibid., p. 189.

76. Herlihy, p. 59.

77. McClure, p. 146.

78. Epperson, p. 19.

79. Rae, John, *The American Automobile Industry: The First Forty Years*, p. 14.

80. Correspondence between Albert Pope and D. J. Post, 1891, Connecticut State Library; Epperson, p. 35.

81. Herlihy, p. 59; Epperson, p. 35; Overman Wheel Co. et al. *v.* Pope Manufacturing Co., Circuit Court D. Connecticut, 1891.

CHAPTER 6

MILKING THE MARKET

I am naturally a lazy man, as far as athletic exercise goes and I think if I can enjoy the bicycle, almost anybody else can.[1]

Colonel Pope

Burned to the ground. Wire instructions.
Albert Linder Pope, Telegram

D. J. POST SEEMED to spend his life on the train. Yesterday in Niagara Falls, today in Detroit, tomorrow in Chicago. His boss, Colonel Pope, called him proudly, "my traveling man." And his fellow travelers regarded him with respect, for Post sold a product that everyone yearned for.

D.J. could tell you the name of the latest model that had just come off the line at the Hartford factory. If he broke bread in the elegant dining car with a couple on vacation, he'd make the man's eyes light up with tales of how fast Columbia's racing safety bicycle could go. As the lurching train jostled the water in their crystal glasses, he would then romance the man's wife by telling her about the smooth ride of the new Ladies' Safety, with cushioned tires. And if he took a shine to you, D.J. might just be able to make you the first in your town to own a Century Columbia.

Then, D.J. might excuse himself to return to his seat, for Hartford headquarters was voracious for news from the field. His job was to set up franchises in new cities, a mission for a shrewd operator, one who could read people instantly and wouldn't be drawn in by a sharpie who later proved to be all sizzle, no steak. Back in his seat, D.J. opened a letter from George Pope, his immediate supervisor and the Colonel's cousin and confidant. And as the train trundled on toward Niagara Falls, Post read about the problems back home.

The company had agreed to let a man named Joyce in South Manchester, across the Connecticut River from Hartford, have a franchise, even though

91

Cheney was selling Columbia bicycles out of his respected department store across town. But now word had it that Joyce was about to skip town with $700 that he owed the Pope company. Let's cut him out, advised George Pope, and let Cheney have the whole territory, so we don't have agents under-cutting each other. On a brighter note, Pope told D.J., "unsolicited orders are coming in every day" with Ladies' Safeties selling at the rate of ten a day.

After reading George's latest missive and taking out his fountain pen to fire off a reply designed to please his boss, D.J. read the daily papers, which newsboys hawked through the railcar at every depot. At train stations, you could find more daily papers than flavors of ice cream, ranging all across the political spectrum. His home town of Hartford, a small capital city, had four dailies and two weeklies.[2]

Not only had Thomas Edison harnessed electricity for the consumer, today's paper observed, but an Auburn, New York, prison had used it for the first time to execute a criminal. Being the first to use the new technology, executioners botched the job and had to give the man a second jolt to finish him off. While public sentiment rose for the repeal of electrocution, the New York Court of Appeals would uphold it.[3]

Leafing through the tabloid, D.J. read that the national population had surpassed 63 million people in the 1890 census. More than 15 million immigrants had entered the country in the last seventy years, a third of them in the last decade. The popularity of such tunes as "Annie Rooney" and "There Is a Tavern in the Town" attested to the numbers, if not yet the buying power, of the new social classes.

Most train stations were downtown, and nearby hotels offered a soft bed and a good meal. Usually, the desk clerk would hand D.J. a letter sent ahead by the plant. "By now, we're turning out 19 one day, 25 another," George Pope informed him, as if to prod his traveling man to get out there and expand the demand to meet production.

Pope Turns Fifty

Pope's cousin, the Colonel, was approaching fifty now, and abundant threads of grey streaked his full beard. He was now firmly at the helm of Pope Manufacturing Company, which had bought out the Weed company for $15.60 a share. Debonair George Day, who had been president of Weed, characteristically deferred to his superior and receded, without complaint, to become vice president of the new outfit.

The two men were firmly ensconced in the top echelons of local business leaders, together with the heads of Aetna and Travelers insurance companies.

Hartford was upbeat as the 1890s dawned, as John Philip Sousa's marches blared out of phonographs in downtown windows, and young people at open-air dance halls did the two-step to Victor Herbert waltzes. Behind the plume of smoke from the carriage clip-clopping along Main Street might just be Mark Twain, attired in a white suit. Harriet Beecher Stowe, now beyond her prime, wandered in her garden from which, if the wind was right, she could hear the clanging of machinery at the Pope factory.[4]

Pope had succeeded admirably in his drive to claim the public roads for bicyclists. Using the roads, he asserted vehemently to anyone within earshot, was a right, not a privilege. What seems to a later gen-

Colonel Pope at age 50, in what must have been his favorite photograph of himself, since it was used from then on in all company literature and press releases. (*The Connecticut Historical Society, Hartford, Connecticut.*)

eration to be obvious was not so apparent to people whose only memories were of animal power—beast and human—on unpaved roads. The notion of a mechanical contrivance having rights equal to God's creatures came under fervid and repeated attack, from the pulpit and from editorials.

But rather than wheedling public officials for permission to ride high-wheelers down Main Street, the Colonel had made a tactical decision to meet vocal opposition head-on, going to court when needed and financing the lawsuits of other defenders of what came to be a perceived right as sacrosanct as breathing the air. A generation later, the nascent highway lobby would leverage the concept that Pope developed into a rationale that government should also build and maintain roads for citizens to use as a matter of right.

It was a startling concept for this earlier generation of Americans. Town roads had long been thought to be the responsibility of those through whose land the thoroughfare passed. If a tree fell across a road, the abutting owners would see to its removal at their expense. Later, a collective responsibility arose, as volunteers and debtors manned "road drags," in which heavy, horse-drawn scrapers, transverse to the line of movement, smoothed out dirt roads.[5]

As part of the Colonel's drive to adapt the public roads for bicyclists, he had local bicycle clubs erect signs to inform riders which roads were bicycle friendly. An arrow parallel to the road sign would signal the road was rideable, while an arrow diagonally across the road warned against taking it. As an incentive for his field representatives, the shiny enameled Pope signs left a place vacant for its agents' names and addresses.[6]

D.J. gleaned from the news this day that Herman Melville, author of *Moby Dick*, had died and that Thomas Edison was tinkering with a device that could simulate motion by speeding up a succession of still photographs. In Springfield, Massachusetts, James Naismith, an instructor at a YMCA training school, had come up with a new game that involved throwing a large ball through hoops mounted on two poles set far apart. Obviously, no competition for the bicycle, D.J. might have thought.

Pressure on D.J.

By 1892, the Pope network had expanded to 600 agencies, which varied widely in size and scope. An established department store might set up a bicycle section under a license with Pope. An agent in another state might set up a storefront and sell only Pope bicycles, while one in a smaller state might sell them out of his house. The agencies were located from coast to coast, in every Western European city of note, and even in such far-flung nations as Russia.

As the network grew, D.J. was drawn thinner and thinner. Not only did he have to solicit new agents, developing a sixth sense about their reliability and cutting off ones who weren't producing, he also had to jolly them into accepting new duties that weren't in the initial contract, such as repairing pneumatic tires that burst.

D.J.'s travels in 1892 would take him, among other ports of call, to Omaha, Detroit, Newburyport (Mass.), Belfast (Maine), Cleveland, Denver, Quincy (Ill.), and Louisville (Ky.). When Post was uncertain about a new agent, George Pope would order a Dun and Bradstreet credit report on him and report to D.J. by telegram.

And while D.J. was trying his mightiest to expand American capitalism, the public sector was embroiled in a battle royal that would leave its mark on the private sector as the years went by. At the Democratic National Convention in Chicago, New York's Tammany Hall crowd took the unusual position of coming out against Grover Cleveland of their own state, a man who ordinarily would have been their favorite son.

Cleveland's nominator at the Democratic Party convention hailed the former president as "the nominee of the people, the plain, blunt, honest citizen, the idol of the Democratic masses." Cleveland was running on a platform promising lower tariffs, and he lashed out at a high tariff proposed by the Republicans as "the culminating atrocity of class legislation."[7] Its Republican sponsor, Ohio Representative William McKinley, would ride his tariff bill into the White House in the next election, as Pope and other capitalists cheered for the protection it would bring their manufactured products.

An 1895 Pope catalog cover. Then, as now, an attractive, well-turned-out woman predictably boosted product sales. *(The Connecticut Historical Society, Hartford, Connecticut.)*

Fat and Not So Happy

If not yet avuncular, Pope certainly spoke with confidence and authority as he turned fifty. In conversation, his eyes locked yours, and his broad-shouldered figure "suggested energy in every movement."[8] But the Colonel belied the notion that Victorian captains of industry enjoyed being ruddy-cheeked and rotund. Two months after his birthday, Pope fired his doctor, who had prescribed a regimen to lose weight. Still at 216.5 pounds and 45.5 inches around the middle, the Colonel blamed Dr. W. H. Bowman for the failure of his diet. In his dismissal letter, Pope didn't mention whether he had ever adhered to it.

Pope had become such a public figure that while a New Bedford jury was considering murder charges against Lizzie Borden for dispatching her

father and stepmother with an ax, the *Boston Post* appointed Pope to a
celebrity jury, which included labor leader Samuel Gompers and author
Edward Everett Hale. While the celebrity and the bona fide jury weighed the
evidence, schoolchildren took up the popular chant:

> Lizzie Borden took an ax
> And gave her mother forty whacks
> And when she saw what she had done
> She gave her father forty-one.

Pope's busy publicity department funneled into the boss's office magazine and newspaper writers eager to profile one of America's most aggressively successful entrepreneurs. Ever alert to dispel the idea of the bicycle as
a dangerous toy, Pope used self-deprecation with a reporter from *Bicycling
World*, as noted in the quotation that opened this chapter.

Pope's reassurances weren't lost on women, who increasingly rode his
products, although the long skirts of the day often caught in bicycle chains.
The company's response was to build a chainless bicycle, in which two wheels
intermesh at an angle to change the plane of rotation. This bevel gear was
enclosed in a solid casing, making the vehicle skirt-safe. Pope doubled the
assurance by covering the rear wheel with wire mesh, lest a flying spoke
entrap the flowing fabric. By 1896, one-third of all bicyclists were women.[9]

One inquisitive reporter asked Pope to identify his best employee. Pope
replied, leaning back in his wooden swivel chair:

> He is the most faithful fellow in the world. He has been in my employ for
> seventeen years, yet he has never even asked for a holiday; he works both day
> and night, is never asleep or intoxicated, and though I pay him more than
> $250,000, I consider that he costs me nothing. His name is Advertisement.[10]

Not content to rely on magazines of his own creation to spread the
word, Pope advertised in hundreds of publications, including some as obscure
as the college journal that carried Sam McClure's senior thesis, which had
brought the bicycle maker to McClure's attention. Every spring, annual catalogs with elaborately designed covers would roll off the press to capture
the imaginations of those looking for diversion after the long winter. When
Thomas Stevens became the first person to ride a bicycle around the world's
circumference, Pope trumpeted that the feat occurred on an Expert Columbia.

But in 1890, few places existed for bicyclists to put their new acquisitions
to the test, for Pope's assiduous nationwide effort to pave the nation's roads
wouldn't bear fruit for a generation. But the Colonel was undeterred. In 1889,
with some other Boston entrepreneurs, he had purchased land in the Back Bay

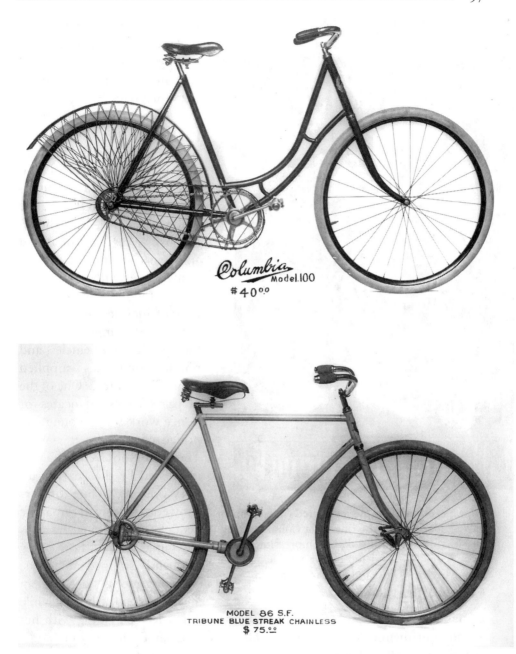

Top: Once Pope had made the move to safety bicycles, he aggressively courted the women's market. Soon sales to females accounted for one-third of his total business. Mesh installed over the chain and rear wheel were designed to protect the long skirts of the day. *(The Connecticut Historical Society, Hartford, Connecticut). Bottom:* Women's clothing often caught in bicycle chains, which also were quick to break, leading Pope to innovate with his Tribune Blue Streak Chainless, which replaced the chain with a beveled shaft. *(The Connecticut Historical Society, Hartford, Connecticut.)*

MARCH. 1882.

Columbia Bicycles

The Pope Manufacturing Co.

Pope bicycle catalogs often pictured young women gazing adoringly at the rider of a Columbia bicycle, leaving the unmistakable impression of the bounty that awaited the reader who acquired a high-wheeler. *(The Connecticut Historical Society, Hartford, Connecticut.)*

to create an athletic park complete with a half-mile track and a grandstand for families to watch their members compete for prizes.[11]

A favorite promotional pastime for the Colonel was to hire a 22-car Boston and Albany excursion train to bring scores of Boston luminaries to Hartford to tour the plant; on board, they dined, in plush velvet seats, on baked shad roe, spring lamb, and strawberries with cream.[12]

As the 1890s wore on, the uses of bicycles proliferated: New York employers used them as delivery vehicles, and phone companies supplied them to inspectors. One of the bicycle's fiercest advocates for police work was a young city police commissioner named Theodore Roosevelt, who was impressed by the "extraordinary daring" his officers showed. One can imagine Teddy's teeth flashing and arms waving as he told how "they frequently stopped runaways, wheeling along side of them and grasping the horses while going at full speed."[13] Stories about actress Lillian Russell riding with her friend comedienne Marie Dressler and the corpulent Diamond Jim Brady, pedaling along breathlessly to lose weight, stimulated readers to do likewise.[14]

Bicycle Railroad

One of the more unusual chapters of the bicycle age began on September 13, 1892, when Professor Arthur Hotchkiss opened his Mount Holly &

Smithville Bicycle Railroad. Its goal was to allow residents of Mount Holly, New Hampshire, to commute to their jobs at the H. B. Smith Manufacturing Company in Smithville nearly two miles away. A devout man, Hotchkiss turned down Coney Island's request to buy his design after learning that the amusement park intended to use it on Sundays.

The contraption resembled a fence more than a railroad, with posts set into the ground and the top rail of the fence serving as a track, capped by an inverted iron T-rail, upon which the grooved wheels of the vehicles rode. Conceived at the time when ordinaries held sway in the bicycle world, the bicycle railroad made sense, particularly for the unathletic or unadventuresome. But once safety bicycles took hold, the restrictive idea of a track doomed the bicycle railroad by 1898.[15]

Pope Buys Out His Suppliers

So heavy was the demand for safety bicycles in 1892 that Albert Pope decided to gather its component makers into his own realm. He bought the Hartford Rubber Works; built the Tube Works, with a capacity of a million linear feet of tubing a year, at the corner of Park and Laurel streets, not far from the Capitol Avenue plant; and for good measure, he purchased a steel company and the largest nickel-plating factory in the world. Rivals might attempt to steal a match on Pope but they'd not now be able to buy off his suppliers.[16] Bringing tubing in-house was the brainchild of MIT-trained Henry Souther, who left the Pennsylvania Steel Company in 1892 to head Pope's testing department and would become one of his most trusted aides in the years ahead.[17]

Technological obsolescence, by which automakers have induced owners to trade in their vehicles in favor of models with head-turning new features, didn't originate in the automobile industry. Early on, Pope discovered that a new color, striping, or perhaps the addition of a warning bell would make perfectly serviceable bicycles obsolete overnight.[18] One such innovation was the carbide lamp, introduced in 1895, which was powered by acetylene gas and threw off illumination sufficient to warn riders of holes and ruts in the road.[19]

While D.J. was on the road, Boston celebrated the anniversary of Columbus's discovery of America with a well-received musical extravaganza at the Globe Theater. He was too busy promoting the Model 30 Relay Century Columbia and its new pneumatic tires to attend.

Since bicycle agents lived for their commissions, disputes about remuneration erupted continuously, and D.J.'s job was to put out the brushfires in the hinterlands. Post had just arrived in Detroit from Chicago when he found a letter from George Pope at his hotel, informing him that Hughes up in Buffalo was looking for a bigger discount. Since agents received bicycles at wholesale prices to resell at retail, a bigger discount amounted to a larger commission.

"I certainly hope that he will not go to the Colonel about discounts," George warned, "for I know that he feels that he has made considerable concession already and to be approached now for a higher rate of discount will not, I believe, result in the best of consequences." As ironic as it appears for George, who had earned a legitimate colonelcy, to refer to his cousin as "the Colonel," it is clear that, at Pope Manufacturing Company, there was room for only one Colonel.

As Albert Pope had proven with McClure, he could be tight with a nickel. So George Pope had to concede to D.J. that Leinbach, their Harrisburg (Pa.) agent, had already jumped ship to sell Wilhelm's competing line of Reading bicycles. "Discount," conceded Pope, "is what is doing it. Either some of the other manufacturers are satisfied with less profit than we are or else they do not fully understand figuring the contingent expense and will find themselves out of the race in the course of a year or two."

D.J. had little time to reply, since he was off the next day on a New York Central train to Grand Rapids, where he learned from George that the company had taken orders for 417 Pattern Cs and Ds and 334 Pattern Es and Fs, the in-house key to production models.

To McClure's Aid Once More

The Colonel's protégé, Sam McClure, in 1893 had launched his own magazine, named after himself, in spite of a technological upheaval that had made it more costly for newcomers to enter the industry. Until then, magazines that wanted a sketch to illustrate an article had used woodcuts, in which an image was carved into wood blocks and the portion in relief inked.

But now, with studio photography a reality, such magazines as *Century* were able to photograph a subject through a wire or glass screen and then record the image on a sensitized copper plate. The screen would break the light rays so that the plate was sensitized in a dotted pattern; larger dots represented darkness and smaller ones, highlights. The finished product was a grainy photograph but light years more advanced than woodcuts, which had been used since the Middle Ages.

The halftone process, as it was called, had first made its appearance in *Century* in 1884. So dramatic in appearance was it that competitors simply had to follow or be left in the dust. Yet the process was expensive, so even *Century* made only one-third of its images halftone by 1893. Digging deep into its resources, *Harper's* used halftones for half of its images, and John Brisben Walker's aggressive and thoroughly modern *Cosmopolitan* used nothing but halftones while it attempted to administer the coup de grace to its competition by serializing Leo Tolstoy's new novel, *Resurrection*.[20]

So while Pope held a tight rein on the commissions his sales agents received, even to the point of watching some of them leave, he came to the aid of his old protégé with a $1,000 advance on advertising. His old friend could now move into the big leagues of magazine publishing, with even larger advances to come.

McClure seemed to be in desperate straits when the Colonel came to his aid. No sooner had *McClure's Magazine* appeared than Walker slashed *Cosmopolitan*'s newsstand price to 12.5 cents, figuring he had greater staying power than McClure, who he expected would have to match his price.

Traveling to London to sign up new writers and massage the egos of existing ones, McClure was besieged by a writer who begged him to pay the $100 McClure owed him for an article. "He said he was about to be put out of his flat," McClure said, "and before he got through talking he actually cried. I cried too, but I had no money to give him from a magazine that was bleeding $1,000 a month."

As competition forced down the price of magazines, it broadened the readership from a monied elite to a much more politically diverse readership base. Attracting workers as well as employers meant *McClure's* readership was now amenable to articles critical of the established order.

Such articles and those who wrote them were in ready supply. If he could hire an established writer on staff, rather than paying freelance fees, McClure figured he could save money. So with his next issue hanging in the balance, he cabled a young woman in her late thirties named Ida Tarbell and sent her $150, asking her to return from Paris, where she was on assignment, to New York to work for him.

While largely unknown at the time, Tarbell would become a household name with her *History of the Standard Oil Company*, a scathing exposé of John D. Rockefeller's operations, which Colonel Pope could not have escaped reading.[21] Exposure of corporate dirty linen was akin to digging in the muck, Teddy Roosevelt would soon declare. And so the practice of sensational screeds against captains of industry became known as muckraking.

McClure would follow up by hiring New York newspaperman Lincoln Steffens, whose serials ended up in a book, *The Shame of the Cities*, which exposed municipal corruption in such places as Minneapolis, St. Louis, Manhattan, and Philadelphia. Ray Stannard Baker followed up with reports on the anthracite fields, which McClure called "an arraignment of the American character," particularly "the American contempt of law."[22]

The Children's Market

Industries from automobiles to tobacco, which have sought to sell their products for decades into the future, have plowed fertile fields by marketing to children. Conditioning the coming generation creates lifelong customers, who may be expected to influence their own progeny. Albert Pope was one of the first to grasp this eternal truth. In one of his more creative exploits of the principle, the high school dropout lectured public school teachers to great effect.

As proprietor of the Boston Athenaeum, a private library and city institution for more than a century, Pope self-published in 1892 a 24-page treatise entitled "Errors in School Books," in which he held forth on numerous pedagogical errors that appeared in textbooks, errors that risked being perpetuated from one generation of students to the next. It might have seemed an odd diversion for an industrial magnate to engage in, but Pope had a method to his madness. In a typical passage, Pope explained that in Harper's *Introductory Geography*, the following statement appears: "For the earth has two different motions all the time. It turns around on itself—so to speak—that is one motion; and it moves in a circle around the sun—this is the other motion."

Pope sagely observed in his preface:

> Every intelligent person knows that the earth's orbit is an ellipse, as was demonstrated by Kepler, whose laws of planetary motion formed the ground work of Newton's discoveries and are the starting point of modern astronomy. It is obviously wrong to teach children things that they must unlearn as they grow older, and school teachers can do no greater service to education than to point out the errors that should be eradicated from text-books.

Pope's exposé of classroom errors turned up ninety, of which textbook publishers owned up to only twenty-three, and Pope offered prizes of Columbia bicycles to teachers who could discover more. By now, teachers were fascinated that this captain of industry would take the time to help mold young minds, and the Colonel's treatise reprints gushing teacher endorsements of his worthy effort.

Having won over his readers with his diligence and sincerity, Pope saved his most severe criticism for the end of the work:

> The greatest error of all those discovered in school books was the omission to teach the great need and importance of the construction and maintenance of good roads throughout the country.... The time has now come when the public demands that there be better roads.... Country life would become far more attractive and abandoned farms less frequent if there were good roads.

Pope exhorted teachers to begin teaching road building in kindergarten, so youngsters could grow up to become highway engineers. His prodigious efforts to enlist such opinion leaders as teachers was a lesson that later generations of highway lobbyists would learn and apply.

To get church ladies on his side, Pope offered $100 at a charity event at the Waldorf Astoria in New York for the best doll dressed in a women's bicycle costume. This gambit won him free media publicity while boosting interest in bicycling among women and encouraging them to create their own ideas of bicycle fashion, rather than imposing it on them.[23]

Good Enough for the Queen to Ride

Once convinced that the safety bicycle was here to stay, the Colonel flogged his troops to promote it as a vehicle for women. George Pope wrote his traveling man in Columbus, Ohio, "Our exhibition machines went off last night and we are not at all ashamed of them. The Ladies' Safety with pneumatic tires is the daintiest and best machine on the market at most any price. It is out to make a great seller and is good enough for the Queen to ride." The image of the stern, septuagenarian Victoria, in a floor-length gown, astride one of Pope's creations, taxes the imagination.

To feed the bicycle frenzy required constant promotion. With the advent of chromolithography, color posters were plastered everywhere, many displaying attractive young people riding colorful bicycles.

Pope and his competitors didn't stop at advertising the bicycle for general use but sought out niche markets to broaden their sales. While police officers welcomed the speed and maneuverability that bicycles gave them, other uses didn't fare as well. The Colonel, for instance, thought that safety bicycles could be adapted for use in the military as mobile artillery units. Harnessing a 100-pound machine gun to a bicycle might offer more mobility, but the heavy weight slowed the vehicle down to a few miles per hour and required its riders to get off and push on slopes. Pope fitted one unit with a small mountain cannon, another with a forward-facing machine gun but, in the end, the obvious problems prevented the U.S. Army from buying the idea.[24]

The craze also produced celebrities, such as a bicycle racer known only as Zimmerman, who in 1893 alone won $20,000 in prizes. Midget Michael, another exhibitionist, boasted that he slept eleven hours a night but on awakening would ride forty to fifty miles "to get up a good sweat." Between rides, he made bicycling paper dolls.[25]

In 1893, Chicagoans rode the voguish bicycles to the World's Columbian Exposition. An elevated railway had been constructed especially for the event and would become a permanent fixture of the city's skyline, but hidden in a corner of the exposition was an exhibit that might give them all pause.

While only one electric vehicle was on display at Chicago's 1893 Columbia exposition, within a few years auto shows were everywhere. Here, Pope (third from left) and his cohorts examine European models to bone up on the competition. *(National Automotive History Collection, Detroit Public Library, Detroit, Michigan.)*

Attached to an ordinary-looking farm wagon was an electric motor, offering the possibility of a driver's moving along a road without pedaling. Pope would be among others examining it. How many perceived its significance?

If viewers had investigated further, they would have found that Karl Benz had sold 300 gasoline-powered motor carriages in Germany already that year. But people tend to rely on what they know, and that year a New York Central locomotive, engine number 999, pulling four heavy cars as the Empress Express, had posted a speed record of 112.5 miles an hour between Crittenden and Wende, New York.[26] The feat would garner far more headlines than European experimentation with a new, noisy, smoky machine.

Just as significant as the electric carriage introduced in Chicago was an enterprise established by Thomas Edison, whose every new creation an eager public awaited. In 1893, he opened in West Orange, New Jersey, America's first movie studio, his Kinetographic Theater, which he nicknamed the Black Maria.[27]

Network Spreads Worldwide

While D. J. Post was racing feverishly from city to city, trying to keep up with Colonel Pope's pace of territorial expansion, his boss's network now reached its tentacles abroad. By 1894, the shiny, enameled Columbia insignia was displayed in Paris, Belgium, Holland, Switzerland, Florence, Milan, St. Petersburg, Vienna, Moscow, Dublin, Hamburg, Breslau, and Athens.

By 1897, the company maintained 2,000 agents. But unlike such retailers as Sears and Singer, which created and maintained their own showrooms, Pope shrewdly leveraged his resources by enlisting existing store owners to carry Pope models on commission, thereby avoiding unnecessary overhead and allowing the Pope label to appear in many more cities around the world.[28]

But Pope wasn't the only bicycle maker in the world, as Chicagoan Ignatius Schwinn and others were proving.[29] And the name Columbia didn't seem to have the same cachet worldwide as it enjoyed in the United States. "The demand in Russia," Pope wrote Post, "seems to be for machines cheaper in price than we can afford to sell Columbias and consequently we do not look for a very large trade."

Writing of Moscow, Pope observed, "Mr. Block has called on us while in this country and we know him to be a shrewd merchant. All attempts to induce him to sell our goods have failed because he can buy English machines on terms which we cannot approach."[30]

The controversial new industry required fighting brushfires on several fronts at the same time. While trying to learn the often-arcane intricacies of foreign markets one day, on the next, Pope moved to counter a dangerous trend at home. Municipalities, which hadn't been able to remove bicycles from the streets altogether, now moved to tax them. When Lowell, Massachusetts, passed a levy on his product, Pope protested that bicycles "are merely machines by means of which muscular power can be used in locomotion to better advantage than in walking." Further, appealing to the concerns of such crowded mill towns, he argued that the bicycle helps solve the tenement house problem "as it enables the workman to live in the suburbs where he has some of the advantages of country life and yet he can ride to his work in the city."[31]

By 1894, George Day prevailed on the Colonel to consolidate his administrative and production operations in Hartford. It would not be a natural move for the Brookline-born entrepreneur, whose family had all been raised in Boston and summered on its south coast, but it made sense for his corporate enterprises.

Day had proved to be an adept and loyal lieutenant over the years and had assimilated into Hartford life in a way that the Colonel never would.

In 1895, he bought a plot of land at 78 Wethersfield Avenue, just south of "Armsmear," the graceful stucco mansion occupied by Sam Colt's widow. Here, Elizabeth Colt maintained an arboretum, which tourists would stop to admire.

To accommodate the Hartford consolidation, Pope engaged prominent architect George Keller to construct a three-story Italian Renaissance structure using molded brick and buff terra cotta, topped by two flagpoles flying colorful banners. British critic John Ruskin had railed against stark factory buildings with chimneys that formed "unsightly, misshapen stacks of blackness against the sky" and that "degrade labor instead of honoring the laborer." But Pope, he enthused, "has done much to remove this reproach ... and has set a commendable example to his neighbors."[32]

Fifth Column at Work

When the plant whistle blew, W. A. Willard quit work and strode down Capitol Avenue with his new coworkers. Perhaps that day they stopped off at the corner bar to hoist a couple of beers and grouse about conditions at Pope Manufacturing Company. But Willard had a mission different from that of his buddies, and when he returned to his rented room, he penned a nearly illiterate letter to his boss.

Frederick Winslow Taylor would read the missive with interest, for Willard was part of his infiltration of the Pope company, seeking to learn close up whether the company had cribbed the process of making ball bearings that had been invented by Taylor's client, the Simonds Rolling Machine Company. If a company turned out a ball bearing using Simonds's process, a large "tit" of metal formed on the ball itself, later to be removed, and was exhibit A in proving that the company had violated Simonds's patent. Since the "tit" was shaved off before the final ball bearing was produced, Taylor needed to put men on the production line to learn all of its steps.

"Well this is the worst job of geting [sic] what you want that could be," complained Willard, "but I don't care to be very bold if I do the fat will be in the fire at once, but I think I shall fix them in the end and that is what I am here for."

While Willard acquired layers of grease on the factory floor, Taylor saved Newcomb Carlton, a graduate of Stevens Institute of Technology, for the white-collar approach. Carlton's job was to infiltrate the books by acting as a front for a nonexistent group of investors; he would suggest that they had big money to buy bicycle companies but, of course, would need to know all the ins and outs of the company's production first.

One victim of Carlton's deception in another city wrote him "two rather savage letters," but by then he was on a train to Hartford, where he reflected, in a letter to Taylor, that "I find that the lying I have lately done has hardened me beyond any ordinary forms of reproach."

Taylor's modus operandi was to construct such a watertight case that, when it was laid before the corporate patent infringer, it would simply bring him to his knees, without the need for litigation. Colonel Pope had been trading on the patent market, so to speak, for nearly two decades, and as a realistic man, he had learned when to hold 'em and when to fold 'em. Confronted by Taylor's incontrovertible evidence that Pope's company had stolen Simonds's patent, the Colonel quickly settled out of court and put the matter behind him.[33]

Gospel of Wealth

In 1889, the steel tycoon Andrew Carnegie wrote an essay entitled "The Gospel of Wealth," which set America back on its heels. The press had lumped Carnegie and John D. Rockefeller into the category of rapacious robber barons, who had milked the nation dry so that they could build gilt-edged townhouses on Park Avenue and 30-room summer mansions in Newport. Wealth, Carnegie asserted, belongs to its owner as a public trust, with a resultant obligation to spend it for the commonweal. Putting his money where his mouth had been, Carnegie then set out to create 2,800 libraries across America in addition to his famous hall in Manhattan and a foundation named for him.

The essay, ruminated over in corporate boardrooms since, helped create a new climate for corporate benefactions. Carnegie maintained he hadn't a charitable bone in his body until he turned fifty and presumably sensed his mortality. Albert Pope dismissed the conversion theory as poppycock; if a man is public-spirited, it will show up early in life and continue throughout or not at all. Pope could employ such a position, of course, to argue that the influential Carnegie essay touched him not at all, that he had been a corporate giver all along, an argument that contains more than a grain of truth.

Back to Nature

In the lives of people, no less than in physics, every action has an equal and opposite reaction. So, as nineteenth-century industrialization made American urban life noisier and dirtier and gobbled up green space, a reaction bubbled up to secure a verdant refuge in the form of public parks, to be designed as a return to man's natural state.

In the forefront of the national parks movement was a largely self-taught landscape planner named Frederick Law Olmsted. Born in Hartford, Olmsted credited the Hartford Public Library with opening his eyes to the wider world. Such esoteric works as the Reverend William Gilpin's *Remarks on Forest Scenery* and Sir Uvedale Price's *Essay on the Picturesque* awakened in the boy a love for the outdoors, not only for its own sake but as a canvas to which he could apply nature's fruit, to create works of art.[34] A far cry from the formal gardens of Versailles, Olmsted's quintessentially American parks would feature broad greenswards and irregularly placed trees, as an antidote against the regimentation and harshness of the industrial age.[35]

Acting on this impulse, Hartford city fathers in the late 1850s replaced a railroad yard, a garbage dump, and squatters' shacks with park land, which gracefully curved along the banks of the Park River and wound from the Connecticut River past the Pope plant and into the city's West End. Olmsted, awash in commissions once he had designed Manhattan's Central Park, evidently recommended a landscape designer with time to complete the park, which was named for Congregational minister and reformer Horace Bushnell.

In 1870, Olmsted returned to the home of his birth to propose a necklace of public parks near the city's periphery. The plan would be discussed and refined over the next generation, but the land required was in the hands of several wealthy businessmen, including Albert A. Pope, who by then owned more than 100 acres stretching north to the New Haven Railroad tracks and south a great distance across the meandering Park River. And so it would remain, until 1894.

In retrospect, Pope's generosity to his community is beyond question, but his giving was inextricably tied to his corporate reputation, so a press release customarily accompanied each gift. Thus, in November 1894, Pope's ample girth didn't prevent him from racing to the head of a parade of those who would create a system of public parks in Hartford to rival any in America.

Charles M. Pond and Henry Keney, two wealthy Hartford businessmen, had recently died. Even before their wills were read, a rumor seeped through the oak-paneled walls of Hartford's gentlemens' clubs that Pond's will had left ninety acres of land and $200,000, nearly half his estate, for a park on the city's west side and that the bachelor Keney had left nearly all of his $1.3 million grocery fortune for park purposes.[36]

Before the estate attorneys could make the gifts public, Pope's publicity department churned out the news that Albert Pope was giving seventy-three acres off Capitol Avenue to the city for a public park. The collective generosity, gushed the *Providence Telegram*, provided Hartford with a park system "which ought to be sufficient for a century."[37]

In typical Pope fashion, the Colonel had not only appeared to be the leading benefactor (an assertion the two dead men couldn't rebut), he had, as well, provided a major source of recreation for his own workers and their families. As if the engineer of the city park system, Pope's letter to the city observed, "Your city is in need of open breathing spaces and pleasure grounds which should be scattered in different regions and so laid out and arranged as to afford the means of recreation and pleasure to all classes of law-abiding citizens."[38]

The Hartford parks system had become a political football, with the Court of Common Council, the city's legislative body, reluctant to give up control of a project full of opportunity for jobs and patronage. But the resourceful Reverend Francis Goodwin, who had coaxed Keney, Pope and Pond to include park land in their wills, now helped force through a city charter revision that gave the city Park Commission control of all park money, the right to name its own members, and the ability to levy taxes to maintain the parks. With Goodwin, George Day, George Fairfield, and Pope's personal lawyer, Charles Gross, on the eleven-member board, the Colonel felt confident that his wishes for the park would be honored.

Knowing that Pope Park would be the major, if not the only, diversion for his workers and their families, Pope encouraged the Olmsted firm to create a variety of settings within it. The bowl-shaped Hollowmead, forming a natural amphitheater, was designed with only a sprinkling of trees around its periphery, to allow workers living in six-family apartment buildings at the park's edge to enjoy the trademark Olmstedian vistas of open space from their windows and front porches. At the highest point, Pope created High Mall, with a semicircular pergola and sunken garden. He built boat landings along the Park River, which hugged the park's southern boundary, and created secluded glades called Nethermead and Thithermead for family picnics.[39]

Pope's benefactions extended to his employees as well. Considered revolutionary innovations at the time, Pope added a well-stocked library, company lunchrooms with hot meals for seven cents, a bike garage, and hot- and cold-water washrooms with lockers.[40] He underwrote the expenses of a 25-member military band, composed of his employees, which marched in local parades under the Pope banner. His customary Christmas present to employees was money, together with a note: "Dear Schofield: I enclose fifty dollars and you can buy your own present. You know what you need most."[41]

More meaningful was his plan to build employee apartments and homes along the park he had created. Reacting enthusiastically to the plan, the Hartford Board of Trade lamented, "Tenements, a disgrace to civilization, have been built here and are rented at exorbitant rates. Women may sicken and children may die, but Shylock pockets his two percent a month."[42]

Change in the Wind

The seeds of a boom's demise are often present at its very height. In 1895, bicycle sales were in the hundreds of thousands; they would top a million by the end of the century, with 300 manufacturers contributing to the total. George Keller, the esteemed architect who designed all of Pope's company housing, complained to his wife that the Colonel "would not let me have a new bicycle as they have orders away ahead for all they can make."[43] The U.S. Census for 1900 reported, "Few articles ever used by man have ever created so great a revolution in social conditions."[44] Yet a knowledgeable observer could sense a sea change, as the prospect of motorized transportation began to loom over the horizon.[45]

Bicycles were still very much in vogue, and their popularity had led Congress and dozens of state governments to surface city streets with asphalt and concrete and to macadamize local roads to meet the public demand. But it was the very success of the bicycle industry in sparking the imagination with dreams of individual travel and in setting off a road construction boom that would ensure the industry's demise.

The industry forecast was not lost on the Colonel, who in 1894 ominously told the *New York Record*, "Bicycle prices will drop when the patents run out, as did the price of sewing machines." That event, he knew, would signal the end of the gravy train.[46]

History teaches that empires often build their most impressive monuments on the eve of their destruction. In an act of corporate schizophrenia, Colonel Pope forecast the decline of his prominent presence in Boston even as construction crews erected an ornate, four-story granite building at 219–223 Columbus Avenue in Boston as the new headquarters of the Pope corporate offices. Within months, he gave in to the entreaties of trusted George Day and moved those offices to Hartford.

Pope had used five buildings as headquarters for the Pope Manufacturing Company in Boston, and the detailing of each telegraphed the Colonel's rising status in the world: from the spartan, boxy location he moved into in 1877 at 45 High Street, with simple four-over-four windows, to the double-cupolaed structure at 87 Summer Street he occupied a year later, to the addition of lintels and pediments on his headquarters at 597 Washington Street, to still more elaborate detailing at 79 Franklin Street. The final headquarters at 219–223 Columbus Avenue, whose six stories were crowned by elaborate cornices set atop rows of huge palladian windows, became Boston's sales offices for Pope bicycles. In charge, he left his oldest son, Albert Linder Pope, then only twenty-two.

Albert Linder was rapidly gaining a reputation as a playboy. After graduating from the prestigious Phillips Andover Academy, he entered Dartmouth but flunked out and went to work for the family business, while taking as much time off as he could to pursue his chief passion, sailing. Believers in primogeniture would have to shake their heads in contemplating the fate of the Pope Manufacturing Company.

Baptism by Fire

The first son had a round face and wore rimless glasses, which ironically lent the young playboy a mien even more sober than his father. Since the Colonel divided his time among Boston, Cohasset, and Hartford, Albert Linder still wasn't out from under his critical gaze, but at least he could sink or swim in his own shop. Above the first-floor glassed-in bicycle showrooms lay the paneled corporate offices, with a rink on the top floor on which members of society learned to ride before offering their skills to public scrutiny.

Prince Albert was working at his desk one weekday afternoon in 1896 about 3 P.M. when he heard a commotion, saw people scurrying down the halls, and heard shouts that the building was on fire. Colonel Pope's private secretary, Robert Winkley, dashed about, gathering valuable papers from cubbyholes in the rolltop desks. "There was no warning," some of the thirty-five to forty employees on hand told the *Boston Post*. "The whole inside seemed to flare up like oil." Six Back Bay matrons, attired in bloomers while riding in the rink, ran down three flights of stairs to escape, along with dozens of workers and secretaries.

Once outside, Pope employees looked to the son and heir, who had escaped with a linen duster and straw hat, looking more like a dandy than a rescuer. His first instinct, understandably, was to seek out his father, said to be in Hartford. "Burned to the ground," his telegram read. "Wire instructions." Yet, as darkness approached, there was no word from the Colonel, who, in fact, was then on a train to Manhattan. Albert Linder realized he was on his own.

After consulting with his uncle Edward, a Pope vice president, and Henry D. Hyde, corporate counsel, young Albert realized that the building was a total loss. They proceeded to contact several vacant stores, into which they might move their operations, and ordered 300 new bicycles from Hartford, which were loaded aboard a Boston-bound train before nightfall. By evening, Albert had engaged a store at 200 Boylston Street, where the Pope Cycle Company would throw open its doors for business the next morning, as if nothing had happened, while on Columbus Avenue, water from firemen's hoses caused rows of bicycle wheels to freeze into eerie sculptures, illuminated by gaslight when the lamplighter came by at dusk to ignite the streetlights.[47]

Newsboys hawked for a penny *Boston Post* headlines that screamed, "Pope Bicycle Building in Ruins." Artists dispatched to the scene depicted tongues of flames licking through the building's upper floors like wings trying to take it aloft. A sidebar noted that the fire was a "pleasing Lenten diversion for Back Bay society," as young ladies gazed "with every evidence of delight at the flaming structures.... A casualty of any sort excites the morbid vein which exists in all the human race, and the upper classes are no exception to this rule."[48]

Albert Linder, perhaps against expectation, had not only survived his baptism by fire but comported himself as well as the Colonel could have. Insurance covered all but about $100,000 of fire losses.

Debut for Margaret

Colonel Pope's attempts to reclaim his family's rightful place within Boston society, diminished by his father's financial disgrace, had evidently paid off. In December 1895, 500 guests attended the debut of Margaret Pope, his only daughter to reach adulthood. Beaming in the bow window of the family's Commonwealth Avenue townhouse, decorated gaily for Christmas, Margaret was "a most pleasing girl of the brunette type," wrote a society reporter, "gowned simply in a white figured chiffon over white satin."[49] "She is not only pretty," said the *Boston Herald*, "but has a charming manner, and a self-possession, unusual for her years."

And so, in 1895, at fifty-two, Colonel Pope had an accomplished wife, had children who were making him proud, and had ascended into the first rank of American industrialists. While the bicycle era was ebbing, another wheeled creation was poised to succeed it, and Pope's legacy to the automobile industry was great. Such contributions as pneumatic tires, wire wheels, ball and roller bearings, differential axles, variable speed transmissions, and steel tube frames would be transplanted directly and smoothly from the bicycle to the automobile.[50]

Allan Nevins, historian of the Henry Ford empire, notes, "Up to 1897, the chain and sprocket were a part of the transmission, and axles and gears both owed much, even though indirectly, to the researches and shop practices of the Pope Company.[51]

But Pope's most significant contributions may have been more intangible. Pope, Nevins notes:

> had been quick to realize that the bicyclist needed a variety of services, among them the establishment of his legal status, the improvement of streets and highways and the construction of special paths along the roads on which he might ride without interfering with or being subject to interference from horse-drawn traffic.[52]

And so, the largest American bicycle manufacturer in 1895 was Colonel Albert Augustus Pope, self-made millionaire. An industry that turned out no more than 300,000 high-wheelers a decade before was now rolling 1,200,000 safety bicycles off assembly lines each year.[53] With 3,800 agents worldwide and 2,000 point-of-sale locations, Pope's plant turned out 600 bicycles each day and had net revenues of $1 million a year.[54]

Looking back years later, Hiram Percy Maxim, the man who nudged Pope into automobile production perhaps more than any other, reflected:

> It has been the habit to give the gasoline engine all the credit for bringing the automobile—in my opinion this is the wrong explanation. We have had the steam engine for over a century. We could have built steam vehicles in 1880, or indeed in 1870. But we did not. We waited until 1895.

Instead, Maxim said, road vehicles did not emerge earlier "because the bicycle had not yet come in numbers and had not directed men's minds to the possibilities of long-distance travel over the ordinary highway. We thought the railroad was good enough. The bicycle created a new demand which it was beyond the ability of the railroad to supply."[55]

Accordingly, once the demand was perceived, it seems natural that bicycle makers themselves would be the first to try to adapt. And among those bicycle manufacturers who turned their talents toward production of a horseless carriage were names today associated largely with automobiles—names such as Opel, Duryea, Morris, Winton, and Willys. And, of course, Pope.

Notes

1. *Bicycling World*, May 1880, p. 9.

2. Hartford dailies included the *Hartford Courant*, the *Hartford Times*, the *Hartford Post*, and the *Hartford Telegraph-Record*. The *Hartford Globe* and the *Hartford Journal* were published weekly, according to the reference department of the Hartford Public Library.

3. Lupiano, Vincent de Paul and Ken W. Sayers, *It Was a Very Good Year: A Cultural History of the United States*, p. 183.

4. Grant, Ellsworth, *The Colt Armory: A History of Colt's Manufacturing Company, Inc.*, p. 67.

5. Goddard, Stephen B., *Getting There: The Epic Struggle Between Road and Rail in the American Century*, p. 53.

6. "Pope Manufacturing Company Correspondence, 1890–94."

7. DiGregorio, William A., *The Complete Book of U.S. Presidents*, p. 345.

8. St. Botolph, June 3, 1893.

9. Dunham, Norman Leslie, "The Bicycle Era," p. 446.

10. Norcliffe, Glen, "Popeism and Fordism: Examining the Roots of Mass Production," p. 275.

11. Ibid., p. 276.

12. "American Cyclist," April 15, 1894.

13. *Wheelman*, 49 (November 1896), p. 14.

14. Ibid., p. 17.

15. Stockinger, Herbert B., "The Bicycle Railroad," *passim*.

16. "Columbia Chronology," p. 22.

17. Epperson, Bruce, "A Model of Technological Dissonance," p. 10.

18. Norcliffe, p. 274.

19. R.F.S., "The Great Bicycle Delirium," p. 71.

20. Tebbel, John, et al., *The Magazine in America, 1741–1990*, p. 75.

21. Lyon, Peter, *Success Story*, p. 131.

22. Tebbel, pp. 112–13.

23. Norcliffe, p. 276.

24. Fitzpatrick, Jim, "Pope's Military Bicycles," p. 68.

25. R.F.S., p. 69.

26. Lupiano and Sayers, p. 191.

27. Ibid., p. 192.

28. Norcliffe, p. 276.

29. Herlihy, David V., "The Bicycle Story," p. 58.

30. "Pope Manufacturing Company Correspondence, 1890–94."

31. Letter from Albert A. Pope to Lowell, MA, tax authorities, May 8, 1893, Albert A. Pope II archives.

32. May 27, 1894, clipping in Albert A. Pope scrapbook, unidentified newspaper II archives.

33. Kanigel, Robert, *The One Best Way*, pp. 277–78.

34. Rybczynski, Witold, *A Clearing in the Distance*, p. 29.

35. Alexopoulos, John, *The Nineteenth-Century Parks of Hartford: A Legacy to the Nation*, p. 11.

36. Records of the estates of Charles M. Pond and Henry Keney, Hartford (CT) Probate Court.

37. "Hartford Happy," *Boston Journal*, November 16, 1894, n. p.

38. Yaindl, Georgette, David Herlihy, and Albert A. Pope II, "The Cycle Capitol of the World," unpublished paper, May 1996.

39. Alexopoulos, pp. 50–53.

40. Ibid.

41. December 23, 1893, letter, Col. Albert Pope, 1893–94 private correspondence, p. 113.

42. Grant, p. 78.

43. Keller, George, letter to wife, Mary Keller, August 9, 1895, George Keller Collection, Harriet Beecher Stowe Center, Hartford, CT.

44. Kelly, Fred, "The Great Bicycle Craze," p. 69.

45. Lewis, Tom, *Divided Highways: Building the Interstate Highways, Transforming American Life*, p. 7.

46. Norcliffe, p. 273.

47. Morison, Samuel Eliot, *One Boy's Boston*, p. 19.

48. "Pope Bicycle Building in Ruins," *Boston Post*, March 13, 1896, p. 1.

49. "Miss Pope's Debut," *Boston Post*, December 11, 1895, n. p.

50. Williamson, Harold F. et al., *The American Petroleum Industry, 1899–1959: The Age of Energy*, p. 186.

51. Nevins, Allan, *Ford: The Times, the Man, the Company*, p. 189.

52. Ibid., p. 256.

53. Musselman, M.M., *Get a Horse!*, p. 29.

54. Epperson, p. 63.

55. Maxim, Hiram Percy, *Horseless Carriage Days*, p. 6.

CHAPTER 7

INDISPENSABLE ROADS

*Notwithstanding the phonomenal crops last season, there
is to-day less grain at railway stations than last year, farmers being unable to haul their crops to the railroad, and
therefore without funds to make purchases, all of which
results in general stagnation and dullness of trade.*
        Stuyvesant Fish, president, Illinois Central Railroad

*I*N THE SAME WAY that skyscrapers remained only an idea until structural
steel and elevators were invented, the notion of a bicycle and an automobile in every garage was but a pipe dream without paved roads. But one
important distinction remains: while the notion of towering buildings awaited
a laboratory invention, good roads awaited the accumulation of political will,
a goal that would daunt the most creative inventor.

A casual observer in 1880 might have concluded that, since bicycles were
all the rage in Europe, they would sell in America at an equal pace. Relatively sophisticated, reasonably prosperous citizenries existed on both sides
of the Atlantic. In this golden age of magazines, spirited accounts of the
great bicycle tours and races being staged without respite on the Continent
stirred the soul of millions of Americans.

But Albert Pope knew better. Europe enjoyed a road-building tradition
harking back to Caesar, who had built a network of stone thoroughfares,
with sophisticated banking, curbing, and drainage, as the spine of his Roman
Empire. Drawing on this tradition, Napoleon in the early 1800s spread paved
roads throughout France, again as a tool of military conquest.

America had no such tradition of road building. The colonies were set-
tled before the great European road builders—Scotland's John MacAdam,
France's Pierre Tresaguet, and Britain's Thomas Telford—had left their mark.
While Paris's Ecole Nationale des Ponts et Chaussées (School of Bridges and
Roads) cranked out highway engineers as it had since the 1700s, no such insti-
tution existed on the west side of the Atlantic.

The United States had experienced a brief spurt of activity in 1806, when the first federally financed turnpike, the Cumberland Road, opened from Baltimore, Maryland, to Ohio, allowing stagecoaches and wagons to haul imports from abroad into the interior, where whole new states were forming. But the competing Erie Canal in the 1820s and the advent of railroads in the next decade quashed what could have become a national roads movement.

A few cities introduced the comparatively primitive technologies of macadamizing and telfordizing roads prior to the Civil War but they did so only sparingly and not under any state or federal government aegis. Invention of the jaw rockcrusher in 1858 and the use of Portland cement to form concrete surfaces after the Civil War caused a modest influx of road activity. But America's vast expanses, contrasting with Europe's compactness, made it clear that a national road network wouldn't get off the ground without federal support.[1]

Government support requires political pressure, which itself demands that sizable constituencies be willing to pay the taxes to pay for good roads. A nation of settlers who shook off the shackles of oppressive authority to come to the land of the free remained to be convinced. Farmer Browns across America, their arms folded across their chests, felt that they and their forebears had gotten along just fine without paved roads so far and saw no reason why they should need them now.

A Foot in the Door

In 1879, the North Carolina General Assembly stuck a muddy foot in the door, when it allowed counties to tax property at the rate of thirty-five cents for every hundred dollars of property value.[2] Common law dating back to Britain said landowners must maintain any public road passing in front of their properties, and most localities let owners contribute either cash or elbow grease to meet their responsibilities. Realizing how much improved roads really cost, Iowa in 1883, followed by other states, decided that road taxes must be paid in cash instead of labor. For the first time, governments began to have a pool of funds with which to make road improvements.[3]

By European standards, the American roads of 1880 were a disgrace. In 1877, workmen had paved Washington's broad, dusty Pennsylvania Avenue with hot asphalt, and similar efforts in New York, Chicago, San Francisco, and Buffalo soon followed.[4] But outside big city limits, mud and dust prevailed, for road building was far too costly for small-town budgets, and the great expanses that had attracted cramped European immigrants made paving exorbitantly expensive.

Albert Pope understood that selling bicycles to everyone required places to ride and, initially at least, they would have to be indoors. But until Pope could offer bicyclists long-distance travel in the open air, he knew his market would be severely limited.

Advent of the safety bicycle in 1884 induced women to join the road advocates. "A frenzy seized upon the people, and men and women of all stations were riding wheels," one contemporary account reported. Samuel Eliot Morison recalled fifty to a hundred young couples passing his Boston door each night, "the girl learning how to ride, and the young man running along and holding on to the handlebar or saddle to prevent her crashing."[5]

Sporting Lobby

Pope had created the League of American Wheelmen in 1880, hoping that dedicated riders would lobby government for better roads. Branching off from the Wheelmen were urban "wheel clubs," which promoted cycling as a sport. But wheelmen alone were insufficient in numbers to overcome the resistance to major road spending. By the 1890s, the Good Roads Movement had widened, as the farmer-led Grangers now joined the chorus, lending the movement the critical mass needed to pass a national roads bill.

Pope's multipronged effort sought to educate the public, to demonstrate how to pave roads, and to educate road builders. First, citizens had to accept smooth roads as a public good. Once convinced, they'd more easily swallow the taxes that roads required. Building on the adage that a picture is worth a thousand words, Pope and his allies from the bicycling community built sections of demonstration roads where none had existed. If people could drive their horses and wagons and, yes, bicycles, onto paved strips as smooth as tabletops, the reasoning went, they'd soon be converted.

Pope soon found an ally in a fellow Civil War veteran. Roy Stone, a white-bearded civil engineer with piercing eyes, gained prominence crusading for good roads in New York state in the 1880s and early 1890s. The reputation of General Stone, as associates called him, eventually reached Congress, which in 1893 called him to head its Office of Road Inquiry but gave him a laughable budget of $10,000. Stone took the job anyway; it was, at least, an opening wedge.[6]

Not waiting for a national effort to get underway, Pope paved at his own expense a stretch of Boston's Columbus Avenue with macadam. Essentially made of layers of compacted small stones, macadam roads didn't offer the smoothness of asphalt or concrete but were light years better than natural dirt roads.

Paying the Mud Tax

As marketers and persuaders, Stone and Pope ran up against resistance to tax hikes time and time again. They argued craftily that citizens were already paying a tax, which the good roads people sought to abolish. They called it the "mud tax," which signified the time and productivity that farmers and merchants lost when rains turned local roads into quagmires, preventing them from moving their products from field and factory to market.

Pope and Stone went so far as to quantify the mud tax in dollar terms, then went on to show how much less taxpayers would have to pay to upgrade their roads. American farmers, they demonstrated, paid twenty-three cents per ton to haul produce to market compared to seven cents paid by British and nine cents by German farmers.[7] The cost above that of their competitors represented the mud tax, which good roads could eliminate. Sleight of hand, perhaps, but the public soon warmed to the idea.

Finally Pope, the high school dropout, financed faculty positions in road engineering at the Massachusetts Institute of Technology and the Lawrence Scientific School. By the time that enough political clout accrued to win legislative majorities for good roads, he reasoned, enough road engineers would have been trained to build them.

Pope and his allies understood that, if they succeeded, the country would have moved forever beyond road drags, in which a horse trailed a heavy wooden plank across the muddy road to smooth it out. The time had come to borrow European technology and experiment with new surfaces, alternative layering techniques, and such modern concepts as curbing, grading, banking, drainage, and traffic control.[8]

Typical of Pope's efforts was his well-publicized drive to set up a Bureau of Road Engineering in the federal Department of Agriculture, a crusade during which he amassed a petition with 150,000 signatures, including those of seventeen governors. Nearer to home, he made Massachusetts only the second state, after New Jersey, to create a highway commission.[9]

Pope had thirsted for learning during his Civil War days, writing home for books and studying subjects new to him, to catch up to his better-schooled comrades in arms. One of his favorite subjects, no longer widely taught in public schools, was rhetoric. The ability to deliver a public talk cogently and self-confidently is a great benefit to anyone who can. But Pope was particularly taken by rhetoric's ability to persuade others, through logical argument, of the rightness of one's position and to bend them to one's will. Now he began to apply that lesson, lecturing in city after city, writing for his magazines, lobbying government, and financing the efforts of others.

European roads, while far better than those across the Atlantic, weren't built nearly well enough for the automobile age. There, as in the United States, a dozen periodicals agitated for better roads. Cycle clubs, including France's Le Vélo, Britain's Cyclists' Touring Club, and the National Cyclists' Union, crusaded as well.[10]

An important distinction emerged at this time between European and American efforts. For European cyclists were not politically influential, whereas in the United States, avid bicyclists included Supreme Court justices, congressmen, and key business leaders. The difference would create a much more potent agency for change on the west side of the Atlantic.[11]

Beating the Drum

In 1892, *Good Roads* magazine appeared, edited by I. B. Potter, a New York lawyer and engineer. Essentially a house organ of the League of American Wheelmen, its stated mission was to persuade the public to pay road taxes. Potter liked to contrast the wretched American roads with those of Europe, particularly France. Whenever a city or county would pave a demonstration road in the United States, his publication would shine a spotlight on it as a model to be followed. The emergence of halftone reproduction was a godsend, letting Potter's readers see the vivid contrast through actual photographs, rather than mere artists' sketches.

Good Roads leaned on the world's first big business to support its roads agenda. The idea that motor vehicles could ever be their competitor dawned late on the railroads, and in 1892, the first American-made car had yet to be sold, so railroads could still be persuaded that better roads were in their best interests. *Good Roads* editorialized that better roads would increase the radius from which the railroad depots could draw farm products. And Colonel Pope urged railroads to lobby congressmen and to strong-arm newspapers in which they advertised to agitate for road reform.[12]

Pope's entreaties won enthusiastic response. Stuyvesant Fish, president of the Illinois Central Railroad, was building his company into an industry giant. Fish, whose legendary New York family produced several generations of public servants, pledged his "hearty cooperation" and shed light on the crisis from one railroad's perspective:

> The present condition of business in the West and South is, perhaps, the best illustration we could have of how utterly deficient this country is in usable highways. Notwithstanding the phenomenal crops last season, there is to-day less grain at railway stations than last year, farmers being unable to haul their crops to the railroad, and therefore without funds to make purchases, all of which results in general stagnation and dullness of trade.[13]

Soon thereafter, the Canadian Pacific; Rio Grande Western; Burlington, Cedar Rapids & Northern; and numerous others fell into line.

Railroads Help Build Roads

Henry Morrison Flagler went well beyond murmurs of support. A preacher's son and chief lieutenant of John D. Rockefeller at Standard Oil Company, Flagler was a dashing rogue with a bushy black mustache and an energetically elegant railroad baron as well. Pushing his Florida East Coast Railway all the way through to Miami had helped transform Florida into a winter vacation destination. Now he offered to haul for free all the road-building material that Pope's men could load onto the railroad's cars.[14]

Entreaties to the nation's newspapers brought a tepid response. Some, such as the *Minneapolis Journal*, saw good roads as largely feeders to the railroads, which had by the 1890s engendered public disdain by overcharging and manipulating stock. If roads are to be built, the *Journal* sniffed, let the railroads build them.[15]

If a road network were ever to develop, Pope realized, states would have to help build roads that passed through multiple towns. The New Jersey Road Improvement Association, for example, demonstrated that most local traffic in 1890 originated from towns outside a municipality's boundaries. Accordingly, it argued, the state should help towns shoulder the load. A state aid bill passed the legislature the next year, requiring abutting property owners to pay one-tenth of the cost of new roads, the state one-third, and the county the rest.

Massachusetts used a different approach, empowering a state highway commission to both plan and pay for new roads. The commission's goal was to link the most important roads within the state into a network. Gradually, state after state fell into line.

But if one state's main road ended at its border and the abutting state chose not to continue the road, long-distance travel would be only a dream. Only Washington could sew the various state patches into one seamless quilt. After a false start in 1892, Colonel Pope waved aloft a petition that measured four-fifths of a mile long and was signed by seventeen governors and 150,000 businesspeople, which called for federal involvement. Congress responded in 1893 by creating an Office of Road Inquiry within the Department of Agriculture, designed explicitly to "get the farmer out of the mud."[16]

The Age of Page

When Logan Page, a 23-year-old Harvard-trained geologist, became testing engineer for the Massachusetts Highway Commission, he copied a tradition that Europe had followed for centuries but that was unknown in America. In 1900, his experiments won him a chance to set up in Washington the nation's first laboratory to test the durability of various road-surfacing materials.

Just as mechanics had tinkered with the bicycle and early internal combustion engines in their laboratories, so too did engineers explore what techniques they might use to advance road building. In some localities, for example, experimenters laid wooden planks lengthwise; others mixed stone and slag from blast furnaces.

Years later, General Roy Stone decided that the future belonged to steel roads. He envisioned two six-foot-wide parallel tracks, laid level with carriage roads at either side, so that wheels might easily pass onto or off of the tracks. In 1898, rapt onlookers at the Trans-Mississippi Exposition in Omaha watched a single horse on a steel track haul an eleven-ton load that would have required twenty horses on a dirt road. Unfortunately, the nation's sheer size worked against laying steel roads coast to coast.[17]

Public-Private Partnership

Pope didn't simply set up a good-government committee to lobby for good roads. That would have provided only an avenue for volunteers to do their civic duty. Instead, he wanted people, such as his Wheelmen, to personally invest in the movement they championed.[18] Owners of horses scared by iron skeletons streaking by had complained to government authorities, which began to ban the ungainly creatures. Pope now realized that if a bicycle craze were to grip the nation, the industry must meet this challenge head on and win the same right to use the roads that horses and pedestrians enjoyed.

Roy Stone became a bedrock ally of Colonel Pope over the years. Unlike the railroads, which considered any ties with government as unabashed socialism, Pope the capitalist and Stone the bureaucrat worked together hand in glove toward a common goal. Their first collective effort was the "good roads train." In 1893, the Massachusetts Highway Commission, trying to increase the bang for its limited bucks, had parceled out some $300,000 among thirty-seven widely scattered road projects, each about a mile long. Once a cross-section of the public could experience the smoothness of paved roads, the reasoning went, the converted would demand more money from their legislatures.

Stone liked the idea but had only a pitiful $10,000 and one clerk to work with. Not to worry, Pope assured him, and together they proved that persuasion helps a good salesperson as much as money: They wheedled road equipment manufacturers into coughing up free pavers and local governments and individuals into underwriting labor and materials.

With barely the funds which a century later would pave a driveway, Stone handed out maps of proposed ribbons of paved roads from Portland, Maine, to Jacksonville, Florida, on the East Coast, from Seattle, Washington, to San Diego, California, on the West Coast, and from Washington, D.C., to San Francisco, California, spanning the country. Such grandiose ideas may have worked against him. Some state officials saw his plan as the opening wedge to a national roads program that would usurp state control.[19]

Stone's first public display was in 1897. At the New Jersey Agricultural College, his crews placed six inches of trap rock macadam eight feet wide on a 660-foot section of the main road to the college; this first "object lesson road" cost a total of $321. This modest project helped set off a century-long feeding frenzy for paved roads, on which Washington has since spent hundreds of billions of dollars.[20]

People at the time learned nearly everything from the printed word, so Pope helped finance the publication of *Good Roads Magazine, Bicycle World, Wheel,* and *Wheelman,* employing such gifted writers and editors as S. S. McClure along the way.

The Movement Expands

In the process, the Wheelmen dovetailed with another grassroots organization, which would broaden its message and strengthen its clout. Joining the Wheelmen's well-heeled easterners were midwestern farmers. They had fallen into poverty at the hands of railroad barons who, in the post–Civil War era, had bankrupted farmers by their monopoly pricing and had diluted the value of stock the farmers had purchased, often with their meager life savings. Promising revenge, the farmers had formed the National Grange of the Patrons of Husbandry.

Unlikely bedfellows, it is true, but both shared a common agenda—to require government to create smooth roads. While local Wheelmen worked the state legislatures, Grangers rode the hated railroads to the nation's capital, where in 1893 they demanded that Congress deliver mail to the nation's farms, an undertaking that clearly would be impossible with dirt roads made impassable by mud and ruts.[21]

Any national movement, from space exploration to civil rights, takes decades to achieve, a fact never lost on Colonel Pope. As America approached a new century, Pope had been working obsessively for road improvement for nearly twenty years. The goal of linking every state capital with paved roads wouldn't be reached until after his death in 1909, when Pope would be heralded as the father of good roads. But, in fairness, the self-effacing George Day should at least rank as an uncle. For the tactful, unobtrusive Day ran the quotidian operations of the Pope enterprises, giving the Colonel the freedom to stage his crusade.

And this fact exposes Albert Augustus Pope's Achilles' heel. For his uncanny ability to hire good managers led him to so rely on them that he failed to keep abreast of changing technology and management trends. Within a few years, better opportunities and the Grim Reaper would strip from Pope the very men who had built his empire. Trying to rebuild from the ground up, Colonel Pope would find himself very much alone.

Notes

1. Nevins, Allan, *Ford: The Times, the Man, the Company*, p. 257.

2. U.S. Department of Transportation, *America's Highways 1776–1976*, p. 41.

3. Ibid.

4. Goddard, Stephen B., *Getting There: The Epic Struggle between Road and Rail in the American Century*, p. 47.

5. Morison, Samuel Eliot, *One Boy's Boston*, p. 29.

6. Goddard, p. 46.

7. Nevins, p. 257.

8. U.S. Department of Transportation, p. 42.

9. Nevins, p. 258.

10. Flink, James J., *The Automobile Age,* p. 4.

11. Ibid.

12. Dearing, Charles, *American Highway Policy,* pp. 227–28; Harrod, Stephen, "Death Wish," p. 5, quoting letter from Colonel Pope to railroad executives in September 1892.

13. Harrod, Stephen, "Death Wish: The Good Roads Trains Impact on American Transportation Policy," p. 4, quoting letter from Stuyvesant Fish to Albert A. Pope, May 9, 1892.

14. Harrod, p. 10, quoting undated letter from Henry Flagler to Albert Pope; Chernow, Ron, *Titan,* p. 106.

15. *Minneapolis Journal*, untitled editorial, October 15, 1892.

16. *Waterbury Republican*, November 19, 1967.

17. Goddard, p. 47.

18. Nevins, p. 256.

19. U.S. Department of Transportation, p. 46.

20. Goddard, p. 51.

21. Ibid., p. 45.

CHAPTER 8

THE WUNDERKIND

Until much improved, go ahead with the electrics. Their [sic] quiet, safe and easily controlled.
Colonel Pope to Hiram Maxim

The Town of Hartford, Connecticut, is the greatest center of activity in the automobile industry today.[1]

OR ALL HIRAM PERCY MAXIM'S prodigious talents, he had one fatal drawback that prevented him from changing the direction of the Pope Manufacturing Company: He was born a generation too late. When Maxim came to work for Pope in 1895 at age twenty-six, he had nearly a decade of engineering experience behind him. Pope was fifty-two and had children nearly as old as his new protégé.

So, when the whiz kid earnestly pleaded his case, insisting that gasoline-powered vehicles were likely to gain the advantage over electric cars, Pope only half listened, patronizingly, as if his son were arguing with him over politics or religion. In short, he didn't take the young man seriously. Had they met as contemporaries and had Pope heeded Maxim, the shape of the automobile industry, then and now, might have been different.

Inventions in the Blood

The Civil War was a vivid memory when Hiram Percy Maxim was born in 1869 into a family of inventors. His father, Hiram Stevens Maxim, had already patented, at age twenty-six, a hair-curling iron and was working on a locomotive headlight when his namesake joined the family in their rented house on Third Street in Brooklyn, New York.[2]

From his early years, the son was called by his middle name, which probably suited his mother well. Calling for "Percy" to come in to dinner would remind Jane Budden Maxim of the hero of a romance novel after whom she had named her child, a fantasy she may have needed to endure marriage to Percy's cruel and mercurial father. While he would answer to "Percy" within the family, he shed the name in favor of Hiram or H.P. once he walked through the factory gates.

Maxim genes bred genius. Percy's uncle Hudson Maxim worked with his brother Hiram in munitions making, and he invented a smokeless cannon powder later used during World War I, amassing a number of patents along the way.

Percy's father was a prolific yet bizarre man. As the son grew, he'd watch his father perfect such diverse contrivances as a steam-powered airplane, a mousetrap, an automatic sprinkling system, steam-powered water pumps, and engine governors. In 1881, he exhibited a pressure regulator at the Paris Exposition. But the invention that had the greatest influence on his son was undoubtedly a gasoline motor.[3]

Flawed Father

Years later, Hiram Percy Maxim would recall his childhood with pain leavened by humor; a whimsical thread lightened a deadly serious life: "I am sure my father merely blundered into fatherhood without giving the matter any serious consideration. He gave every evidence of conceiving fatherhood to be a means provided by nature for perpetrating humorous misconceptions upon young and inexperienced offspring."[4]

Disdainful of household help, all of whom he labeled "stupid," the elder Maxim would experiment on them for his own entertainment, if not edification. Hiram had read, for example, that the sensations of extreme cold and extreme heat are the same. One day, in view of a kitchen maid, he heated a poker red hot and cooled another to below zero. As soon as her back was turned, Maxim "slapped the cold poker on the back of her neck while talking about the intense heat of the cold poker." The young girl shrieked as Maxim "dissolved in laughter," then gave her notice "in a fit of frenzy."[5]

Soon, the indifferent and often cruel parent became an absent one as well. In 1881, at the Paris Exposition, he wrote home boastfully to his family: "You know of course that I am a Sir Knight now. Having been made so by the French President. I have the decoration of the Cross of the Legion of Honor. I may be able to get another decoration in Spain."

Hiram never returned from his visit abroad and soon settled in London. Three years later, he implored his son to visit him there, but the teenager's abandonment had taken its toll, and Percy, who then was only two years away from graduating from MIT at age seventeen, wrote a reply that displeased his father. While Percy's letter has been lost, his father's reply remains:

My Dear Son Percy

Your curt letter to me is at hand. So you choose to disobey the commands of your Father do you? Well it is not such a soft snap as you might suppose to drop into a first class position.... However you will find this out for your self later. Who ever advises you to take the course you have taken is doing you a great injustice.

Your Father Hiram S. Maxim

P.S. This will be a good letter to keep and read when you are about 25 years old.[6]

At the time, Percy did not travel to London, and father and son never met again. The son would read in the public press of his father's achievements, including inventing the machine gun, which made him wealthy. Later, he became a British subject and was knighted by the British Crown.

Percy longed silently for his dad. Much later, in 1898, newly married, Percy took his wife to London on their honeymoon. He quite unexpectedly came upon his father in a public building but, rather than approaching him, simply peered at him a long while from behind a column, hungry for the sight of Hiram yet unable to call out to him, perhaps fearing yet another rejection.[7]

MIT's mechanical arts course at the time required only two years' study, which Percy completed at age seventeen. With barely a beard, young Percy embarked on an engineering career, taking four different jobs with companies in Indiana and Massachusetts before landing one with the American Projectile Company at Lynn, Massachusetts, thereby consciously or unconsciously following his father's interest in munitions. By age twenty-one, he had become its superintendent, the equivalent of plant manager.

One weekend afternoon, Maxim pedaled his bicycle over rutted dirt roads from Salem to Lynn, Massachusetts, to visit a girlfriend. On his return home, his aching legs told him there had to be a better way, and a concept began to take root in Percy's fertile mind.

Out of the Loop

By the early 1890s, experiments with internal combustion engines were taking place in dozens of shops and garages in America and Europe, where men with names such as Benz, Peugeot, and Opel linked their motors to crude chassis in attempts to create a new form of locomotion. To those who kept up with the publications burgeoning in this new industry, the buzz of inventive talent was evident, yet, in spite of his natural acumen, the trend was somehow lost on Maxim, who recalled in his celebrated autobiography, *Horseless Carriage Days*:

> As I look back, I am amazed that so many of us began working so nearly at the same time, and without the slightest notion that others were working on the problem. In 1892, when I began my work on a mechanical road vehicle, I suppose there were fifty persons in the U.S. working on the same idea.... It has always been my belief that we all began to work on a gasoline-engine–propelled road vehicle at about the same time because it had become apparent that civilization was ready for the mechanical vehicle.[8]

In truth, most inventors came to work on the ground-breaking concept because they had read about others doing so; they did not reinvent the wheel themselves. Maxim, however, continually worked to fix problems that had long since been solved by other designers. Automotive historian James Flink says the predominant pattern of automobile development was for a single source of technological innovation to spawn imitators rather than for simultaneous independent innovation to occur. The Duryeas, for example, were first motivated to design an automobile after reading a description of the Benz tricycle in the 1889 *Scientific American*.[9]

As a result of his isolation, Maxim had no idea that his engine would need a cooling system and carburetor. "He was deeply shocked to find the amount of waste heat he had to get rid of, but hoped, when the engine was fixed to a bicycle, that the current of air on the naked steel cylinders would suffice to keep them cool."[10]

Had Maxim been more in touch with the developments of his competitors, he would have known that George Lewis had invented a system of water cooling and that John Wilkinson of the Franklin Company of Syracuse had divided the engine into four small elements, which gave it a larger radiating surface to keep it cool; he had also invented an auxiliary escape valve to expel burned-out gases, which otherwise heated the engine.[11]

Meeting with Disaster

The first trial of Maxim's fledgling motor was connected to a "rather decayed, tandem bicycle." He found he couldn't pedal fast enough to start the engine, so he disconnected the driving chain and pushed the bike to the top of the steepest hill around, hitched up the chain, and set off downhill. He met half his objective. The engine started, but the vehicle careened out of control when its front wheel struck a rut, hurling its navigator over the handlebars into a ditch and leading him to conclude that a sturdier, four-wheel vehicle might be more practical. The experience also taught him that he needed a workplace home that was further ahead on the learning curve.

In 1894, Maxim visited Hartford and dropped in to inspect the impressive Pope complex. He was already well aware of Pope's success in the bicycle industry, and the plant he visited was by then an industrial giant. Pope, in the words of one writer, was "a self-made millionaire, who had built his company into the largest in the world and who always had a sharp weather eye on the horizon in search of a new way to pick up another million or two."[12]

Pope by now was well aware of what his domestic and foreign competitors were up to, but he didn't share their faith in the internal combustion engine. Electric storage batteries had only recently been developed; to Pope, they were quiet, smooth-running, and clean. A buckboard fitted out with electric batteries in an enclosed box had been exhibited at the Columbia Exposition a year earlier, and Pope was inclined toward electric locomotion as the standard for the industry-to-be.[13]

Yet Pope was a realist and understood the unpredictability of the market. While tinkerers labored to put together working models, Pope had a big league industrial plant at the ready. When the small fry were ready to begin production, he knew they would have to turn to him or someone like him or they would advance very slowly.

Calling on the Duryeas

In this spirit, Pope approached some neighbors to the north in Springfield, Massachusetts, brothers Frank and Charles Duryea, and suggested producing the gasoline-powered vehicle they had been developing. He'd give them, Pope promised, $5 royalty per car. They countered with a demand of $50 per car. "Highway robbery!" huffed Pope and stalked from their plant.

Dismissed by the Duryeas, Pope fell back on the methodology that had served him so well in the bicycle era. He decided to bring outside expertise into his plant. So when Maxim got up the nerve to approach the Pope company in 1895, he met a receptive ear.

Percy, too, was ripe for a change. After having spent most of his career in Lynn, he had resolved to broaden his horizons. The young bachelor posed for his picture during that time with chin down and eyes cast up eagerly, emphasizing his poorly hidden ambition. Determination emanated from him, in spite of his mischievous eyes, a smile that played at the corners of his mouth, and porcupine-quill hair sticking up all over his head, which he often covered with a derby.

The Hartford visit was arranged by Hayden Eames, who as a naval lieutenant had inspected projectiles at Maxim's Lynn plant before retiring to manage the Tube Department of Pope Manufacturing Corporation. A tall, profane man of military bearing, "he stood erect, looked you over in a stern way, and had you on the defensive in the first few minutes," Maxim recalled later.[14] Yet Eames came to think well enough of Maxim to soon arrange a match with his wife's sister, one that would end in marriage.

It must have cheered Maxim to know that the one person at the Pope plant to whom he was a known quantity thought well enough of him to plead his case with management. But when they chatted at the Tube Works in May 1895 and Maxim told him about the gasoline-powered tricycle he was working on, Eames told him flatly he was wasting his time. The success Pope had had with the bicycle, Eames ventured, resulted from the physical exercise it involved. A motor would destroy the vehicle's chief advantage. Obviously, he had missed the young man's point entirely.

Maxim had been having second thoughts himself about his tricycle but not for the reasons that Eames expressed. To be suitable for a motor, he concluded, a vehicle should be four-wheeled, providing room to put things and "room for one man to adjust the machinery while the other steered."[15]

Likely Prospect

Eames introduced Maxim to George Day, who headed Pope's local bicycle operations and whom Maxim found to be "quiet, approachable and sympathetic, with a cordiality which was irresistible."[16] Day and Eames liked Maxim well enough to dispatch Henry Souther, also an MIT graduate engineer, to visit Maxim's factory in Lynn.

When Percy told his mother of Souther's approaching visit, he wrote, "She unconsciously added to my panic by asking how in the world I ever dared to have an expert from a great company come all the way from Hartford to Lynn to look over anything that I could have made. That was precisely the way I regarded the matter." But when Maxim met the tall, mustachioed Souther at Boston's North Station, they soon became fast friends, a relationship that would last for the rest of their lives.[17]

Souther returned with rave reviews of Maxim's tricycle, leading the Colonel to offer Maxim a job developing a motor vehicle for the Pope Manufacturing Company. Maxim wound up his affairs in Lynn and in July packed his belongings onto a Hartford-bound train.[18] As a bonus, Pope let Maxim bring along Herbert W. Alden, his aide-de-camp. Pope also recruited Frederick W. Law, an experienced gasoline automobile engineer and inventor, to head the new division's model room.[19]

Within a month, Maxim had designed the Crawford runabout and took it out for a test drive on nearby Park Street, hoping to drive it on a 3 percent grade for fifteen minutes to "the smallest possible audience."[20] To get it outside, they had to carry the flimsy contraption down a flight of steps. While Maxim drove, machinist Eugene Lobdell ran alongside, carrying a leather traveling bag filled with copper tubing, wire, screws, and nuts should the machine malfunction.[21]

Maxim's penciled engineering notes on the Crawford Wagon, maintained a century later in neat ruled notebooks, show the grade location, road condition, average pounds pulled, distance traveled, time taken, approximate rate of speed (from three to twelve miles per hour), foot pounds of energy expended, corresponding horsepower, and total weight of the wagon and load. He made sure, in testing the vehicle on nearby streets, to drive it over pavement and through sand and mud.[22]

Standing beside a Ton of Dynamite

To say George Day was unimpressed would be an understatement, although his characteristic tact would have made him choose his words carefully, so as not to offend his naive charge. Entreating his boss to ride in the runabout, Maxim said, "He acted as though he were standing beside a ton of naked dynamite. I think he expected the contraption might burst at any moment and rend him. He made me drive it around the yard a great many times before he could bring himself to venture in it with me."[23]

Maxim was not unsympathetic to Day's reaction and had the perspective to see things through other's eyes. "It shook and trembled and rattled and clattered, spat oil, fire, smoke and smell, and to a person who disliked machinery naturally, and who had been brought up to the shiny elegance and perfection of fine horse carriages [as had Day], it was revolting."[24]

A few days later, Maxim succeeded in luring the Colonel himself for a ride:

> I asked him to note the safety plug and the controller handle, but I was wasting my breath with him. He was not interested. I drove him around the yard as I had Mr. Day, noting with interest that Mr. Day had gathered Lt. Eames and himself at the appointed spot.
>
> The Colonel asked questions about how much the machine had cost and how much cheaper they would be were they to be built in quantity.... After explaining the backing I performed the turning-round evolution. The Colonel was not impressed even a little bit. He took it all for granted. What he was interested in was talking with Mr. Day about manufacturing, costs, prices, etc.[25]

Pink Slip for Maxim?

Maxim was lighting no fires, or so he thought. The Colonel was known to be committed to electric automobiles, and Maxim had built for him the Mark

I and Mark II electric models, but the latter, a two-cycle motor, had failed.[26] Late in 1896 his mentor, Eames, summoned Maxim to Pope's office, where Maxim anticipated his dismissal. Instead, Pope said he wanted him to build a small gas tricycle package carrier, which merchants could use in deliveries. In those days, muddy streets were packed with teenage boys delivering merchants' goods on foot-pedaled tricycles, and Pope saw a market if he could promise to increase the speed with which those packages would reach their destinations.[27] As far as gasoline passenger cars, Pope's avuncular advice was: "Until much improved, go ahead with the electrics. Their [sic] quiet, safe and easily controlled."[28]

To elude competitors eager for inside information, Maxim purposely scheduled test rides at night, so as to attract the least attention. After one jaunt in a Mark VII to Springfield, thirty miles north of Hartford, he wrote, "In addition, it was now dark and all we had to pick out rocks and chuck holes in the gloom was the little kerosene bicycle headlamp."[29] The trip took nine and a half hours, and, as he was to learn, the Duryea brothers had already completed a round trip to Hartford.[30]

Powered vehicles on the streets of Hartford weren't exactly new. In 1797, Dr. Apollos Kinsley had kicked up clouds of dust as his steam automobile rumbled down the city's Main Street. A man named Christopher M. Spencer "was annoying the farmers hereabouts with his roaring steam car along the highways in the early 1860s."

The model that Maxim tried out on city streets in 1895 was a three-cylinder, four-cycle engine, with no brake or reverse gear. Pope's increasing faith in Maxim had led him to build a new motor carriage division of the Pope Company nearby at 1 Laurel Street. "Those first miles," recalled Maxim, "were filled with adventure and the spirit of conquest," though the carburetor was "a nightmare. Fortunately there were jounces enough to keep the engine from stalling." Yet, within the year, the car was running a hundred miles to New York and to Boston.[31]

Maxim's Scrapbook

History is indebted to Hiram Percy Maxim for keeping a scrapbook of everything he read on the burgeoning industry. In it, he detailed advances in motor vehicles from all over the world, dating to his first interest in 1893. Press coverage of the day was rife with excitement about this development, which was likely to transform everyday life. For example, an 1893 *New York Sun* article breathlessly described in headlines a new product that had taken Germany by storm: "The New Propelling Power that Has Come Out of Poetic

Hiram Percy Maxim, still in his 20s, sits in his first commercial creation for Pope Manufacturing Company, the electric-powered Mark III Stanhope. *(Courtesy John Lee and Percy Maxim Lee.)*

Germany. It Is Independent of Rails, and Can Fly over Country Roads at Thirty Miles an Hour.... No Noise, No Smoke, No Steam, No Odor. Any One Can Handle It."

New York Central Railroad President Chauncey Depew is quoted on railroad speed records set that year, with the prediction that "before the new year has been ushered in we may have more surprises on land and water." One article reported that the first motor-wagon was shown, in crude form, at the Munich Exposition in 1888 and that by 1893, Benz had already sold 300 carriages.[32]

Maxim's scrapbook belies the contention in his autobiography that hundreds of early automakers innovated in a vacuum, each ignorant of the progress or discoveries of the others. The facts, of course, were quite different: mechanics of the era were quite aware that others were inventing, and many kept abreast of their competitors' progress through industry publications.

Competition at Work

Charles Duryea had begun to experiment in Springfield in 1888, Henry Ford in Detroit in 1896, although he would later claim he had done so as early as 1892.[33] In 1894, Henry Morris and Pedro Salom had produced in Philadelphia an electric car they called the Electrobat.[34]

"After the Paris Exposition of 1889 virtually no development of importance in automobile technology went unreported in one or another of the engineering journals, bicycle periodicals, auto trade journals, newspapers and popular magazines of the day," observes auto historian James Flink.[35]

Why Maxim would choose to suggest otherwise is a conundrum. Would his advances seem more impressive if his readers thought they had sprung full blown from his own mind? As a member of a family steeped in invention, did he seek to romanticize the process by suggesting that many separate minds evolved solutions on parallel tangents?

Maxim had been in Colonel Pope's employ only a few months when he attracted the attention of the *New York World* in an article that described "Young Maxim's Motor Tandem Tricycle." The piece described Maxim as the son of the inventor of a flying machine and the nephew of a man who invented a gun "which is calculated to work such terrible slaughter, amounting practically to annihilation that it is expected to make the bickering powers of Europe come to terms and live hereafter in peace."[36]

Free Media

As a sign that the horseless carriage was here to stay, the prestigious *Scientific American* ran a special supplement on auto carriages and the Paris-Bordeaux auto race. A page of accompanying cartoons spoke only half facetiously to the dizzying trend of industry supplanting nature. In one, entitled "When the Horseless Carriage Comes In," an old hen says to another, "They don't use horses any more and I see they are shooting clay pigeons, and it wouldn't surprise me to see them manufacture eggs and spring chickens soon."[37]

Automobile races had become the rage, and Maxim or an assistant dutifully clipped into his scrapbook coverage of them, such as the *Chicago Times Herald* article containing pages of rules. In the 1895 Thanksgiving Day race, only two of eighty-three entrants were able to complete the 55-mile race, won by a Duryea car, followed by a Benz driven by Charles Brady King, mentor to a 31-year-old Detroit engineer named Henry Ford. The winning time averaged less than eight miles per hour.

Thomas A. Edison, whose reactions to events in the news always made good copy for a hungry press, told a reporter from the *New York World* that "the horseless vehicle is the coming wonder.... It is only a question of time when the carriages and trucks in every large city will be run with motors."[38] He didn't specify whether the motors would be electric, steam, or gasoline.

By 1896, electric phaetons and runabouts, carrying the label of the Columbia Electric Vehicle Company, were rolling off the assembly lines at 1 Laurel Street, a couple of football fields from the Pope main offices. But Maxim had finally convinced Pope to let him also produce a few gasoline-powered cars. During 1897, the year that Charles and Frank Duryea sold the first commercially produced automobile in America, Hiram Percy Maxim followed suit with ten of his own.[39]

Yet when George Day dropped by Percy's experimental room later that year to see what his young charge was up to, Maxim recalled:

> He spied the gears in a box all of them swimming in black oil. In a shocked sort of a way he asked me what all the cogwheels were for. I told him they were the change gears.
>
> He looked at me a moment, shook his head and walked away. After a few minutes he beckoned to me. I went over to him and he said, "Maxim, is it necessary to have all those gears in a carriage?" I repeated that there was no possible escape as long as a gasoline-engine was used. He went on to ask, "And you have to have all that oil?" I explained that the gears ran more quietly in oil and that the bearings also needed oil.
>
> Again shaking his head sadly, he announced emphatically, "Well, then, Maxim, let me tell you something. We are on the wrong track. No one will buy a carriage that has to have all that greasy machinery in it."[40]

Three Modes in Play

Duryea and Maxim were hardly alone among auto producers in that early year of 1897. Francis and Freelan Stanley that year began to produce steam vehicles under their own name in Newton, Massachusetts, burning kerosene or gasoline to heat the boiler. The engine operated at pressures of up to 600 pounds per square inch, making them highly efficient. Their drawback was the twenty minutes required to work up a head of steam and their need for frequent servicing.[41]

While New England inventors concentrated primarily on electric and steam vehicles, most midwesterners worked with internal combustion engines. Ransom E. Olds in Michigan and Alexander Winton in Ohio were among the leading gasoline-automakers. Yet, among them all, only the Pope company could be considered a major auto manufacturer, turning out 500 electric and 40 gasoline carriages in the next two years.[42]

Electric carriages were powered by heavy accumulator batteries, each

Apprehensive secretaries from Pope's Hartford plant ride an early Pope model in the late 1890s. Note how much of the wheels and frame is borrowed from bicycle design. *(Courtesy John Lee and Percy Maxim Lee.)*

of which weighed some 750 pounds. Quiet and fast as they seemed, their drawback was being able to travel only forty to fifty miles without a charge. Yet the Colonel believed in the technology and let Maxim build gasoline-powered cars only as a sideline.

With so many small-scale manufacturers churning out new products, the public was awash in marketing. How could a consumer decide?

Industry Innovation

On May 13, 1897, Pope, who had initiated so many innovations and felt he had a finger on the public pulse, introduced a marketing tool that would soon become an industry standard. Calling together members of the press, Pope, with much hoopla, unveiled his new models for 1897. Not only did he let press members peek at his shiny new cars, he let them be the first in their towns to operate one, and he gave them photographs they could take home to their newspapers for publication. Soon, manufacturers were bringing in reporters from long distances, realizing that train fare and a lavish buffet were small prices to pay for the "free media" that would follow.[43]

Accordingly, in 1897, Pope produced the world's first public demonstration of a production model electric automobile, even testing its endurance through mud and water. The local *Hartford Courant*, with great prescience, remarked that the day "would mark the inauguration in Hartford of an industry which will surely develop into great proportions and add to the fame the city already has for first-class mechanical productions."

The car demonstrated was the Mark III Stanhope, and it drew engineers as well as reporters from all over the world. Its battery accounted for nearly half of its 1,800-pound weight, and its two-horsepower motor could accommodate four speeds, from three to fifteen miles an hour, with a 30-mile range.[44] A British technical paper editor, who had come to Hartford after touring Britain, France, and Germany, where Daimler and Benz were experimenting, declared, "The Town of Hartford, Connecticut, is the greatest center of activity in the automobile industry today."[45] As Colonel Pope stood among the bunting decorating the plant for the new model unveiling, Maxim and his minions spared barely a glance through the towering front windows at company executives pumping the hands of imported dignitaries before they bent over their drafting tables once more.

Against the backdrop of Sousa marches playing outdoors, Maxim refined calculations for next year's model: "Assume push on pedal to be 100 lbs.," he penciled in his notebook. "Pull on chain would be $6.75/3.25 \times 1 = 207$ lbs." Another day, he recorded, "Decided to abandon continuous flame method and return to intermittent explosive principle similar to sketch dated Dec. 11, for the reason that means have been found to probably make explosive method self-maintaining and to avoid having to pump in the fresh supplies of air against 'boiler' pressure."[46]

Life with Mother

In 1898, Percy lived with his mother and sister Florence on Hartford's Main Street, less than a mile from Pope's auto works, in a fashionable new hotel of Romanesque design called the Linden, whose top floor sported an ornate cupola with panoramic views of the expanding city. Before zoning stratified neighborhoods, lower Main Street featured a melange of uses, with a flour mill, tobacco shop, dye works, two saloons, brass mill, and livery stable. If Percy sought a personal attorney, he may have steered clear of his neighbor William J. Hamersley, whom Mark Twain publicly blamed for driving him to bankruptcy in his futile attempt to manufacture a printing compositor: "Of Hamersley, about 2/3s of him is knave and the other is fool."[47]

Test runs to measure the effectiveness of new components ruled Maxim's day. Excerpts from his diary for early 1898 illustrate the differences in automobiling then and now:

> 1-16: Took Mother [for a ride]. Scared horses in front of Linden. Made bad fall in street. ... Made run on tri [gas-operated tricycle] out to West Hartford and back. First long run made by gasoline Pope vehicle.
> 1-19: Took tri over to Main works and showed it. [Henry] Souther ran it. ... Broke fork South Wethersfield and came home to fix it. Left tri in barn.

In run after run, Maxim sought to work the bugs out of his motorized tricycle, which Pope had seen as an ideal delivery wagon, since it would carry more than a simple bicycle. "Went out on tri in evening," Maxim reported on February 10, "getting confidence enough to stop in street anywhere now, that is, almost anywhere."

On March 4, Maxim wrote: "Made a try at run to Springfield with Lobdell [coworker]." Runs were often at night, so as not to attract the notice of competitors as the Pope team sought to iron out the kinks in their machinery. "Started at 9:45 P.M. Moonlight. Got to Stony Hill near Windsor and found roads impassable and gave up. Broke little tube leading to burner and had to put up in a shed over night."

He reported auspiciously on March 11: "Took Miss Julia Hamilton out in Mark III at noon. Her first ride ... lunched at Eames house." (The wife of Hayden Eames, his supervisor, was Julia's sister.) Not to play favorites, he took Julia's sisters Leonore and Josephine for rides later.

About to enter his thirties and still living with his mother, Percy had begun to think seriously about his domestic future. In the next few weeks, he would size the three Hamilton sisters up as he went for rides with one, then another. On March 26, he observed that Josephine was older than he (she was thirty-two) "and very conventional. Mighty fine girl, but cold, I guess."

"A Rather Fine Girl"

Two weeks later, in spite of her spurning a ride in his Mark IV model (she thought it too plebeian, he guessed), Percy reported, "Coming to the conclusion that Miss Josephine Hamilton is a rather fine girl." They rehearsed together for an upcoming amateur theatrical, *A Cup of Tea,* and the next day, an obviously lovestruck Percy wrote, "Miss Hamilton *smiled* on me. Gawd!"

In 1898, Hiram Percy Maxim basks under the adoring gaze of sister Florence, as overprotective mother Jane Budden Maxim appears to ward off anyone who would stand between her and her son. When he asked Josephine Hamilton to marry him soon thereafter, his mother told him the marriage would cause her death. She actually lived for 13 years. *(Courtesy John Lee and Percy Maxim Lee.)*

"Funny why I enjoy rehearsing with Miss Hamilton," he reported on Easter Sunday. "How she does drink water and how she does abuse mankind! I look forward for some unknown reason to taking her home." So much did he appear smitten that his sister Florence, the bespectacled family eccentric, bet her brother shortly thereafter $100 that he'd marry Josephine.

Things had progressed enough that in May, Percy was invited to Hagerstown, Maryland, to meet the family of his new girl, an occasion during which, Percy wrote, he "didn't sleep hardly any, could scarcely down my breakfast." Meanwhile, in Hartford, the prospect of losing her son to another didn't sit well with his mother, who was "awfully upset," a concern he was able to assuage a few days later during a long ride with his mother in his Mark III.

But business wouldn't wait for romance. On July 13, Maxim "found burned field trouble with Mark VI motor. Pope returned and thinks water cooled tri engine necessary" to cure the overheating. By month's end, he had "a very frank talk" with Josephine about "our love and marriage" during an excursion to an amusement park in which their trolley car broke down and they had to help push it back to Hartford.

The Colonel Mellows

Maxim's boss was gradually mellowing to gasoline vehicles. On Aug. 18, Percy recorded, "took Col. long ride down town on Quad [quadricycle]. Worked well. Our first gasoline pleasure vehicle a success." Percy's dogged efforts had brought Pope around to manufacturing a few gasoline vehicles but couldn't dissuade him from his belief that electric cars were a cut above.

In spite of his British knighthood, Percy's father was gaining a notorious reputation abroad. On October 9, "Article came out in papers about old man's bigamy charge. Terrible shock. Makes me feel terribly about Josephine. ... Can't express poignancy of regret." The next day, he received a letter from Josephine, which said, "She would stick by me but I can't get over the awful suffering it must be causing her." In desperation, he observed, "I ought to change my name, it seems to me"; he actually went as far as writing the governor for information on how to go about it.

Wedding plans accelerated, although Percy's sister Florence declined the honor of serving as a bridesmaid at the wedding "because she must wear pink!" Percy's mother was still giving him fits about the marriage, telling him she wouldn't live two years more (she lived thirteen). "Depresses me to have her feel so about our marriage." This marked the last entry in the diary, which he discontinued upon his December 22, 1898, marriage in Hagerstown; the happy couple sailed thereafter for a European honeymoon on the *Statendam*.

Aboard ship, Percy wrote his new sister-in-law Julia:

> There are a few people on this earth who have been true friends to me. You stand in the first row in their list. I hope from the bottom of my heart the occasion will arise when I can show my gratitude. It may only come in the opportunity to be the husband that Josephine, your sister, deserves.

Back to the Lab

While motor vehicles borrowed much from the bicycle, the automobile was a wholly new invention. Metallurgy had refined the bicycle frame, which Maxim and others used in early models, for example, but the stress of engine vibration required stronger, more resilient frames. So, after settling his bride into a new Pope-built brick townhouse at the corner of Park Terrace and Capitol Avenue, next door to the Eames family, Maxim headed back to the lab.[48]

Creating the template for others to follow "was a tremendous task," Percy recalled later in *Horseless Carriage Days*. "Everything had to be created. There were no suitable bearings, suitable wheels, tires, batteries, battery-handling equipment, battery-charging equipment, gasoline engines, carburetors, spark plugs, brakes or steering gears."[49]

Transmissions, clutches, and drive shafts are taken for granted today, but their evolution and refinement a century ago was a subject of pitched competition among automakers. Whether Maxim was reading popular magazines on the subject or not, others were, and a solution posed to a dilemma raised in one issue would be answered several issues later by another reader/mechanic. Indeed, the cross-fertilization of ideas sped the development of the automobile along at breakneck speed.

How, some inventors pondered, could power travel from the engine to the wheels? Many of the early tinkerers were farmers who had worked with farm machinery, so they borrowed the principle of a belt run from a stationary engine to a factory machine. Others borrowed the bicycle principle of a chain drive.

In 1894, one inventor presaged modern times by introducing a friction disc, which could be connected to a drive shaft to propel a vehicle. Two years later, Ohio's Alexander Winton introduced a propeller shaft from the engine and bevel gears in the car's rear axle.

These devices worked well on level surfaces, but how could the vehicle be made to climb hills? The solution lay in developing a transmission, with gears of different sizes for hills and grades.

How could the drive shaft disengage from the engine when the driver wanted to shift gears, without having to get out of the vehicle? Soon Detroit's Charles Brady King developed the air clutch. Refining that idea in 1898, J. W. Packard produced the spring clutch.[50]

The vibrations of a gasoline motor were so violent as to rend apart a flimsy metal frame, so metallurgical labs began experimenting with strong yet light alloys. In 1896, Ransom Olds introduced a new spring frame construction to cut vibration. And placing the engine in front rather than under the seat let a driver stand up to repair his vehicle rather than groveling in the mud beneath the car.[51]

By 1898, Maxim had worked out many of the bugs that had plagued early tinkerers and produced a vehicle that bears, in its essentials, remarkable resemblance to automobiles produced a century later. His Mark VIII, Lot 4, was the first to incorporate a shaft drive to a live rear axle. Its single-cylinder engine was now mounted in the front, not under the driver's seat. The Mark VIII featured an electric ignition with automatic advance-and-retard mechanism, and its wheel steering column could be tilted forward to give better access to the front seat.[52]

Reasons to Celebrate

As Maxim neared his thirtieth birthday, he had every reason to celebrate. He headed his own automotive division, he had persuaded the Colonel to let him produce a few gasoline automobiles along with many more electrics, he had won the hand of a beautiful woman, and Pope Manufacturing

Company stood on the brink of becoming the world's largest car manufacturer. Yet around the corner lay big trouble, disguised as a magnificent opportunity.

Notes

1. Dean, Clarence, "Pope-Hartford Started Auspiciously in Auto Field," p. 1.
2. McCallum, Iain, *Blood Brothers: Hiram & Hudson Maxim, Pioneers of Modern Warfare*, p. 22.
3. *Encylopaedia Brittanica* (1978), Vol. 6, p. 712.
4. Lee, Percy Maxim and John Glessner, *Family Reunion*, p. 179.
5. Ibid.
6. Ibid., p. 183.
7. While no record exists that Percy and his father ever met again, in 1914, he wrote a ten-page letter to Sir Hiram after representing him at a commemoration in the latter's home town of Sangerville, Maine. He recounts meeting his father's friends, climbing the old rock his father climbed, drinking at the spring his father drank at, and concluded, "The experience was one of two of the most profoundly impressive events of my life. The other one was the death of my dear Mother," whom Sir Hiram, of course, had abandoned many years earlier. While doing his father's bidding, Percy speculated waspishly that his lengthy report might not be up to his father's expectations, for "I never remember doing a job to your satisfaction in all my life." Yet he closed by suggesting that he might buy an acre at his father's birthsite at which he, his father, and Percy's son, Hiram Hamilton Maxim, might "spend a couple of weeks in the summer time, When we feel so inclined." The record is silent on whether such a rendezvous ever occurred. The letter is in the collection of Percy's grandson John Lee.
8. Nevins, *Ford: The Man, the Times, the Company*, p. 133.
9. Flink, James J., *The Automobile Age*, p. 13.
10. Bird, Anthony, *The Motor Car, 1765–1914*, p. 171.
11. Oppel, Frank, ed., *Motoring in America: The Early Years*, p. 88.
12. Musselman, M.M., *Get a Horse!* p. 29.
13. Oppel, p. 83.
14. Maxim, Hiram Percy, *Horseless Carriage Days*, p. 28.
15. Ibid., pp. 29–32.
16. Dean, p. 1. Day's writings oozed gentility, a valued commodity in his day. In acknowledging a request for information from local artist Katherine Seymour Day (no relation), George Day replied, "I fear that you could get but very little information from me on the subjects in which you are so much interested, altho I am much interested in them. And I hope, sometime not very far away to have the pleasure of listening to more of your questions as they are based upon such an intelligent understanding of the subjects and are so instructive." Letter from George Day to Katherine Seymour Day, December 29, 1901, in Katherine Seymour Day Collection, Harriet Beecher Stowe Center, Hartford, Conn.
17. Interview with Percy Lee, Maxim's daughter, September 29, 1999.
18. Ibid., p. 35.
19. Cave, Henry, "Chronological Hartford Auto Happenings," February 1947, unpublished, p. 1.

20. Ibid., p. 42.
21. Ibid., p. 43.
22. Maxim, Hiram Percy, Scrapbook, August 28, 1895.
23. Maxim, Hiram Percy, *Horseless Carriage Days*, p. 47.
24. Ibid.
25. Ibid., p. 67.
26. Schumacher, Alice Clink, *Hiram Percy Maxim*, pp. 23–27.
27. Ibid., p. 74.
28. "Hartford Was Cradle," by Hermann Cuntz, *Hartford Times*, September 16, 1947, p. 1.
29. Maxim, Hiram Percy, *Horseless Carriage Days*, p. 87.
30. Ibid., p. 91.
31. Burpee, C.W., *History of Hartford County*, p. 528.
32. Maxim, Scrapbook, 1893–95.
33. Oppel, p. 85.
34. Rae, John, *The American Automobile Industry: The First Forty Years*, p. 16.
35. Flink, p. 13.
36. *New York World*, September 1895.
37. Maxim, Scrapbook.
38. Flink, p. 23.
39. Musselman, p. 31.
40. Nevins, p. 290.
41. Finch, Christopher, *Highways to Heaven: The AUTObiography of America*, pp. 41–42.
42. Rae, p. 11.
43. Flink, p. 30.
44. Schiffer, Michael Brian, *Taking Charge*, p. 49.
45. *Hartford Courant*, August 28, 1958.
46. Maxim, Hiram Percy, Workbook, vol. 1, August 8, 1896–January 23, 1897.
47. Henry, Carl, "Buckingham Square," n.p.
48. Schumacher, p. 39.
49. Maxim, *Horseless Carriage Days*, p. 174.
50. Oppel, p. 87.
51. Ibid., p. 88.
52. Bird, p. 171.

CHAPTER 9

A PATENTED FORMULA

He acquired the reputation of making money faster, and disposing of it faster, than any man of his day.
    Biographer's description of William Collins Whitney

The scheme was a very broad one, promising all manner of possibilities in the way of stock manipulation. Whether it was intended to develop profits out of earned dividends or by unloading the stock on the public, I will not venture a guess.

    Hiram Percy Maxim

SILENTLY THEY STOOD, perhaps even side by side, on a summer day in 1876 and gazed upon the ungainly contraption that would change both their lives. Albert Pope and George Selden, unknown businessmen in their thirties, couldn't have realized as they attended the Philadelphia Exposition that they would become household names and that their paths would intersect fatefully before the century was out.

Albert Pope was an importer and small manufacturer, ever on the lookout for products made abroad that would sell at home. The velocipede was all the rage in Britain and France. Pope would cross the Atlantic, bring velocipedes by steamship to America, set up a production line, and in a few years become the biggest bicycle manufacturer in the world.

George Selden would look at the same product and see an entirely different vision. Already familiar with gasoline motors from farm machinery, he looked at this comparatively light, wheeled vehicle and wondered what would happen if engine and bicycle could be linked together into a powered conveyance that the driver could steer himself. He'd spend the next years of his life obsessing over the idea and trying to sell it to investors. Then he'd meet Albert Pope.

Tabula Rasa

Old Bessie still pulled farm wagons in 1877 America, while popular European bicycles had begun to arrive at America's eastern docks. Steam engines ran America's railroads, and a motor powered by igniting a mixture of gasoline and air was already in wide use on midwestern farms. It didn't overly tax an intelligent person's deductive powers to imagine hitching up an engine to a wagon. But even most intelligent people weren't law school–trained patent engineers. Selden was a recent graduate of Yale's prestigious Sheffield Scientific School, but the most he had come up with was a patent for barrel hoops, and that was nothing to write home about. If his latest idea panned out, though, he could write his own ticket.[1]

To appreciate what Selden faced at this juncture, the reader must erase from his mind all knowledge of motor vehicles. Selden wrote on a tabula rasa. He realized that a motorized vehicle could be configured in any number of ways—the engine might be in front or in back or under the seat. The fuel tank, likewise, could be located in one of several places. And he knew enough patent law to realize that a patent on a specific working model would protect only that particular configuration. But Selden also knew that one can patent a process as well as an object.[2] If he could patent as general a concept as possible, he'd build a giant umbrella and become, in effect, the gatekeeper for a new industry—one which, if it caught on, could transform the way people thought about time and space. If Selden won his patent, anyone trying to sell a gasoline-powered vehicle of any description would have to deal with him. He could reap massive profits from making horseless carriages himself, and at the same time exact tribute from competitors.

Accordingly, Selden decided shrewdly not to make a working model of his invention to accompany his patent claim, but that didn't mean he was unable to do so. At the Philadelphia Exposition, he had first seen a two-cycle engine, patented by George B. Brayton of Boston.[3] This led him to create a working three-cylinder internal combustion engine. His claim to the U.S. Patent Office, elegant in its simplicity, encompassed any vehicle that used a "hydrocarbon engine of the compression type" with a disconnecting device between the engine and the vehicle and a place to hold liquid fuel. Thus Selden gathered under his umbrella a spectrum of models that might yet be invented.

As clever as his gambit was, Selden soon learned that actually manufacturing such a vehicle would require backing far beyond his meager savings. And what shrewd investor would sink money into such an untested product? It began to dawn on Selden that if he won his patent and took ten years to secure financing, he'd have used up more than half of the seventeen years the law shields a patented idea from competitors. And so, to prevent the clock from ticking, George began to file amendment after amendment to his patent, each delaying the date of its granting, while he beat the bushes for financing.

Years passed, as Selden moved from eager youth to frustrated middle age. Approaching potential investors, he said later, usually resulted in "getting them to express a kind of commiseration for my family." The total fruit of his labors was one $25 option on his patent, which ran out, unexercised.[4] By 1895, events forced Selden's hand. Although the idea of delaying applications to fend others off while gaining additional protection time didn't originate with Selden, the U.S. Patent Office caught on to the practice and began to tighten up its rules against those who tried to manipulate the system. But by then, such European automakers as Benz, Daimler, and Peugeot had each sold hundreds of vehicles a year, awakening investors' interest in matching them on American soil. Now, with Wall Street purse strings loosening, Selden submitted the final version of his patent, and on Nov. 5, 1895, the U.S. Patent Office granted patent 549,160.

A Capital Idea

By 1895, the chance of George Selden having heard of Albert Pope far outweighed the possibility that the Hartford manufacturer had become aware of the Rochester attorney and engineer. For all Selden had was an idea, while Colonel Pope had already built an empire. Few towns existed in America where a Columbia bicycle didn't sit in someone's shed. As New England's largest manufacturer and point man for the national Good Roads Movement, Pope was a bona fide celebrity.

Pope added an automotive division in the summer of 1895, in part because bicycle sales had nose-dived. Two years later, as the Colonel was poised to move beyond design into producing and selling motor vehicles, a young in-house patent attorney named Hermann Cuntz found a directive in his in-box to research what automobile patents existed that might tie Pope's hands. Albert Pope had already sued thirteen bicycle manufacturers for patent infringements and, understandably, wanted to avoid becoming a defendant in such a lawsuit

While Pope had put most of his eggs in the electric car basket, he had saved a few for what he considered a riskier venture, gasoline-powered cars. Accordingly, when Cuntz's research turned up U.S. patent number 549,160, his blood ran cold. Selden, it seemed, held a monopoly on building and selling any gasoline-powered carriage.

But when he ran down the hall and told his tale breathlessly to the chief of the new automotive division, Percy Maxim told Cuntz that Selden's claims

The gold-domed state capitol provides a backdrop for the front of Pope's Capitol Avenue factory, while at right are some of the early housing units built for employees. *(The Connecticut Historical Society, Hartford, Connecticut.)*

were ridiculous. Still in his twenties, the wunderkind had won the respect and admiration of his colleagues, who routinely addressed their memos to "Mr. Maxim," so he had the authority to reject Cuntz's claim without fear of retribution. Cuntz was aghast at Maxim's flippant attitude, knowing that one who violates a valid patent is liable to its owner for damages. So he proceeded up the chain of command—first to brusque Hayden Eames and then to gentle George Day—but got the brush-off from both. As Maxim observed later, "Cuntz's story ... was too awful to be believable."[5]

Pope by the 1890s had constructed a company town with four-story, smoke-stacked factories stretching nearly a mile along the tracks of the New York, New Haven & Hartford railroad. Across Capitol Avenue, the Colonel had built two streets of attractive, tree-shaded brick row houses, which he rented to workers to keep them near the factory. There, when first in Hartford, Maxim lived with bachelors such as Cuntz, who now played Cassandra to coworkers into the night, taking them by the lapels to warn of the perils that would befall their company if it blithely drove off the Selden cliff. But, Maxim observed later, Cuntz was left to stew in his own juice.[6]

Progressive Employer

Pope's home building for his workforce wasn't without precedent among American employers. In probably the most notable example, railcar manufacturer George Pullman had built an entire town hard by his factories and named it after himself. By furnishing shelter, entertainment, and access to food and clothing and discouraging the use of alcohol and violent behavior, his heavy-handed planning encouraged a lifestyle that held the greatest promise for his employees to arrive at work well-fed, rested, and sober.[7] Just a mile away from Pope's plant, bushy-haired Samuel Colt had created Potsdam Village, a community of detached homes with balconies and gingerbread detailing, to make his European workers comfortable.[8]

To build the Columbia Street–Park Terrace neighborhood, in 1890 Pope bought more than a hundred acres of land, spread across several city blocks. A Pope-controlled corporation, the Hartford Real Estate Improvement Company, with George Day as its treasurer, constructed the dwellings and rented them to workers and executives alike. Pope engaged his favorite architect, George Keller, to install state-of-the-art kitchens and bathrooms with copper bathtubs set atop Italian marble slabs.[9] Maxim's and Eames's families occupied next-door units at 1 Park Terrace, which allowed the Hamilton sisters to remain close together even after marriage. The Eameses also kept a country house in Farmington, a ten-minute ride by interstate highway a century later but then a good hour-long trek over rutted dirt roads.[10]

The Colonel considered himself among the more enlightened manufacturers of the time and was as proud of his seven-cent hot lunches, employee library, and locker rooms as he was of the latest Mark III emerging from the production line. Hearing that an office worker planned a bridal shower, Pope offered the use of his lavish fourth-floor suite for the event. When some lovesick workers complained of the difficulty of bicycling over rutted roads to their lady loves who lived in New Britain ten miles away, Pope offered to build a bicycle path between the two cities but withheld ten cents a week from their pay as a contribution to its cost.[11] His gift to the city of Hartford of seventy-three acres worth $100,000 for a municipal park was civic-minded but also self-interested, since it offered Pope's employees a place to relax in a neighborhood close by their workplace.

Pope was happy to attend the 1897 annual supper of the Church Association for the Advancement of the Interests of Labour, at which he expected to impress his audience with his solicitude toward his employees and, perhaps, wonder aloud why trade unions were necessary anyway. But before he could deliver his peroration, Pope was blind-sided. Rising to speak was Bishop Potter, who attacked mechanization for "turning the laboring man into a simple idiot." As the audience edged forward on its chairs, the bishop added his criticism of "the manner in which the capitalist looks down upon the men who labor for him" and castigated machinery as "the great cause of the general ill-feeling and uneasiness among the laboring classes."

Pope grew hot under the collar during the verbal assault and ignored the speaker's clerical collar when it came his turn to speak. "The Bishop is doing a great harm by widening the breach between labour and capital," said the Colonel, noting that white-collar workers did as much monotonous work as production-line laborers. But, striking the right Horatio Alger tone, Pope pointed out that a young man, "if he has the right kind of fiber in his makeup, can develop and rise to better and larger things."

An Example to Follow

Characteristically, Pope's up-by-the-bootstraps homilies used his own experience as exhibit A: "As a boy, I, myself, worked under the sidewalk in a dark hole stirring up barrels of varnish. It was monotonous and exceedingly tiresome, but ... I do not know that any harm has come from it." As to the idea that machinery would reduce the need for employees, Pope said experience has shown that technology only boosts the numbers of workers and raises their salaries.[12]

Such broadsides against capital increased in the 1890s as the excesses of unchecked capitalism loomed into view. The mantra of reform became a drumbeat for the proliferating ten-center magazines, which now could add photographs to their purple prose of scandals and oppression. Teddy Roosevelt, who never hesitated to hoist the reform banner when it suited him, would coin the term *muckraker* early in the new century, a pejorative term denoting journalists who writhed in the mud to get a story and sell magazines or newspapers. And yet, when it suited him, Roosevelt didn't hesitate to rub elbows with such muckrakers as Lincoln Steffens.

Ironically, the magazine which brought muckraking into full flower was *McClure's*, edited by Pope protégé S. S. McClure. As the Colonel read Ida Tarbell's scathing assault on John D. Rockefeller's Standard Oil Company and Steffens's exposés of municipal corruption, could he feel the noose tightening? For Pope's dealings, as Frederick Winslow Taylor had demonstrated in a patent context, weren't entirely beyond reproach.

But would Sam McClure bite the hand that had fed him when his magazine was on the verge of financial collapse? Pope would find out in 1899, when McClure's pit bull, Ray Stannard Baker, who had already eviscerated coal-mining companies and the railroads, took on the fledgling automobile industry in an article which marveled at the $388 million of capital that U.S. automakers had attracted in practically no time. One unidentified company,

Baker foreshadowed in a reference to a forthcoming Pope venture, was rushing to completion an order for 200 electric cabs "to supply the popular demand for horseless locomotion." One can see the corpulent Colonel, his heart quickening, moving his finger down the text to see if his name appeared. But Pope had not yet embarked on the course that could indeed subject him and his partners-to-be to the kind of scrutiny that fed circulation. The article, by Baker's standards, proved to be temperate, even positive. For now, Pope had dodged the bullet.[13]

Death in the Family

Elizabeth Bogman Pope's strong determination that her husband, Charles, would not live upon the sea was insufficient to protect their progeny from Neptune's wrath. It is difficult to be raised within sight of water and not be drawn to it, if not for a livelihood then for recreation. Albert Linder Pope had given his heart to sailing early on, so it was natural that the Colonel's other children would follow suit, including Charles, his fifth-born. In 1898, at age sixteen, the second-youngest child was sailing off the coast when, in an accident whose details are uncertain, he drowned. Albert and Abby were devastated at the premature loss of another child; Mary had died many years earlier, in infancy. And while few families escaped a visit from the undertaker in a day when medical care was primitive, nothing grieves a parent more than the death of a child.

The Popes' response was to find something positive in the event by constructing a small stone church, with bell tower and rose window, on Jerusalem Road in Cohasset, beside the marshes that led to the ocean that claimed their son. The Pope Memorial Church, dedicated in July 1900, is revealing of Albert's and Abby's philosophy of life. Presented for the use of the people of Cohasset, it expressly disavowed any particular creed or religion. Engraved on the exterior wall of its double-arched entryway are the words "Love to God and love to man." Anyone with a religious belief, whatever it might be, was welcome.[14]

Enter Whitney

When Grover Cleveland lost his bid for reelection as president in 1888, William Collins Whitney, his secretary of the navy, left to seek or, more accurately, to augment, his fortune in the private sector, somewhat to the dismay of his wife, Flora Payne Whitney. A striking woman, with limpid eyes and hair in the kind of artistic disarray that suggests a libertine streak, Flora

The death of teenage son Charles in a sailing accident off Boston's south shore led Colonel Pope to build the Pope Memorial Church near his Cohasset estate. Purposely eschewing a creed, its welcoming words etched above the front entrance, read simply: "Love to God and love to man." *(Courtesy William Pope, Sr.)*

Whitney entertained so lavishly and frequently at their mansion on the out-skirts of Georgetown that she was credited with receiving more than 60,000 guests during their four years in the nation's capital, incurring the ire of the Woman's Christian Temperance Union.[15]

The Whitneys returned to their Fifth Avenue townhouse in Manhattan, and William Whitney set out to wring profit from the hyperactive private sector, through shrewd investments in street railways and utilities. Born to wealth and the son of a Civil War general, Whitney didn't need money, but the challenge of a new age excited him. "He acquired the reputation," said one biographer, "of making money faster, and disposing of it faster, than any man of his day."[16] The motorized vehicle was as powerful an idea in the late 1800s as silicon chips would be a century later, and Whitney, a tall, good-looking man, whose high forehead rose haughtily above the pince-nez he customarily wore, determined that his future lay on the open road.

Electric cabs captured Whitney's imagination during the harsh winter of 1898, after taxis manufactured by Henry Morris and Pedro Salom came to the rescue of New York City during a severe blizzard. The electric cabs managed to run on city sidewalks even though most city streets were impassable.[17]

Isaac Rice, president of the Electric Storage Battery Company of Philadelphia, had seen electric taxicabs largely as a way to sell his batteries. Soon, he bought out Morris and Salom and expanded their fleet from thirteen to about a hundred and reincorporated as the Electric Vehicle Company. This bold move led Whitney to Rice's door, and ultimately he bought both concerns at a "handsome profit" for Rice.[18]

Soon Whitney had put together a syndicate to merge the Electric Storage Battery Company of Philadelphia with the Electric Vehicle Company, setting out to manufacture 2,000 electric taxicabs to run on Manhattan's streets. But that was just for starters; his sights lay far beyond Manhattan, and his goal was to expand the fleet into most major American cities.[19]

While Whitney's Wall Street contacts filled his pockets with backing capital, few industrial plants had the horsepower to fulfill such a contract. One that did, Whitney discovered, lay a hundred miles northeast in Hartford. What drew Whitney to Pope Manufacturing Company was not that he filled orders in such numbers for automobiles but because his monumental bicycle production had created the expertise and capacity needed to turn out automobiles in volume.

Had Whitney wanted to make gasoline-powered cabs, he never would have gone to New England, whose manufacturers were committed to steam and electric power. Instead, he would likely have chosen Michigan or Ohio, whose experimenters—often local farmboys with experience in operating gas-powered farm engines—used the technology they knew to make motor vehicles. While Pope Manufacturing Company made both gas and electric vehicles, it had found electric models the biggest seller, probably because Pope promoted them more.[20]

The electric taxicab, of course, had a glaring drawback: a cruising radius of only forty miles before it needed a new charge, sending the cabs back to the barn far sooner than the workday ended. Skilled workers at a central charging station, which were common in cities of any size, would spend eight hours hoisting the 1,200-pound battery out of each vehicle, charging it, and reinserting it in the vehicle. But a downtown taxicab, moving perhaps six miles an hour, could still make many trips before running down.

Family Connections

Pope wasn't entirely an unknown quantity to Whitney, whose brother, Henry Payne Whitney, was the Colonel's next-door neighbor and dinner guest

Figuratively sticking his finger in his father's eye, young Harry Whitney bought this Pope Mark III gasoline car, even as his father, William Collins Whitney, was staking his future on joining Pope to make electric vehicles. *(Courtesy John Lee and Percy Maxim Lee.)*

at Cohasset and had likely whispered in William's ear in behalf of his friend. Both Albert and William were Republicans of the mugwump reformist stripe, who had jumped party lines to support Democratic Buffalo Mayor Grover Cleveland in 1884.[21] And Colonel Pope's name was at least as well known as Whitney's. *Horseless Age*, "delighted with the prestige the Pope organization brought to the auto industry," devoted a lavish center spread to his first vehicles in 1897, and in 1899, the Colonel was the only automaker listed in *Who's Who in America*.[22]

Whitney, in targeting Pope in the spring of 1899 as the industrialist who would manufacture his taxicabs, found the Colonel especially willing to listen, for the bicycle boom was now on the wane, the victim of its own success. With the market for new sales saturated, Pope found himself with excess production space, the same fix he had discovered Weed Sewing Machine Company in twenty years earlier on his first trip to Hartford.

As Whitney prepared to board the New York, New Haven and Hartford steam train in April to meet with the Colonel and argue his case, George

Selden, near despair, continued to knock on doors, seeking backers for his gasoline-powered car but finding the doors slammed in his face. He had already approached Pope, who had dismissed him out of hand.

Pope's delegation met Whitney and company at Hartford's Union Station one April day in 1899 and drove them by carriage to the plant. They had facts and figures at the ready, as befitted businessmen who try to stay ahead of the competition. But then Whitney threw in a curve. He asked Pope directly whether any patents existed which might give them problems. Hermann Cuntz found himself summoned to the front office, where Hayden Eames and George Day urgently debriefed him on what the Selden patent was all about. It was Cuntz's moment in the sun, and he succeeded in convincing his superiors that they'd better look into the matter, particularly since Whitney let it be known that he'd be willing to commit $1 million in cash only if the Selden matter was disposed of. Enough was at stake to dispatch Percy Maxim, chief of the automotive division, to Rochester to meet with George Selden.

Cuntz had gotten wind of a story, almost surely circulated by Selden, that five Wall Street investors were ready to advance a total of $250,000 for Selden's patent.[23] But Selden reportedly had told the investors that he wanted not simply money men but a manufacturer who could ensure that the car would be put into production. While Maxim went to Rochester to negotiate with Selden, Cuntz called on others in the industry. William B. Greeley, a patent attorney, sailed to England to discuss the patent with Dugald Clerk, then regarded as the foremost authority in the world on gasoline engines. Was Selden's patent sound? Greeley asked. Oh yes, came the resounding reply.[24]

Patent without a Model

When the 28-year-old Maxim arrived in Rochester to check out the working model that underlay the patent, he found it didn't exist. All the white-haired, mustachioed Selden had was a piece of paper. One might have expected Selden to be defensive when confronted by the representative of a potential competitor, but instead, the inventor was open and engaging.

He had been a patent solicitor in 1870, the lanky inventor told Maxim expansively, and when refining technology produced gasoline that year, he conceived a way to explode gasoline vapor and develop power the way illuminating gas was exploded in gasoline engines. Rushing to patent his idea in 1877, he told Percy, he decided he'd better hold off, so the seventeen-year protection period the patent granted wouldn't expire. He kept amending his patent, "asking for one impossible thing after another."

The careful reader will wonder why Whitney and Pope were going to such lengths to acquire a patent which wouldn't have prevented manufacturing electric cars. And here lies the first hint of the ulterior motive that Whitney and Pope were conjuring: not merely to win the market for a mode of cars they made but to control, indirectly, the market for a mode they did not.

In May 1899, Whitney, his investors, and Pope incorporated the Columbia and Electric Vehicle Company, uniting deep-pocket financing with a name that had become in two decades nearly synonymous with bicycles. Its $5 million capitalization included the entire plant capacity of Pope's Capitol Avenue facility, Whitney's Electric Vehicle Company, and Whitney's cash infusion in the new company.

The timing of Whitney's move was propitious. Pope's strategy of touting Columbia quality while keeping bicycle prices high had begun to have disastrous results in the mid–1890s. While he had sold a cut-rate bicycle sub rosa under the label of the Hartford Cycle Company, he still had to discount his beloved Columbia in 1897 from $100 to $75, setting off an industry-wide price war. While British bicycle makers used profits to finance their automotive production, Pope's bicycle operations were bleeding cash profusely. The million-dollar cash infusion had come in the nick of time.[25] Pope's great-grandson Albert recalls that the Colonel's children especially favored the Pope-Whitney linkage, feeling that it signaled an upgrade of the family from the minor to the major leagues.[26]

Warring Technologies

With steam, gasoline, and electric each vying for a foothold in the automobile market, investors had to worry not only about whether motorized vehicles generically were the wave of the future but whether they had put their money on the right horseless carriage. The automotive press was filled with charges and countercharges by representatives of each mode. When Percy Maxim wrote, "The storage battery is advancing more rapidly than the gasoline, steam or other systems," the editor of *Horseless Age*, which had staked its future on gasoline models, branded the remark "an unqualified falsehood" and its author "a discredited expert."[27] With so much at stake, it is hardly surprising that competitors resorted to means foul as well as fair, to protect their interests.

As William Collins Whitney set about to sink millions of dollars in electric vehicles, he faced a potential embarrassment from within his own family. His son, Harry Payne Whitney, a genial, open-faced young man, had met Percy Maxim and had become so enthused about his plans for gasoline-operated automobiles that he bought one of the first Mark VIII carriages, which he intended to use to commute between Manhattan and his Long Island estate. The Whitneys provided constant gossip for the society pages, particularly through the activities of flamboyant Flora Whitney and her parties. If it became known that young Harry was successfully operating a gas-powered car while his father had banked his all on electric cars—well, the feature story writes itself.

Soon after Harry's purchase, Maxim got word that the Mark VIII had "failed utterly" and was now garaged at a streetcar barn on New York's Fourth Avenue, to which Percy immediately traveled, only to find that someone had filled the gas tank with varnish—and not accidentally. Another time, Maxim was called in to diagnose the cause of gasoline-engine failure, spotted by two automotive experts. He sprang to attention on discovering that the experts were the same ones used widely by the Whitney interests. After closer examination, Percy found that a copper rivet had been purposely introduced into the carburetor, which had stopped the flow of gasoline. In still another instance, someone stuffed a man's shirt into a car's crankshaft, soon bringing the car to a halt.

These incidents underscore the amount at stake in the turn-of-the-century automobile wars. Of the three competing modes, one would prevail, and if matters foul as well as fair helped bring about that outcome, so be it. However, so delicate and treasured were the relations between Whitney and Pope that it appears likely that the Colonel never confronted the patrician Manhattanite about the incidents. After all, the clever corporate sabotage was directed at a mode which, in Pope's view, was going nowhere.[28]

It is difficult to overestimate the credibility that Thomas Alva Edison brought to the marketplace as the century neared its end. Carefully cultivating his image as an eccentric wizard, he held court to trainloads of curiosity seekers, who swarmed over his laboratories at Menlo Park, New Jersey, seeking to touch the hem of the inventor of the phonograph, motion picture, and electric light. So when he called for the abandonment of the lead-acid battery, on which electric vehicles were based, he gained an immediate audience. Edison determined to build a nickel-iron alkaline battery without lead, reasoning that it would give batteries a higher energy density, lengthen battery life, and ease their maintenance.[29]

Searching for a Successor

At age fifty-six, with his robust health waning just as his interests were widening, the Colonel faced a decision crucial to both his family and his empire. George Day, for some time, had been the go-to man at the Columbia and Electric Vehicle Company, leaving Pope free to pursue his writing and lecturing. But the time had come to tap a permanent successor. "I am fifty-six years old. I have no desire to assume new responsibilities," Pope wrote, in a tone that seems older than his years. "Presidents can be hired and no man living can pay me a suitable wage at my time of life."[30]

It would not be an easy choice. Primogeniture, the doctrine that the eldest child inherits his father's estate, was weakening but not without cultural force at the turn of the twentieth century. Prince Albert, now twenty-seven, had acquitted himself famously in handling the fiery debacle at the Columbus Avenue headquarters three years earlier. Expelled from Dartmouth, he had worked off and on in the Hartford operation and had been a white-collar executive there for the past two years. But no one knew better than the Colonel that young Albert's heart lay in sailing, a pastime he pursued passionately and which gave coworkers the sense that he didn't have his mind entirely on business. Albert Linder's divided loyalties were, by one account, a bone in the throat of his nose-to-the-grindstone father.[31]

But if not Albert Linder, then who? Pope's loyal cousin George Pope knew all the facets of the business, but George was only a year younger than the Colonel. Hayden Eames, Columbia's general manager, at thirty-four, seemed a tad too young, and his fiery temper and brusque manner made him not a natural choice for the job. Harry Pope, who the Colonel had taken under his wing since his brother's untimely death, was a capable inventor and engineer but had little management experience or inclination. And the brilliant Percy Maxim was barely thirty. Which left 48-year-old George Day, the quintessence of capability and charm, with a soothing temperament, the logical choice.

Yet by now, Albert Linder had begun to press his advantage in the Hartford plant as the boss's son. Aside from the Colonel's reservations about his grit lay the threat of internal dissension, which would likely result if the young executive were to assume the helm. No one knew better than the Colonel that he couldn't have built his empire without the likes of Day, Eames, and Maxim. Were they to leave in disillusionment, the carefully erected Pope tower could shudder and fall.

Pope went to the mountain and returned with what seemed to be a win-win solution: to divorce the bicycle operations from the automotive operations, putting Albert Linder in charge of the bicycle division, which would be known as the Pope Manufacturing Company, and letting Day head up the automotive enterprise. Pope built a seventeen-acre plant in Westfield, Massachusetts, on donated land to expand his bicycle operation so his son would feel well-utilized, while the capable Day would have a firm hand on the wheel of the venture that Pope expected would become the most profitable.[32]

Merge or Die

The sharp decline in bicycle sales in the mid–1890s pressured Pope to lower prices, as some 700 manufacturers competed for a declining market. His reaction was the same as those of the railroad barons when competition threatened their monopolistic prices: consolidate the industry, thus weeding out competitors.

A. G. Spalding, already the head of a proliferating sporting goods empire, had taken advantage of the advent of parcel post to develop a giant mail order catalog business. He and Pope were both being hurt by the bicycle price war, so Spalding set out to win options to buy bicycle operations and quickly secured 107. He exercised options on about twenty, offering to pay either in cash or in stock in the new consolidated enterprise, which Spalding called the American Bicycle Company. When he convinced the father of the American bicycle to join in, his mission was complete. Spalding would head the new company, with George Pope as vice president, and the Colonel as a director.[33] But an ominous storm cloud hung over the venture, for nearly all acquired companies chose to accept cash, which signaled that the industry, as a whole, was ready to cut and run and which also left the new company more than $9 million in debt.

With bicycle manufacturing in secure hands and young Albert off his back, the Colonel could turn his attentions to the automotive enterprise. Envisioning a national operation, Whitney now sought to make the Electric Vehicle Company a holding company for the anticipated branch operations In June 1900, dapper George Day took the helm of the new company formed by the merger of Columbia and Electric Vehicle Company and the Electric Vehicle Company.

Increasingly, Pope found his mind on other things than manufacturing. The Good Roads Movement cried out for someone to shepherd it to the critical mass of public support it needed, to induce state and local governments to absorb it as an obligation, which would create one of government's first entitlement programs. Nearer sixty than fifty, Pope felt as well the need to explore new fields while he was still able. And the death of his son Charles, only two years earlier, may have been a reminder of his own mortality.

So, when the opportunity presented itself, he let the Whitney interests buy him out, thus severing the twenty-year tie between Pope and Day. In the process, the Electric Vehicle Company swallowed up several small competitors; as the new century dawned, it could claim nearly a monopoly in the electric car industry.

Just Another Day

"Jan. 1, 1900" read the matter-of-fact first entry in Percy Maxim's engineering notes for the first day of the new century. While Hartfordites were sleeping off New Year's champagne toasts to the new century, Maxim was hard at work, calculating the cost of charging the batteries of Mark III carriages and making detailed tire calculations for the front and rear wheels of a Hansom cab. With a sanguine and flexible temperament, Percy had thrown himself into arguing the case for electric vehicles.

The most frequent question doubters of electric vehicle technology asked was, understandably, what could be done to make cars run longer before their batteries died. In a day before gasoline stations existed on every corner, Maxim, in speeches and articles, championed the idea of central charging stations. While most individual homeowners would have been hard pressed to afford electric-charging equipment, residential car parks with a central charger could allow vehicles to charge while their drivers slept. If downtown employers installed charging hydrants next to parking spaces, their commuting employees could plug in before work and leave to find their vehicles reenergized.[34]

Missed Opportunity

John T. Rainier set out to organize a chain of garages, particularly in New York, allowing motorists to get skilled aid when in trouble. Scores of millions of dollars had by then been invested in electric cars, but the battery issue proved to be their Waterloo, as two $25 million–companies went belly up in 1900 and another cut its capital from $25 million to $5 million.[35] A century later, after scientists had sent a man to the moon, they still labored over the practicalities of electric motors for automobiles.

No sooner had electric trolleys been introduced in 1887 than electric companies began to buy them up as a reliable source of electricity sales, particularly at peak commuting times when home use of electricity was down. With the advent of a new industry, the utilities again saw the chance for new profits. Early Maxim associate H. W. Alden, who came with Maxim to Hartford from Lynn, Massachusetts, suggested in retrospect that electric companies were, in fact, very much involved:

> The Electric Vehicle Company finally was controlled by the electric power and lighting interests and they decided to inaugurate a system of city transportation units. These would buy vehicles from Hartford, batteries from the Electric Storage Battery Company in Philadelphia, motors from Siemens-Halske in Chicago. As usual the public would furnish the cash at $100 a throw. This

was a beautiful set-up, if only the transportation companies made money. Companies were organized in Boston, New York, Philadelphia, Buffalo, and Chicago. All went fine until it became evident that the companies couldn't make money. When they went into the red, the whole venture just folded up and, while some investors got out on a $3 basis, most people lost all they had put in. ... Therefore both the private investor and the New England banker wrote the automobile business off as a flop and concentrated on machine tools and insurance.[36]

Alden's thesis is supported by a 1907 publication of the Pope Motor Car Company, which blames utilities for charging insupportable rates for electricity sold to charging machines, at a time when gasoline vehicles had become increasingly popular and a boom in oil wells had made gasoline dirt cheap. "The result was that the electric carriage vehicle garage, far less expensive to start, became the more profitable." One can only speculate on the result if a visionary in the electric power industry had decided to subsidize networks of electric-charging stations in the short term as the oil industry did with gasoline stations, so that electric vehicles could gain a foothold.

Taking the Wrong Turn

Students of nineteenth-century industry have marveled at what possessed Colonel Pope, then one of the country's most prosperous and established industrialists, to merge with, in the words of automotive historian John B. Rae, "an enterprise which was at best a technological and commercial gamble."[37] Several reasons suggest themselves.

Pope had an unwavering belief that electric cars would, after an industry shake-out, carry the day. They were clean, safe, and quiet, unlike the smelly, noisy, and greasy gasoline automobiles. But would not the limited range of travel that storage batteries allowed be a fatal defect? The nation in the 1890s was awash in transforming new inventions—from the electric light and phonograph to the typewriter and the linotype machine to the pneumatic tire and the telephone. Could Colonel Pope be forgiven for feeling that the battery problem was just one more hurdle that technology would leap easily? Or should he have heeded the ominous 1897 prediction from no less an expert on electric power than Thomas Edison that the horseless carriage, once perfected, would likely run on gas or naphtha, not electric power?[38]

At first dismissive of the idea of safety bicycles, Pope embraced these user-friendly machines once he understood that women could ride and enjoy them; by the mid–1890s, women accounted for one-third of the bicycle market. And while even men were breaking their arms in using hand cranks required by gasoline autos, women could ride electric cars without fear for their safety. So, Pope realized, electric vehicles offered a promising dual-gender market that gasoline automobiles seemed to lack.

The fact remained, however, that electric cars were considerably more expensive to manufacture and some three times as costly to operate as gasoline vehicles. Even as late as 1910, electric vehicles could run no more than fifty to eighty miles without charging their batteries, which added such weight to the car that hill climbing was challenging. Then, too, storage batteries deteriorated quickly, and charging stations were few and far between.[39]

Could Pope have been dazzled by the Harvard- and Yale-educated patrician, who swashbuckled into town, offering $1 million in cash to build 200 taxicabs? As much a success as Pope had become since his days in Boston, he lacked a college education and Beacon Street polish. Was his head turned by a man who had the refinement he lacked and who, in the process, might also connect him to Wall Street?

More than One Way to Make a Buck

Some historians have suggested another, more sinister, motive. Through exploitation of patents as well as manufacturing wheels, Pope had learned that more than one way exists to make money. Rae theorizes and finds supports from no less a Pope cohort than Hiram Percy Maxim that perhaps Pope thought he had found a third way: manipulation of company stock.

In Maxim's recollection, "The scheme was a very broad one, promising all manner of possibilities in the way of stock manipulation. Whether it was intended to develop profits out of earned dividends or by unloading the stock on the public, I will not venture a guess." As the venture's chief automotive engineer says modestly in his diary, "I was just a hired man." But he recalls, "In those days of wild finance, unloading on the public was very fashionable."

It was the day of "watered stock," a term coined for the railroad industry a generation or two earlier. Robber barons had won the enmity of western farmers in one-railroad towns by luring them to invest in the railways, then diluting their stock holdings by artificially raising the value of the company stock, which left the farmers with a smaller share of the corporate pie. Such machinations led to the Granger movement in the 1870s and 1880s and the populist revolt, which created state railroad commissions and the federal Interstate Commerce Commission.

Now invidious stock watering was rearing its ugly head once more. While Whitney's 1899 plan called for $3 million of contributed capital, by 1902 the Electric Vehicle Company would inflate that to $20 million in issued stock. By then, some 2,000 electric taxicabs were ferrying passengers to and fro, not only in Manhattan but in Boston, Washington, Philadelphia, and Chicago.

Had electric vehicles proved to be the mode of choice, the rising tide of company prosperity might have absorbed the stock watering. But while the Electric Vehicle Company managed an 8 percent dividend in 1899, the next year it had to go, hat in hand, to State Trust Company for a bailout. The handwriting was on the wall. The century was not more than a year or two old when it became clear that electric vehicles simply weren't sending out any sparks. By now, financial manipulations had led the muckraking press to refer to the Electric Vehicle combine as the "Lead Cab Trust."[40]

Whether Pope knew what he was getting into, he helped create one of the most tumultuous sagas in American industrial history. An industry was about to be born, and the Whitney-Pope forces determined to shape it, not merely by producing more cars than anyone else but also by blocking anyone else from horning in on the act.

Selden's Audacious Gamble

With so many alternative configurations of motor vehicles in play, it was quite bold for a patent owner to claim that anyone making any kind of gasoline automobile would infringe on his patent. Yet, in a calculated gamble, that is just what the Electric Vehicle Company set out to do. Would the scores of small shops and tinkerers producing early motor vehicles fall in line or would they simply ignore Pope and Whitney? The future of automobiling depended on the answer to that fateful question.

The Pope-Whitney forces' shot across the bow came in a suit against Alexander Winton's Motor Carriage Company in Cleveland, which at that juncture made more gas-powered engines than any other company. They brought Winton to his knees, winning a court judgment that held that, indeed, he had violated the Selden patent.

Because of the obvious implications, competing manufacturers, such as Packard Motor Company and Olds Motor Works, hung on every bulletin from the courthouse. While they were competitors, it was clear that the Electric Vehicle Company wore the black hat in this battle, and the enemy of their enemy became their natural friend. Following the judgment, the smaller automakers huddled with Winton as he tried to decide whether to mount an appeal. After all, they and Winton were all potential victims of this looming corporate bludgeon. Packard's Henry Joy and Olds's Frederic L. Smith convinced Winton that wisdom lay not in pursuing a winner-take-all appeal but in meeting with Pope and Whitney and trying to carve up the pie so that everyone got something.

The defendants' gambit was as wise as it was logistically brilliant. For the mechanics building early automobiles typically were barely able to finance car production, let alone a costly patent suit. But they also knew that, for the Pope-Whitney forces, compromise meant not risking a judge throwing the Selden patent out of court. In that case, the Electric Vehicle Company would be simply one of dozens of auto manufacturers scrambling for market share. Once both sides understood each other on these terms, they shook hands and agreed to construct a fortress that would protect them all. The Association of Licensed Automobile Manufacturers (ALAM) would represent a wide moat across which anyone seeking to produce motor vehicles against its will would have to swim.

Of the sales price of each car its constituent members sold, the Electric Vehicle Company demanded 5 percent. Yet, while the Joys and the Smiths, with their calloused hands, could never match the sophistication of their manicured opponents, neither were they rubes. They recognized the vulnerability of the Pope-Whitney forces and bargained them down eventually to a royalty of a mere 1.25 percent for each car manufactured under the Selden patent. Of this, three-quarters would go directly into the Electric Vehicle Company, with the rest paying ALAM's lawyers and administrators to beat down those who sought to play by their own rules. The Whitney forces ended up buying Pope out before the deal was struck. While Pope watched the machinations long distance from Cohasset and Boston, his key aide, George Day, ascended to the helm of the Electric Vehicle Company.

Thirty manufacturers had joined ALAM by 1904, fledgling producers such as Studebaker, Cadillac, Olds, and Packard—not a household name among them, certainly no name with the recognition of Pope. ALAM's success wasn't surprising; smaller producers could hardly counter the might that the Electric Vehicle Company could bring to its litigation. Quality control in the automotive industry was nonexistent before ALAM, with small machine shops each turning out mere handfuls of cars, some of them lemons, which would damage the reputation of the industry. Invoking the Selden patent as a paradigm for production wasn't simply an economic weapon but, in fact, set quality standards for the industry.

Pulling up the Drawbridge

Now that he was a member of the in-crowd, Alexander Winton closed ranks: "We had to pitch in and fight the wildcat automobile companies on the outside," he later recalled. "Orphan cars were numerous and always were a 100 percent liability, because it was impossible to get replacements for broken parts."[41]

Why would the Pope-Whitney forces accept one-fourth of their original demand and a minority position of only one of five members on the ALAM board? If smaller automakers were in no shape to engage in prolonged litigation, it appears that neither was the foe they feared, as it blew smoke like the Wizard of Oz behind a curtain. "Since Day himself was none too certain that the patent would survive a full-fledged test in court, it was plainly wise for the Electric Vehicle Company to make the best deal it could with the gasoline automobile manufacturers."

Pope's chief engineer, Percy Maxim, served in the same capacity in the new venture. The 2,092 vehicles which Pope manufactured in 1899 accounted for nearly half the total number of cars made in America that year and made him, at the dawn of the new century, America's leading automaker. As historian John Rae observes, the decline of auto manufacturing in New England should not have been fatal, since Pope also maintained auto plants in Toledo and Indianapolis. But while ALAM became the backbone of the ascendant gasoline-powered industry, the drive for electric cars withered on the vine, and its participants lost their shirts. Rae concludes:

> The worst casualty was the Pope Manufacturing Company. Here was a concern which had done some valuable pioneering work with highway vehicles, both gasoline and electric, and possessed the organization, financial resources, and technical skill to become a major automobile producer, but which lost its opportunity because its officials allowed themselves to be tempted by an alluring get-rich-quick scheme. No other explanation is sufficient to account for the Pope catastrophe.[42]

Pope's engineers and managers applied the same techniques to making and selling automobiles that had worked so well for them in selling bicycles. Yet the automobile had far larger commercial applications than did the bicycle, so it's not surprising that, when the industry took off like a rocket, the old methods simply couldn't keep pace. Hindsight is twenty-twenty, of course. Who could have foreseen in 1900 that brash upstart Henry Ford would win his challenge to the automotive oligopoly? Who could have known that the Spindletop oil well in Texas was about to open up apparently limitless supplies of gasoline or that refining the technology of storage batteries would daunt generations of engineers? Had the Pope-Whitney forces not let their energies be drained by a patent suit that was little more than a power grab, could they have created a national network for electric vehicles the way Pope had created the Good Roads Movement?

"All they accomplished," concludes historian Rae in a harsh analysis, "was to offer a demonstration that in business, there is no adequate substitute for the production of goods and services."[43]

Notes

1. Lacey, Robert, *Ford: The Men and the Machine,* p. 99.

2. Conversations on various dates with Kenneth Dusyn, patent specialist of Hartford, CT.

3. Flink, James J., *The Automobile Age,* p. 51.

4. Greenleaf, William, *Monopoly on Wheels: Henry Ford and the Selden Patent Suit,* p. 51.

5. Maxim, Hiram Percy, *Horseless Carriage Days,* p. 165.

6. Ibid., p. 164.

7. Sclereth, Thomas, *Victorian America: Transformation in Everyday Life,* p. 97.

8. Grant, Ellsworth, *The Colt Armory,* p. 144.

9. Agreement between Weed Sewing Machine Company and George Keller, dated September 1889, George Keller Collection, Harriet Beecher Stowe Center, Hartford, CT.

10. Land records, City of Hartford, Office of the Town Clerk.

11. Norcliffe, Glen, "Popeism and Fordism: Examining the Roots of Mass Production," p. 277.

12. Ibid., p. 271.

13. Greenleaf, p. 53. Albert Pope II maintains the Colonel actually had pro–Union sentiments, once personally broke a company lockout, and induced his suppliers to unionize as well.

14. Gay, John Curry, "1912 Pope-Hartford Model," p. 17.

15. Kahn, E.J., Jr., *Jock: The Life and Times of John Hay Whitney,* pp. 9–12.

16. Nevins, Allan, *Ford: The Times, the Man, the Company,* p. 10.

17. Rae, John, *The American Automobile Industry: The First Forty Years,* p. 16.

18. Ibid., chapter 5.

19. Corrigan, David, "Corporate Genealogies," Appendix II.

20. Gelderman, Carol, *Henry Ford—The Wayward Capitalist,* p. 28.

21. Chernow, Ron, *Titan,* p. 291; May 8, 1999, interview with Albert A. Pope II.

22. Lewis, D.L., *The Public Image of Henry Ford,* p. 16.

23. Nevins, p. 288.

24. Ibid., p. 289.

25. Epperson, Bruce, "A Model of Technological Dissonance," p. 57.

26. Interview with Albert A. Pope II, May 8, 1999.

27. "A Discredited Expert," *Horseless Age* 5, no. 3 (Oct. 18, 1899), p. 3.

28. Maxim, pp. 150–161.

29. Schiffer, Michael Brian, *Taking Charge,* pp. 68–69.

30. Hirsh, Mark D. and William C. Whitney, *Modern Warwick,* p. 557; *Hartford Times,* August 4, 1899, p. 1.

31. May 8, 1999, interview with Albert A. Pope II.

32. Columbiamfginc.com/historydoc.htm.

33. Epperson, p. 76.

34. Maxim, untitled article in *Horseless Age* (May 1899), pp. 17–19.

35. Oppel, Frank, ed., *Motoring in America,* p. 90.

36. Lee, Percy Maxim and John Glessner, *Family Reunion,* p. 190.

37. Rae, John, "The Electric Vehicle Company," p. 302.

38. Ibid.

39. Flink, p. 10.

40. Rae, p. 303.

41. Ibid., p. 305. Respected historians differ in their interpretations of Winton's and Whitney's bargaining skills. James Flink holds that Winton "capitulated" in 1903, just before a court decree entered in the case that the Pope-Whitney forces had brought against him in 1899 for enforcement of the Selden patent. John Rae, on the other hand, is astonished that the Electric Vehicle Company agreed to settle the case on terms so favorable to Winton and his allies, accepting a massive reduction in the royalty that manufacturers would have to pay for the privilege of manufacturing cars under the Selden patent.

42. Ibid., p. 311.

43. Ibid.

CHAPTER 10

LIKE A DOG
WITH A BONE

I felt perfectly certain that horses, considering all the bother of attending them and the expense of feeding, did not earn their keep. ... To lift farm drudgery off flesh and blood and lay it on steel and motors has been my most constant ambition.

Henry Ford

We will protect you against any prosecution for alleged infringement of patents. The Selden patent does not cover any practicable machine, no practicable machine can be made from it, and never was so far as we can ascertain.

Henry Ford

AT THE TURN OF THE CENTURY, to be seen at the Pontchartrain Hotel in downtown Detroit was to matter. Decorated in high Victorian splendor, its builders had not stinted on marble, mahogany, or plush carpeting in creating an elegant setting in which the city's elite could entertain and present their daughters to society at lavish debutante balls. But then a curious invasion took place. Prominent local attorney Peter Drexelius began inviting to the rococo barroom a rougher class of men, with calloused hands and dirt under their fingernails. Not just one or two but dozens.

If you sidled up to the bartender through the cigar smoke to ask who these people were who looked so out of place, you'd learn that they belonged to a new industry, one that hoped to put men behind the wheel of a conveyance that ran not by pedaling, but effortlessly, through a series of tiny explosions that happened when gasoline and oxygen were set on fire in a closed chamber. The men Drexelius had gathered were clearly about business—they moved, spoke, and acted with intensity. They were the designers, inventors, engineers, promoters, and salesmen of the new automobile industry.

Although they were potential competitors, they were here to put their heads together, as they tested out self-starters on marble-topped tables, no doubt to the consternation of the Pontchartrain's management.[1]

Hiram Maxim would write three decades later that early automobile experimentation took place within a vacuum, so that inventors, over and over, had to reinvent the wheel. Such, of course, was not really the case. Trade magazines were a great clearinghouse for experimenters, and developments in drive-shaft technology, carburetors, engine cooling, and brakes reported there allowed inventors to bypass intermediate steps and give birth sooner to the final product. The cross-fertilization of ideas taking place at the Pontchartrain would spawn the Society of Automotive Engineers. No chowder and marching society, the SAE proved itself to be an immensely important trade organization because it set standards for making cars, allowing parts from one to be used on another, for instance, thus cutting the price to consumers.

This was the world of Henry Ford. To understand him is to understand midwestern farmboys in the waning of the nineteenth century. Far more agrarian than their contemporaries in the East, they were comfortable around farm machinery. Steam engines had long been used to power such farm devices as threshers. Indeed, Ford in later years would take great delight in hosting threshing picnics every September, firing up an old Westinghouse steam engine and threshing clover while his guests munched on sandwiches and ice cream.[2]

Since Frenchman J.J. Etienne Lenoir had invented a double-acting, spark-ignition internal combustion engine in 1859, farmers had used the smoky device out in their fields. So when Ford devised a gas-powered vehicle in the 1890s, he wasn't exactly starting at ground zero.

Midwestern Populism

The second strain that set midwestern farmboys apart was that many distrusted and even hated eastern capitalists. These were the sons of men drawn west in the glory days of American railroads, who had been plied with free government acreage and seduced by railroad agents to invest their meager savings in the world's first big business.

Sophisticated enough to realize their vulnerability, farmers found themselves hopelessly outpriced in the market because railroads customarily demanded monopolies in the territories they operated in and set rates accordingly. Monopoly pricing wiped out thousands of farmers and led them to create in the 1880s the National Grange of the Patrons of Husbandry, whose thousands of chapters would storm the state capitals and eventually Congress to throw a noose around the runaway railroads. "The Grange championed temperance, staging teetotal square dances and hoedowns to prove that farming—and virtue—could be fun."[3]

Against this backdrop, young Henry Ford strode onto the world stage at the dawning of the automobile age. His hard-won lessons in machinery and finance led him to identify with the man on the street rather than in the country club and to resist at all costs any encumbering ties to big money. In an odd way, the antipathy of Ford and his midwestern brethren to Wall Street capital worked in their favor, by making them rely on their own resources in financing their ventures. Eastern capital, with the industrial revolution in full bloom, didn't need to risk investments in chancy propositions such as the automobile, a fact that would help seal the fate of Atlantic seaboard automakers such as Duryea and Pope.

As late as 1907, when William Crapo Durant predicted to a House of Morgan financier in Manhattan that automakers would soon sell a half million cars a year—more cars than there were horses on the street—the financier showed him the door. For in the pre–Model T era, "cars were rich men's toys, plagued by unreliability and poor roads, an attitude that rankled Henry Ford and reinforced his contempt for Wall Street bankers."[4]

Engine for the Farm

Henry Ford didn't start school until he was seven and a half, which wasn't unusual for his day. Nor was his mile-and-a-half walk to the red brick Scotch settlement schoolhouse with its stove and two-seater desks facing the teacher at the blackboard. "We started school off with a song or a prayer," recalled his sister Margaret later. "There wasn't any set schedule. It depended on the mood of the teacher."[5] Ford's aptitude for the mechanical showed itself early, both at home and at school, where students and teachers alike soon looked for answers to the young boy, who seemed blessed with an unusual gift. Ford's parents had widely differing temperaments. Mary Litogot Ford, with an open friendly face crowned by black hair parted down the middle, was a sharp contrast to her husband, William, whose goatee and severe, deep-set eyes seemed ready to sit in judgment.[6]

The reality of Ford's early years led him to dream not of creating ways for people to get around more easily but rather of how he might lighten the back-breaking drudgery that characterized farm work of the day. "The idea of a 'horseless carriage' at first did not seem so practical to me as the idea of an engine to do the harder farm work ... a tractor to attend to the excessively hard labour of ploughing," an activity the young farmboy felt in his bones from having done it. "I felt perfectly certain that horses, considering all the bother of attending them and the expense of feeding, did not earn their keep. ... To lift farm drudgery off flesh and blood and lay it on steel and motors has been my most constant ambition."[7]

While immersed in things electrical as a young engineer with the Detroit Edison Company near Detroit's city hall, Ford found himself lured to the possibilities of the internal combustion engine. One of the bricks of the monument Ford built to himself so assiduously in the public mind is his building of an internal combustion engine in 1893, but he appears to have set the clock ahead three years. Ford put together his first vehicle in 1896, which was still before the great multitude of automakers; they soon would flood the market, only a year after Percy Maxim had turned out for Pope his first production model.[8]

Through the years, Ford's version of reality has been that he brought into his family's Christmas Eve kitchen in 1893 a simple experimental engine and hooked it up on the sink, so he could use the newfangled electric house current as a primitive spark plug. Lacking even a carburetor, the mustachioed Ford asked his wife, Clara, to pour some gasoline into a metal cup, which served as a carburetor, the story goes, and to feed it into the intake valve by turning a screw. When Henry spun the flywheel, gas and air entered the cylinder and mixed, and soon flames burst from the exhaust valve and the sink began to shake.[9]

Shading the Truth

For decades, historians have argued over which date—1893 or 1896—is correct, but the weight of the evidence points to 1896. For one thing, no one beyond Clara has ever corroborated Henry's story. And given Henry's passion for auto racing, it strains credibility that the highly competitive Ford possessed a working automobile in 1895 and failed to run it in the well-publicized Chicago auto race on Thanksgiving of that year.

However, the only person Ford really cared about proving he had beaten was inventor George Selden, with whom he would be embroiled for years over whether Selden's patent required Ford to pay royalties. If Ford could show that he had a working model of Selden's concept before Selden patented it, he might convince the court that he was immune from such royalties. With his future on the line, Ford had every incentive to offer perjured testimony and it is not hard to imagine that he did.

What most historians believe happened is related by Robert Lacey in his Ford biography. In January 1896, the young engineer visited the Detroit office of his friend Charles Brady King, who he had met in 1893 or 1894.[10] On King's desk, Ford spied two copies of *American Machinist* magazine, one for late 1895, the other for early 1896. Oliver Barthel, a King associate, later reported that Ford told him, while pointing to the magazine, "I want to build one of these."[11]

The first public witness of a horseless carriage on Detroit streets was on March 6, 1896. A *Detroit Free Press* reporter gushed, "When in motion, the connecting rods fly like lightning, and the [three-horsepower] machine is capable of running seven or eight miles an hour."[12] As a test run to win public notice and, therefore, public backing, the experiment was less than front-page news. The biggest coverage was a six-inch story in the *Detroit Journal*.

The vehicle that Ford experimented with, whether during 1893 or 1896, was a four-cycle motor with two cylinders of two-and-a-half-inch bore and a six-inch stroke, which gave off a modest three to four horsepower. He built the chassis and body of the quadricycle at the shop next to his Bagley Avenue home. The automobile was capable of two speeds—ten and twenty miles per hour—as well as a neutral gear, but it had no reverse. The clutch lever tightened or loosened a belt. Pulled back, it put the car in low gear; erect, neutral; and forward, high. The motor had a flywheel, which was spun in neutral to start the engine. To stop it, one had to go back to neutral and apply the brake.

Now or Never

By 1899, Ford realized he'd better jump into the new industry with both feet or be left behind. But his backers failed to grasp Ford's dream of a cheap car for the common man, rather than cars for the wealthy elite, as Colonel Pope had decided to do in Hartford. This led Ford to go it alone, entering his cars in popular races of the day to gain what later marketers would call free media.[13]

In August 1899, Ford, now a husband and father, left the security of a stable position with Edison to leap into the void of the unknown. Offering to take carriage blacksmith David M. Bell into business with him, Ford reassured the Edison employee, "You'll grow with the business."

"What business?" his dubious colleague asked.

If he had been asked the same question in the same year, Pope could have answered with confidence. While Ford was both unknown and untested, the father of the American bicycle had two months earlier merged with the Whitney interests, forming a $3 million combine that was the biggest of its kind in the world. The Colonel stoked the fires by telling the press that his 15,000 bicycle agents around the world were "fairly howling" for automobiles to meet "an enormous demand."[14]

Pope and Ford stood at the head and the tail, respectively, of a pack of

57 automakers, which that year would produce 3,723 cars. As bewildering as the plethora of producers seems, it would pale against the figure for 1919, when 2,830 automakers would turn out 1,934,000 automobiles, a year before the shuddering shake-out of the 1920s began.[15]

Ford called his first venture the Detroit Automobile Company, which he joined as superintendent. During the ensuing three years, the company would turn out about twenty gasoline autos, an average output among his competitors. But when financial backers nixed Ford's plan to produce more cars at a cheaper price, the company closed its doors in 1901.[16]

A Pope for a Friend

Among Ford's early admirers was Colonel Pope, a man old enough to be his father. When Ford visited Pope at the Capitol Avenue plant while gearing up to go into business, "the Colonel admired his spirit of enterprise," reports Pope's great-grandson Albert. Pope could never have conceived how their paths would intersect in a few short years.[17]

While Whitney was pleased to have Pope as a nominal partner in the electric taxicab operation, it was clear from the time that the Colonel delegated control to George Day that Pope's mind was largely elsewhere, even though the popular grey eminence would still make appearances as needed. His Delphic predictions about the future of the automobile rang with a credibility that the newcomer, Whitney, lacked. "Inside of ten years," Pope forecast, "there will be more automobiles in use in the large cities of the United States than there are now horses in these cities."

By the time Ford's first venture had failed, Pope had effectively distanced himself from the day-to-day operations by selling out to the Whitney interests in 1900, indulging in his own single-minded pursuit—good roads, on the success of which would depend the entire automobile industry. During his leisure time, his thoughts turned toward the prospect of silver in them thar hills.

Historian Allan Nevins observes that Pope was nearly alone among automakers in working for legislation to pave America. Most simply accepted conditions as they were, striving to strengthen their vehicle designs to withstand the rigors of muddy, rutted roads. Pope's vision was much more fundamental. If government could be persuaded to surface roads, the market for automobiles would soar, and all automakers would benefit.

Pope had been preaching his gospel of good roads for nearly a generation now, and while the fruit of his labors included the federal Office of Road Inquiry and highway commissions in many states, the miserable state of public roads remained largely unchanged. As late as 1904, when the Office of Road Inquiry took the first American road census, it would find that barely 7 percent of the nation's more than two million miles of highways and byways had been improved beyond their natural state; even the surfaced roads consisted largely of primitive gravel or macadam.[18]

Railroad Allies

Ironically, it was the railroad industry, not his fellow automakers, which came to Pope's aid. His friend Stuyvesant Fish, president of the Illinois Central Railroad, was not only supportive of Pope's cause but agreed to send trains to haul road-building equipment. Loaded with eight railcars full of rollers and bulldozers, the convoy set off from Chicago to New Orleans as the first buds appeared on Chicago trees in the spring of 1901. The train stopped at communities in five states, giving how-to demonstrations to county road supervisors and, perhaps more important, paving short strips so that Farmer Brown might drive his horse and wagon on the tabletop-smooth surface and feel as if he were walking on the moon. By 1905, Good Roads trains had barnstormed thirty-six states.

Railroads intuitively embraced the Good Roads Movement, knowing that their chronic shortage of railcars resulted from traffic being compressed into the few months of the year in which dirt roads from farm to depot were passable.[19] Year-round accessibility would spread out deliveries over twelve months, allowing more cargo to be carried with fewer cars. The November 1901 edition of the *Railroad Gazette* described a Good Roads Train's consist (a railroad term for the composition of cars linked together into a train):

> There are two traction engines and three crushing plants with a combined capacity of 150 cubic yards a day. Here are also distributing cars to surface the earth road with stone, gravel, chert, slag, tar, macadam or oyster shells, such as the various communities furnish. There are bins and screens for separating the various size[s] of materials. The train carries wheeled scrapers, flat scrapers, disc harrows, plows, shovels, picks; in fact, everything needed to build early macadam or gravel roads.[20]

While the railroads couldn't then see the monumental irony, their road-surfacing campaign also paved the way for public subsidy of what was to become their competitor. As people took to the new object lesson, roads activists agitated for government to do more: They established good roads as a right as basic as breathing clean air. Anesthetized against impending doom by the profitable short-term business of hauling road-building materials, the railroads, in essence, carried the coffin to their own funeral. Only decades later, they would howl that they had to construct and maintain their own railbeds while government gave the truckers the equivalent as a public right, an inequity they had helped to create.

Those who had the most to gain from good roads, of course, were the automakers. Yet, aside from Pope, few showed any enthusiasm for the effort. Most turned a deaf ear and threw their efforts into designing cars that could withstand the rigors of muddy, rutted roads.[21] Unlike the railroad behemoths, turn-of-the-century automakers were small fry, the majority of them located in garage workshops, where they turned out a mere handful of automobiles in a year. They had all they could do to keep the wolf from the door; they had no time to fight national crusades.

Good roads had been but an idea when Pope began his crusade in the 1880s. But the escalating popularity of automobiles held out a practical application for all to see. In 1901, when Pope's League of American Wheelmen invited 200 businesspeople to participate in forming a Road Builders Association, only three showed up. A mere two years later, the National Good Roads Convention, meeting in St. Louis, boasted among its speakers President Theodore Roosevelt and William Jennings Bryan. And by 1904, attendees at its annual convention numbered 1,129 from twenty-nine states.[22]

Silver in Them Thar Hills

Good roads might not bring home the bacon immediately to Colonel Pope, but silver might. William C. Whitney, his friend and former business partner, had by 1901 made a killing in western silver mines. His mine at Tonopah, Nevada, had yielded a staggering $125 million in gold and silver, netting Whitney a $32 million gain, Gatesian profits even in his day.[23]

And so, in 1901–2, the bicycle and automotive pioneer became a silver miner, buying the Hot Pot mine in Leadville, Colorado. In what proved to be a brief excursion into the extractive industries, the Colonel also displayed dramatically and perhaps puckishly what journalists of the day might have labeled "derring-do." A Worcester, Massachusetts, associate, G. Henry Whitcomb, had joined Pope in the venture and knew they would need to create a settlement for the miners, including hotels, dormitories, restaurants, saloons, and, given the proclivities of single men on the frontier, perhaps a bordello as well.

Having acquired some fifty acres of land in Custer County near the Bassick mine, in which both men had an interest, the idea occurred to them to build a town in a single day. Why? Just to see if they could do it. They had houses and stores constructed in movable sections in Pueblo and on the evening of June 9, 1902, had them carted to their new location, which they decided would be called Custer, after the American general whose forces Chief Sitting Bull's warriors had beaten so thoroughly at Little Big Horn. By the dawn's early light, sides of houses cast long shadows as they rose into place, while carpenters joined them together and installed roofs. By day's end, the Colorado governor had conducted a ceremony dedicating the new town.[24]

Will Steam, Gas, or Electricity Win?

In 1901, each of the competing technologies of steam, gasoline, and electricity had a potentially fatal Achilles' heel: steam, for the length of time needed to stoke up an engine; electricity, for the limited range its vehicles could run without a charge; and gasoline, for the inadequate supply then available. The first mode that managed to solve its dilemma would gain a giant edge over its competitors.

The thousand-horsepower Corliss steam engine showcased at Philadelphia's Centennial Exposition in 1876 was representative of steam engines at industrial plants across America that, in turn, drove smaller machinery. Portable steam engines were hauled from farm to farm, particularly in the Midwest, to supply the muscle for heavy tasks. It was natural that, in designing road vehicles, steam would come to the fore, and even Henry Ford spent time learning to repair steam engines. However, the key to individual motor transportation was convenience, and a twenty-minute wait for one's engine to come up to speed didn't sit well with an increasingly impatient populace.[25]

Purveyors of early electric vehicles marketed a variety of home-charging kits, but most homes still lacked electricity, and difficulty in adapting home voltage to vehicle needs soon made it clear that the future of electric cars depended on central power stations, which already powered businesses and residences. A few stations and entrepreneurs created hydrant-like "electrants," which allowed electric vehicles to charge at the office or at home. Producing them in sufficient volume to enable drivers to venture beyond their home cities proved a chicken-and-egg proposition. Electric companies weren't willing to invest in charging stations until many more electric vehicles were on the roads, and auto companies had difficulty selling vehicles in volume to consumers who lacked reliable sources of power, particularly since other dealers were clamoring to sell them gasoline or steam vehicles.[26]

Against this backdrop, a Baptist Sunday school teacher in Beaumont, Texas, amused his students by lighting gases escaping from the ground in 1899, a development that drew frenzied speculators to the area. After months of aimless drilling, they struck pay dirt on January 10, 1901:

> Mud began to bubble with great force from the well. In a matter of seconds, six tons of drill pipe catapulted out of the ground and up through the derrick, knocking off the top, and breaking at the joints as the pipe shot further upward.

The well at Spindletop Hill was the first of thousands of gushers in Texas alone and gave instant assurance that gasoline-powered vehicles would no longer have to worry about supply.[27] If Spindletop represented the lid for the coffin of the electric car industry, the addition to gasoline-powered cars of sturdier cylinder castings, spark plugs, and electric ignitions were the finishing nails.[28] And the silver rails through which the electric vehicle began its descent into the grave may well have been Thomas Edison's vaunted nickel-iron alkaline battery. For two years, he had held the industry captive, arguing that the conventional lead-acid battery was doomed to failure. In 1901, the Wizard of Menlo Park gathered the press and announced that "a near-miraculous product" was imminent, a tactic he had used earlier with other inventions when they were nowhere near the stage of unveiling.

Edison threw the industry into an uproar. Hayden Eames, by now employed at Westinghouse, debunked the Edison battery and bemoaned the fact that prospective purchasers of electric cars were immobilized by uncertainty just at the time when the Spindletop well left no uncertainty of a fuel supply were they to purchase gasoline vehicles. The Wizard's product turned out to be unrealistically costly, and ultimately, he ceased production. If the foremost inventor of his age couldn't master the storage battery problem, many consumers concluded, why should they risk purchasing a problematic product?[29]

The industry Ford joined in 1899 still measured its production in the thousands, not even the tens of thousands, but it had sprung from nothing in just a few years. As Ford contemplated his prospects in Michigan, he had to know that New England had leaped far ahead of the rest of America in steam vehicles (1,191 to 470 for the rest of the country). However, New England had already begun to fall behind the rest of the country in electric vehicles (734 to 841). And, ominously, only 171 gasoline-powered vehicles were produced in New England of a total of 936.[30] Still leading all automakers in production was the Pope Manufacturing Company of Hartford, which by then was churning out both its favored electric as well as Percy Maxim's prized gasoline-powered carriages.

If New England automakers were shortsighted in not grasping the ultimate popularity of the gas-powered automobile, most also failed to understand that cars were not merely the latest fad but rather a tectonic shift in popular culture as well. Having watched two tides of bicycle sales crest and ebb, it was not unreasonable, perhaps, for them to take the conservative course of limiting production to a relatively few costly automobiles for the country club set.[31] Many of New England's early auto manufacturers sprang from an industrial tradition that placed them among society's elite, and if they specialized in high-end vehicles, it may have been because that's what their country club associates told them they wanted. But Henry Ford, unlike Albert Pope, belonged to no country club; his buddy was the man on the street. And there were vastly more laborers than millionaires.

Not just by numbers was the motor industry growing. Clearly, the new machine had caught the public's imagination in the same fashion as the computer would captivate citizens a century later. The phenomenon evolved into a rush just to keep up. Races in America and abroad proliferated and were wildly popular, stirring the blood of both potential customers and investors. As production soared, unit prices lowered, so that Alexander Winton by 1899 could sell a machine for $1,000 while the Knox Automobile Company sold a "tricycle" for $750.[32]

The Automobile Club of America formed in 1899, and national auto shows exhibited the manufacturers' wares at stylish exhibits in such venues as Madison Square Garden. Ever on the lookout for more showy displays, entrepreneurs such as John Brisben Walker, the publisher of *Cosmopolitan* and key rival of S. S. McClure, promoted his Gasmobile by constructing a wooden hill atop Madison Square Garden and employing a stunt driver to show off his car's ability to climb, brake, and—no small feat in those days—back up.[33]

Henry Behind the Wheel

Within this milieu, Henry Ford turned his attention to building a race car with two opposing horizontal cylinders. He eventually developed twenty-six horsepower, a quantum leap from his original three-horsepower motor but not particularly impressive stacked up against his racing competitors, some of whom had attained forty miles per hour. By 1901, Ford was ready to try his vehicle in public, entering an October race in his home town of Detroit. Such attention did the media pay to the event that local courts shut down for the afternoon, so the judges, bailiffs, and attorneys could watch local "chauffer, Henry Ford" vie with the far better known Alexander Winton in a ten-mile race at the Grosse Pointe race track along the Detroit River.[34]

Cleveland's Winton was the sure favorite, having won most such races and holding the mile record on a circular track. Charles B. Shanks, Winton's sales manager and a promoter of the Detroit race, had selected a lavish punch bowl for the winner's prize, "because he figured it would look well in the bay window of the Winton dining room."[35]

As was common then, numerous entries had been eliminated in earlier heats of the race because of mechanical failure, leaving Henry Ford's 26-horsepower racer alone at the starting line next to Winton's celebrated 70-horsepower machine. No contest, it appeared. But on the eighth lap, blue smoke rose from Winton's vehicle, and Ford rolled to victory. Amid the ensuing pandemonium, Ford declared he never would race again. Had he not consciously cast himself as David against Goliath up to then, he now understood the full value of such a contrast. It was a lesson he would apply to great advantage in a few years.

Sadder but wiser from his experience with the Detroit Automobile Company, Ford entered talks in mid–1902 with Alexander Malcomson, a dealer from whom Ford had bought coal while he was employed by the Edison company. In return for a modest capital contribution by Malcomson, Ford agreed to sign over a half-interest in all his patents, models, tools, and drawings. Given Ford's previous business failings and the fact that associates described Malcomson as "opportunistic, restless and compulsive," the new venture lacked any earmarks of promise.[36]

"Asinine Folly"

Malcomson's job was to raise capital for the new enterprise. He approached the Daisy Air Rifle Company for financing, but its attorneys turned him away. He knocked on the door of banker friend John Gray, who said, "Invest in a horseless carriage? Asinine folly." But when Malcomson stuck his neck out and agreed to guarantee payback within a year, Gray anted up $10,000. Daisy's Charles Bennett, who had had a change of heart, contributed a similar sum. Another $10,000 went into the pot from two attorneys who had collected bad debts for Malcomson. The collective infusion allowed the company to be incorporated, with Ford and Malcomson dividing equally 51 percent of the stock.[37]

When the business was only a few weeks old, Ford's financial chief, James Couzens, opened a letter which contained an ominous warning: "United States Patent No. 549,160 granted to George B. Selden Nov. 5, 1895, controls broadly all gasoline automobiles which are accepted as commercially practical."[38] The letter went on to list the manufacturers which Selden had managed to bring to their knees and which had agreed to secure a license in return for granting royalties to the holders of Selden's patents. Its message was clear: Join up or get ready for a brass-knuckled fight.

The letter met with ridicule from Ford and the blustering Couzens. With the welter of competing concepts in play for the gasoline-powered automobile, how could one inventor—let alone one who had yet to produce a working model—dare to monopolize an industry on the strength of one patent? They were not alone in their condemnation. The new auto publication, *Motor Age,* called the ALAM putsch "an audacious but dangerous attack." Philadelphia patent attorney R. M. Hunter derided the Selden claims as "too preposterous to merit serious consideration."[39]

Armed with Selden's patent, the ALAM was attempting to corner the still-developing market, and smaller manufacturers fell quickly into line. By

February 1903, the ALAM appeared so formidable that a meeker Ford and Malcomson approached Pope's Hermann Cuntz at a Chicago convention to discuss throwing in the towel. Their new posture may have come from learning that Winton, the main protagonist in the suit involving ALAM, was on the verge of capitulating.[40]

Fateful Rebuff

Several months later, Ford approached Fred L. Smith of Oldsmobile, ALAM's president, only to be told brusquely that ALAM was unlikely to accept his application, that Ford's was "really nothing but an assemblage plant," an allegation that could have been leveled at some ALAM members themselves. ALAM's inner councils knew well that Ford was far more than "an assemblage plant," that his increasing numbers of lower-priced vehicles threatened to change the industry standard of high-priced vehicles for the upper class. Pope, whose great-grandson says had met Ford and taken his measure, argued for bringing the young man into the fold, but with his sellout to Whitney, Pope's time had passed, and he was unable to persuade ALAM.[41]

History does not recall Ford's reply to Smith, but he was livid, at least privately. Ford had brought along his aide-de-camp, James Couzens, essentially Ford's chief financial officer. The bearish Couzens was a dour man, who one writer says flashed "an annual smile." After hearing ALAM's case and the warning of Ford against making cars in violation of their patents, Couzens told Smith, "Selden can take his patent and go to hell with it!" Smith looked to Ford, seeking a more temperate response. The lanky Ford, his chair tilted back against a wall, told Smith coolly, "Couzens has answered you."

"You men are foolish," said Smith. "The Selden crowd can put you out of business—and will."

Couzens laughed unpleasantly, and Ford jumped to his feet, now as hot under the collar as his assistant. Pointing his finger at Smith, he cried, "Let them try it!" and stalked from the room.[42]

The die was cast.

On October 22, 1903, the Electric Vehicle Company and George B. Selden filed suit in U.S. District Court for the Southern District of New York against Henry Ford. Ford may have gotten wind that ALAM sought to pressure him by threatening his dealers themselves with suit, so several weeks before the lawsuit, Ford bucked up his franchisees with a notice in the *Detroit News* promising:

> We will protect you against any prosecution for alleged infringement of patents. The Selden patent does not cover any practicable machine, no practicable machine can be made from it, and never was so far as we can ascertain.[43]

To keep afloat, the Ford-Malcomson forces had to keep churning out automobiles with one hand while they were waging legal wars with the other. Yet by 1905, Ford and Malcomson were heading toward a falling-out. Malcomson had joined the ALAM crowd in believing that the biggest profits lay in making heavier, more expensive touring cars for the elite, while Ford pursued his grand vision of what he called "a car for the great multitude," a strategy which he felt would be equally financially successful. He would sell many more cars at a substantially lower unit cost.[44] Finally, in 1906, Ford agreed to buy out his partner. The Model N that Ford then began producing went on the market for $600 in an era when some luxury cars, including Pope's, were selling for as much as $10,000.[45] Ford also put in place a network of branch sales outlets and agencies in prime urban locations. Transportation historian James Flink observes that these were often set at strategic geographical points at which freight rates changed, showing how finely Ford calibrated his efforts to cut shipping costs to the bone.[46]

For Albert Pope, the years 1900–1903 had been a lengthy and productive sabbatical. He had made great progress in conditioning the American public to pay for the highways that lay in their future, and he had enjoyed a change of scene through his western mining operations as well as the cattle ranches he picked up along the way in California. But it was far clearer to Pope now that the automobile was here to stay and that potential profits far outstripped those that had been available to him in the bicycle industry. Four years earlier, he had seemed ready to retire. Now sixty and not in the best of health, the Colonel surprised his colleagues and family by summoning his strength for one last major undertaking.

Notes

1. Denison, Merrill, *The Power To Go: The Story of the Automotive Industry,* pp. 111, 125.

2. Finch, Christopher, *Highways to Heaven,* p. 67.

3. Lacey, Robert, *Ford: The Men and the Machine,* p. 59.

4. Chernow, Ron, *House of Morgan,* p. 221.

5. Nevins, Allan, *Ford: The Times, the Man, the Company,* p. 45.

6. Ibid., p. 47.

7. Lacey, p. 40.

8. Finch, p. 67.

9. Nevins, p. 143.

10. Lacey, p. 148.

11. Ibid., p. 41.

12. Nevins, p. 150.

13. Finch, p. 67.

14. Flink, James, *The Automobile Age,* p. 27.

15. Peterson, Joyce Shaw, *American Auto Workers, 1900–1933,* p. 4.

16. Nevins, p. 191.

17. Clues to a Pope-Ford linkage bedevil the historian. Rumors abound that Henry Ford visited Hartford several times to learn more about volume production and interchangeability of parts, that he met with Colonel Pope, even that he worked briefly as a bicycle mechanic in Hartford. Each lead runs into a dead end. Albert Pope II says the Colonel wrote an unpublished autobiography, which he saw before it was lost. In it, he says, a link is described between the two men. One searches in vain through indexes of Ford biographies for such a link, and the efforts of researchers at the National Automobile History Collection in the Detroit Public Library are unavailing as well. That having been said, it is perhaps unlikely that Ford, as a notorious self-promoter, would give public credit to one who had taught him how to mass-produce cars. And Pope's failure to mention Ford in his writings isn't remarkable, since the Model T had been launched only months before Pope's death and Ford was largely unknown at the time. This issue is discussed in further detail in Appendix I.

18. Nevins, p. 258.

19. U.S. Department of Transportation, *America's Highways,* p. 49.

20. *Railroad Gazette,* November 8, 1901, pp. 769–70.

21. Nevins, p. 259.

22. Ibid.; Dearing, Charles L., *American Highway Policy,* p. 228. Pope had lobbied to create the Massachusetts Highway Commission. Yet in 1903, when he sought to obtain its first issued plate, historian Kevin Burke says he was "cruelly rebuffed."

23. Hirsh, Mark D., *William C. Whitney: Modern Warwick,* p. 562.

24. "Was Leader in Good Roads Movement," *Boston Globe,* August 11, 1909, p. 1.

25. Schiffer, Michael Brian, *Taking Charge,* pp. 11–13.

26. Ibid., pp. 65–66.

27. Yergin, Daniel, *The Prize,* pp. 82–87.

28. Greenleaf, William, *Monopoly on Wheels: Henry Ford and the Seldon Patent Suit,* p. 71.

29. Schiffer, pp. 80–90.

30. Nevins, p. 194.

31. Greenleaf, p. 63.

32. Nevins, p. 196.

33. Ibid., p. 197.

34. Ibid., pp. 202–4.

35. Simonds, William Adams, *Henry Ford—His Life, His Work, His Genius,* p. 69.

36. Lacey, p. 68.

37. Collier, Peter and David Horowitz, *The Fords: An American Epic,* p. 44.

38. Ibid., p. 53.

39. Nevins, p. 290.

40. Ibid., p. 295.

41. Interview with Albert A. Pope II, May 8, 1999.

42. Nevins, p. 297.

43. Collier and Horowitz, p. 54.

44. Flink, p. 33.

45. Ibid.

46. Ibid., p. 57.

CHAPTER 11

TRIUMPHANT RETURN

I have never had 2 percent of my employees in my life that ever asked me to raise their pay. ... I hold them because of mutual interest, and I mean to treat them as well as I can.

Albert A. Pope

H ARTFORD'S HABERDASHERS, dry goods merchants, bicycle dealers, insurance executives, carriage makers, restaurateurs—gathered as the city's Business Men's Association—were upbeat and jubilant this evening, not about the upcoming Fourth of July holiday but because tonight's event spelled profit for all of them. For three years now, they had buzzed about the future of Colonel Albert Pope, and to speculate about him was to contemplate the future of their city, for until 1900, he had been its largest employer.

When, at age fifty-seven, Pope had sold out his share of the Electric Vehicle Company to William C. Whitney, rumors flew that the Colonel was ill, that he planned to move back to Boston, that he had lost interest in the motor industry. Indeed, he hadn't spent much time in Hartford the past three years; he had been silver mining in Colorado, lobbying nationally for better roads, and relaxing at his seaside compound in Cohasset. But on July 2, 1903, he was back. And back to stay. Happy days were here again. Tonight Colonel Pope would stick out his chest and talk of "coming into my own again."[1] Waiting for him on the dais was a giant silver loving cup, bestowed on him as a symbol of the association's gratitude for his return and the hoped-for boon that fact would confer on the city.

The graceful Allyn House on Hartford's Asylum Street, a block from the state capitol and a mile from the Pope factory complex, sported the finest ballroom in town. And tonight, Governor Abiram Chamberlain and Mayor Ignatius Sullivan bounded up its steps, past colorful floral tributes sent by well-wishers and through potted palms whose leaves gleamed under the new incandescent lights, which in their brightness seemed to usher in a new era.

The hotel's finest china was set for the testimonial dinner at eight, and the last speaker didn't wind up until three in the morning, hours after waitresses had cleared the dessert dishes. All eyes were on the Colonel, seeking some sign from him of renewed purpose, which would put the unemployed back to work and create new business opportunities for the community. As they basked in the glow of his return, dinner guests traded reports about the first transcontinental automobile trip, which had begun in San Francisco on May 23 and would reach New York in several weeks.

At last, Colonel Pope, the man who had elevated Hartford to the top rank of industrial centers, rose to speak, and his audience inched forward on their seats. "Gentlemen," he intoned after pausing to accept applause from the male audience, "let me tell you that the automobile is as much bigger than the bicycle as it weighs more than the bicycle."

As often as Pope spoke to groups around the country, the self-taught orator was given to fractured syntax from time to time. But he could have been reading the telephone book as far as his audience was concerned. As Pope's listeners struggled to define his meaning, he added words of clarification: "The day is coming when you lovers of the horse won't see him in our streets. Horses have got to go just the same as they went from the street cars." Buggy whip and harness manufacturers in the room perhaps suppressed an instinct to challenge the speaker from the floor; as they looked around, they knew they were outnumbered in this changing world.

The evening was waning, and everyone ached to go home. But when Pope made the prophetic statement that the time will come when he'd become "old and feeble" and someone else "would take over," his colleagues rose in self-interested cries of "Never! Never!" His words were truer than his associates realized, and Pope, as he smiled at their loyalty, no doubt knew that he was already a doomed man.[2]

Back in the Saddle

Albert Augustus Pope had returned to the fray. But the landscape before him had changed almost beyond recognition during the past three years. He had left the Electric Vehicle Company when it still had high hopes of dominating the market for electric vehicles directly and for gasoline types indirectly. The *Hartford Globe* had run a massive illustrated section on the automotive industry in April, upon word that Pope was returning to Hartford, with a full-page ad from downtown department store Brown, Thomson & Co., which was offering several gasoline models for sale, including the low-priced Cadillac.[3] By 1903, it was becoming apparent to industry insiders that gasoline autos were gaining in popularity at the expense of electric vehicles, and ALAM was gearing up to embark on a lengthy, draining patent battle with Henry Ford.

When Pope had left Hartford in 1900, industrialists were still generally revered for their enterprise and as community employers, in spite of the disrepute attached to a few notorious railroad robber barons. But by 1902, the bloom was off the rose. S. S. McClure had begun to publish exposés on the oil industry, the railroads, and municipal corruption. *Everybody's* magazine and *Collier's* added broadsides against the insurance industry and the beef trust. Keeping up the drumbeat of bigness as badness was Frank Norris's *The Octopus*, which dramatized the alleged exploitation by the railroads of midwestern wheat farmers. And soon to follow would be Upton Sinclair's powerful novel *The Jungle*, which uncovered abuses in Chicago's meat-packing industry. In reaction, Jack London's socialist novel, *Iron Heel,* propounded an alternative, more citizen-friendly polity called socialism. While Colonel Pope had yet avoided the lash, the climate for big business was clearly becoming less sunny.

On a more personal scale, Pope was returning to economic circumstances much cloudier than when he had left in 1900. The American Bicycle Company, formed from the remnants of forty-five bicycle makers, had been capitalized to the tune of $80 million. But now the media had dubbed it the "bicycle trust," and it sank into receivership in 1902, with Colonel Pope named as its receiver. Whether receivership resulted from the popularity of the new automobile or from the ineptness of Albert Linder Pope's leadership is debatable. American Bicycle groaned from its inception under a mountain of debt and a perception by many of the acquired bicycle manufacturers that their industry's future looked bleak. Offered the choice of stock in the new venture or cash, most took the money and ran.

In truth, Prince Albert had one hand tied behind his back from the beginning. When most of the acquired manufacturers insisted on cash instead of stock, which was quite unexpected, the new combine had to make regular payments on a debt of $9.3 million, quite apart from its operating expenses. To keep afloat, American Bicycle began to liquidate assets. By 1902, only two years after its organization, creditors closed the company down when it defaulted on its debt.

Spalding and the other investors could walk away from the ruins, chalking it up to a failed experiment, but Pope had a deeper stake. Quite aside from personal pride in protecting the integrity of the Pope product, he knew that thousands of men and women depended on him for their livelihood, people with whom he had passed from youth to middle age. In 1903, he bought the tattered remnants of its production capacity.[4] He would fold it and his new Pope Motor Company into the Pope Manufacturing Company, which would produce both bicycles and automobiles.[5] While one of his plants

Teddy Roosevelt becomes the first president to ride in an automobile during the Hartford parade in 1902 in a Pope car. Alongside, astride Columbia bicycles, are members of the Secret Service, formed the year before in the wake of President William McKinley's assassination. *(The Connecticut Historical Society, Hartford, Connecticut.)*

would continue turning out electric vehicles, the Colonel had seen the handwriting on the wall and now concentrated primarily on gasoline models.

Tilting with Teddy

Soon after Pope's triumphant return to Hartford, the visibly aging Colonel became embroiled in one of the few political turmoils of his life. A Republican who had associated in the 1880s with the reformist mugwump branch of the party, Pope was a great friend of General Nelson Miles, a Civil War general from Boston with whom he had served and whose friendship had lasted for decades after. General Miles took a leading role in the Indian wars in the American West in the declining years of the century. In 1899, when beef packers challenged the general for proof of his charge that they treated beef chemically, Pope shot off a telegram, directing the general to count on him for $1,000 to prove that chemicals were used to embalm beef furnished U.S. soldiers. It was not the last time Pope would stand by his Civil War colleague.

In September 1903, as a member of the Commercial Travelers' Sound Money League, Pope joined in endorsing President Theodore Roosevelt for the presidential nomination and was named as a member of the committee designated to present the resolution to Roosevelt at the White House. Roosevelt had ridden in an Electric Vehicle Company car when he visited the city in 1902, and his friendship as the nation's chief executive could do Pope nothing but good.

When he became convinced that Teddy Roosevelt had insulted his friend General Miles, however, Pope faced the choice of personal loyalty or opportunism. As a mugwump, apostasy wasn't foreign to Pope, so he cast caution to the winds and abruptly resigned from the committee and the league itself, saying, "President Roosevelt insulted my friend, Gen. Miles, and I would not go near him on any errand. I hope the democrats will have the sense to nominate Gen. Miles, and republican as I am, I will go on the stump to help elect him."[6] History does not record the nature of the alleged insult.

Risky Business

Pope's decision to leap back, at age sixty, into a market far more competitive than the one he had left three years before brims with pathos. Whether he knew the nature of his illness or not, it was a progressive disease, so his strength was gradually ebbing. His able lieutenants, on whom he had depended so much, were gone: Day, to ALAM, then to an early death in 1907; Maxim, to Westinghouse in Pittsburgh; and Eames, to Studebaker. Henry Souther and nephew Harry Pope left for other positions as well.

"Scientific management," a revolutionary advance in industrialization championed by Pope's nemesis, Frederick Winslow Taylor, was replacing the industrial paternalism of Pope's golden years. At Harvard, Professor William Z. Ripley pioneered in transportation economics, indoctrinating such students as Franklin D. Roosevelt in the fine points of a new science, which Pope might have found incomprehensible.[7] Having said four years before that he was too old for new challenges, why did Pope feel the need to take on such a seemingly overwhelming risk?

The record is silent on Pope's reasoning. Yet how could a man of pride, who had restored luster to the family name after his father's business failures, let the financial ruin of both his auto and bicycle enterprises be his lasting legacy? No, the Colonel was embarked on a course of personal vindication, and to show his seriousness of purpose, he removed such names as "Electric Vehicle," "Columbia," and "American" from his business standard.

From now on, the corporation would be known as the Pope Manufacturing Company, and models would bear his own surname. Succeed or fail, Pope's last hurrah would be an intensely personal venture.

Even with the experience and acumen that Pope possessed, the odds against success in this rough-and-tumble field were daunting. Between 1902 and 1907, 287 automakers began making vehicles, then went belly up.[8] By 1906, 146 separate companies turned out $65 million worth of cars.[9] It seemed like every manufacturer with a track record of success in its field was drawn to automobile manufacturing—like moths to a flame. The American Locomotive Company, whose hard-charging vice president at the time was young Walter Chrysler, began adding automobile carriages to its line of rail carriages. The White Sewing Machine Company, perhaps recalling the precedent of the Weed company, diversified into automobiles. The Peerless Company left clothes wringers for motors, and the Stanleys jumped from making dry plates to building cars.[10] Most would find that the capital requirements and skills required far exceeded those in the field they had left.

Choice of Four Models

The reorganized Pope company offered the public four models, ranging widely in price and styling. They were made in far-flung company plants—the Pope-Toledo luxury car in Toledo, Ohio; the medium-priced Pope-Hartford in Hartford; the compact Pope-Tribune in Hagerstown, Maryland; and the Waverley electric, which was named after the Indianapolis company that sold out to Colonel Pope.[11] Since the Electric Vehicle Company was still manufacturing cars a stone's throw away from his Hartford plant, Pope was now going head to head with his former colleagues.

In 1904 the company produced its first one-cylinder Pope-Hartford, and it soon expanded into four- and six-cylinder engines. Swelling with pride that the Colonel was back in town and that the city was once more on the move, Hartford executives vied to buy one of the early gas or electric models and could be seen wearing scarves and goggles, putt-putting past the plant and ascending Capitol Avenue past the ornate domed state capitol. Attempting to work the bugs out, Pope's test drivers drove farther and farther, down the Berlin Turnpike, out fifteen miles into rolling farmland, and fifty miles along the Connecticut River to the shore.

Pope formed the International Motor Car Company from those affiliates of the American Bicycle Company that also made automobiles. Using this shell as a base, Pope now changed its name to the Pope Motor Car Company.[12] The unused capacity of the Pope Manufacturing Company was reconstituted as a $6.5 million New Jersey corporation, which held the remaining

The Pope Tribune (center) was manufactured for the economy market at Pope's Hagerstown, Maryland, plant. Henry Ford's Detroit location, at the center of the national market, gave him a natural advantage over Pope, who had to pay greater shipping charges for raw materials and for finished products. *(The Connecticut Historical Society, Hartford, Connecticut.)*

Pope and American Bicycle Company assets, with operations in Hartford and Westfield, Massachusetts.[13]

Colonel Pope resumed weekend residence in his Capitol Avenue penthouse in the three-story, buff-colored, brick office building. Its lush green front lawn, punctuated with manicured shrubs and flowerbeds, was an elegant counterpoint to the clattering factory next door. There, amid lavish facilities for entertaining, Pope stood again at the wide arched windows of his chandeliered corner office, behind his heavy oak worktable with its white wicker desk chair, and gazed across Capitol Avenue to the tree-canopied brick townhouses he had built for his staff in his halcyon days. From this aerie, Pope was again at the helm of the remnants of his bicycle and automobile empire. By telephone, telegraph, and personal visits, he kept a constant finger on its pulse.

The Westfield bicycle factory was strikingly similar to the home office in that, like in Hartford, the first building a visitor on the street encountered held the gracious, homey company offices, which sat in the shadow of the

1903 MODEL-B.

Pope was quick to marry the best of the bicycle and the automobile in his 1903 Model B motorcycle, which maintained the bicycle chain in place, in case of failure of the gasoline motor which was installed under the seat. (The Connecticut Historical Society, Hartford, Connecticut.)

utilitarian three-acre brick factory complex, whose five ells each stretched longer than a football field. In discrete factory departments, thousands of blue-shirted workers engaged in their specialized activities of nickel-plating, wheel assembly, enameling, framing, brazing, and gear-cutting, forming the rudiments of a production line that others would later refine.

In Elyria, Ohio, Pope had founded the Columbia Steel Company in 1892, a ten-smokestack facility which supplied open-hearth steel in strips and sheets for the Pope bicycles and automobiles. In Indianapolis, the Waverley plant of Pope Motor Car Company kept the Colonel's vision of electric motoring alive for the present, its plant churning out more electric vehicles than any other in the world. To counter the competition from gas-powered vehicles, the company had decided to concentrate on sales to local governments, which could install centralized charging stations. Company literature boasted that the average travel radius had nearly doubled from its earlier models to thirty-three to thirty-five miles per charge and, on occasion, up to eighty. Before the era of smooth roads, eighty miles would cover the great bulk of daily jaunts. Woodworking was a priority in Indianapolis; poplar was used for veneers and paneling; ash, maple, and second-growth hickory for wheels and top bows. Pope installed the largest elevator Elisha Otis had ever installed in the West to carry the finished vehicle to the ground floor shipping platforms.

Pope had acquired the handsomely landscaped Toledo factory at the turn

In an era before PCs, office workers at Pope's Capitol Avenue plant make hand-written entries into company ledgers under the glow of early electric lights. *(The Connecticut Historical Society, Hartford, Connecticut.)*

of the century. The Pope-Toledo, the crème de la crème of Pope production, used alloyed steel for strength and reached a fuel efficiency of nearly sixteen miles per gallon, besting all comers for a car of corresponding weight. Pope's brother Harold, sitting at a paneled rolltop desk beside a long cluttered worktable, ran the Hagerstown factory's production of Pope-Tribunes. Company literature made sure that readers, who were above all, potential customers, knew that the big boss had been a Civil War hero, serving but a few miles from the plant during the battles of Antietam, South Mountain, and Gettysburg.

Drafting and design functions for all factories resided in Hartford, where engineers and draftsmen with eyeshades bent over row on row of tilted tables, refining concepts they had developed and altering them to keep ahead of the galloping competition and to work out bugs. Laborers in its boiler room, their bare arms glistening with sweat, stoked huge furnaces to power engines with a total of 775 horsepower, spread throughout the 400,000-square-foot plant, where hundreds of people toiled amid a riot of belts, pulleys, whirring wheels, and grinding machines. Company publications touted the raw muscle of its machinery, of 3,000-pound hammers used in drop forging.

"The Most Perfect Automobile"

A flight of stairs above Hartford's factory floor labored the sales, advertising, and publicity departments. In a day before the science of public relations had evolved, Pope publicists honed self-serving pronouncements: "The Pope Manufacturing Company has earnestly set itself the task of producing the most perfect automobile in existence, ... a fact which immediately becomes self-evident to the intelligent visitor at the Hartford factory."

Robert Winkley, the Colonel's former personal secretary, who had saved valuable corporate records from the Boston fire in 1896 and who now headed the publicity department, was such a trusted Pope aide that he would become a beneficiary of his will. The PR staff spun with great élan the moral homilies which were the fashion of the day: "The man who works diligently, plays hard, fights to the finish and stands privation with a smile is the kind of character that wins out in business campaigns and economic reforms." Keeping things in the family, Albert's younger brother Arthur and uncle George also served on the board of directors of Pope Manufacturing Company.

Pope reverted to the schedule he had maintained before leaving Hartford in 1900. Each Saturday morning, he'd hoist his increasing bulk onto a Hartford-bound train, which was met at noon at Union Station by the driver of a smart carriage. While Abby attended the symphony and directed the lives of the children still at home in Boston, taking them by train to Cohasset on sunny weekends, the Colonel would oversee the Hartford operation on Saturday afternoon, then break out the liquor, and, as one participant recalled, "keep the young men up til midnight." After a Sunday in the shop, Pope would return to Boston on the 7:15 evening train.[14]

Only then could Albert Linder Pope loosen his tie. "My father had the feeling," William Pope recalls, "that the Colonel came on weekends largely to check up on him." Why did he do his partying away from his family in Boston? "I really think," William says, "that he didn't want Abby to know what was going on."[15]

One of Pope's strengths had always been his skill at identifying capable young workers and giving them their head. Quietly, uncomplainingly, they had wrestled with the myriad of details necessary to run New England's largest industrial plant. But in so doing, they unwittingly did Pope a disfavor, for once he was left to handle alone the quotidian duties of an auto manufacturer, he learned how much he didn't know. Pope had stayed on good terms with William C. Whitney, who had linked him to Wall Street financing, which he would surely need in his new venture. Though nominally competitors, Whitney had continued to manufacture electrics while Pope's Hartford operations, at least, were committed to gasoline power. But, unknown to them both, Whitney had but months to live.

In a few years, Ford's car for the common man would eclipse Pope and all other early automakers. Two decades later, William Durant and Alfred Sloan's concept of "a car for every purse and purpose" would outpace Ford. Ironically, Pope was the first to recognize the public's desire not only for a choice of price ranges but also for a chance to demonstrate their own success by the kind of car they drove. In 1899, social theorist Thorstein Veblen had bestowed a lasting label—conspicuous consumption—on this phenomenon. And while New England Calvinism had preached that one's good works are evidence of predetermined salvation, a wide choice of styles and prices offered consumers a sort of materialistic Calvinism as well.[16]

Since no capable right-hand man such as George Day was available to take the helm, the Colonel appointed himself president, tapping his son Albert Linder as vice president and cousin George Pope as treasurer.[17]

Magnificent Obsession

Like a dog with a bone, Henry Ford chased his vision of a car for the common man, an obsession that by 1905 threatened to drive out his partner, Alexander Malcomson, who saw big profits instead in catering to the carriage trade. In the East, auto touring had caught on among the smart set as a leisure diversion. Promoting the trend most avidly was millionaire auto enthusiast Charles K. Glidden, who organized "reliability tours," which in the days of rugged terrain combined sport, adventure, and travel. Glidden's only stipulation was that the auto must be driven by its owner. In July 1905, the Colonel not only entered but won the first Glidden tour, a grueling nine-day event, in a 45-horsepower Pope-Toledo driven by Albert and his brother Arthur on a seven-hour jaunt from New York to Hartford. Fittingly, Pope served as toastmaster of a dinner that evening with 150 Hartford motoring enthusiasts. The press and motor magazines duly noted the event and Pope's prominence in it, which certainly did the brand name no harm.

The next day, the group set off for a 122-mile run from Hartford to Boston, leaving at 6 A.M. A tour participant noted:

> The weather was fine, the scenery beautiful; and from Worcester to Boston is encountered the best stretch of highway in the U.S. It has proved that Amer-

Eddie "Cannonball" Ball, goggles at the ready, prepares for 1906 automobile race in a Pope racer as bowler-hatted judges wait to officiate. *(The Connecticut Historical Society, Hartford, Connecticut.)*

ican cars are durable and efficient. It has shown the few who took part how delightful their short vacation may be, and it has strengthened our belief in the permanence of the automobile.[18]

Henry Ford wasn't putting together vacation tours for the glitterati. His target market didn't often take vacations, but given the automobile's role in expanding their lives, they might soon be able to afford one. In the 1904–5 season, Ford's new company introduced the Model C at a sticker price of $800; with a tonneau cover to keep out the weather, its price rose to $900. Ford's Model F touring car sold for $1,000, and the Model B four-cylinder touring car for the better off had a sticker of $2,000. By comparison, a seven-passenger, 24-horsepower Packard cost $7,000, and even the mid-priced Pope-Hartford sold for $3,200. More ominously, as the decade wore on, the lights burned into the night at Ford's three-story plant at 411 Piquette Street in Detroit. There, in a third-floor office in the building's northeast corner, Ford

As with the bicycle, press coverage of auto racing and touring gave valuable free publicity to automakers. Here, a Pope pilot car prepares to advance racers to the starting line of a weekend race. *(The Connecticut Historical Society, Hartford, Connecticut.)*

and his engineers were designing, in secret, yet another model, one that would shake the automobile market to its roots.[19]

Pope, however, was not about to abandon the economy field to Ford, and he managed to bring in the Tribune for a competitive price.[20] But the Colonel's choice to manufacture a car for the man on the street in coastal Hagerstown was a tactical error. The one- and two-cylinder Pope-Tribunes featured a six-horsepower engine and went on the market in 1904 for as low as $650.[21] In a highly price-competitive market, freight haulage of raw materials to factories and of finished automobiles from factories to showrooms was a major line item. Had Pope chosen to make Tribunes in the geographical middle of the market—in his Toledo plant, for instance—such a choice would have substantially reduced his shipping costs. [22]

In 1906, presaging the Model T he would introduce in 1908, Henry Ford put on the market his Model N, a four-cylinder runabout, whose $600 price undercut Pope's Tribune.[23] Partly because of the shipping cost differential and its relative lack of power, the one- and two-cylinder Tribunes turned out to be money losers, and within a year after Ford introduced the Model

Unlike Henry Ford, who marketed his Model Ts to farmers, Pope catered to the carriage trade. This early Columbia electric allowed riders the privacy of an enclosed compartment while the chauffeur rode in front, exposed to the elements. *(Courtesy John Lee and Percy Maxim Lee.)*

N, the Tribune ceased production, leaving economy production to the man from Detroit.

The Pope-Toledo, an elite automobile evolved from the Toledo steamer, survived two years more. With peaked bonnets and four-cylinder, water-cooled engines, the Pope-Toledo was top of the line, aside from Pope's addition of limousines and seven-seat touring cars. The longest survivor was the mid-priced Pope-Hartford, which the company cranked out in the city of its birth until 1914.[24]

Read All about It

It was evident to anyone watching the industry in 1903 that the automobile had come to stay and that the public's interest was keen and sustained, so a market opened for specialty magazines. *Horseless Age* had made its debut as early as 1895, and *Automobile* and *Motor Age* joined the fray by century's end. Soon *Motor World* and William Randolph Hearst's *Motor* crowded them for space on the newsstands, following up on the success that Pope had enjoyed with bicycle magazines in the 1880s and 1890s.[25] Yet they were still far outnumbered by the dozens of trade journals, popular magazines, and railway guides promoting still-popular train travel.[26]

Even before the nation's railroads reached their peak trackage in 1916, their new competitor dogged their steps; American life was about to be transformed forever. In what could serve as a symbol of the passing of an era, the colorful Elizabeth Hart Jarvis Colt, the widow of gunmaker Samuel Colt, neared the end of her life in the summer of 1905. She had been the next-door neighbor of George Day for many years. As remembrances to her closest friends, Elizabeth prepared small gifts and gave Sam's gun collection and Dresden china to Hartford's Wadsworth Atheneum. She then left orders for her five horses to be shot and buried, before passing away at her niece's home in Newport. [27]

In 1906, when it became apparent that the Electric Vehicle Company's days were numbered, Hiram Percy Maxim and his best man, T. Wells Goodridge, went into business together. Ironically, in spite of Maxim's passionate championing of gasoline vehicles and the general failure of electric vehicles to win a foothold in the markets, their Maxim-Goodridge Electric Company turned out a vehicle called the Lenox Electric. "In those days, he was struggling to make a living," recalls his daughter Percy Lee, born that year in the family's home at 550 Prospect Street on the city line.[28] When, predictably, the venture failed, Maxim turned his attention to developing the silencer, for which his name would be best known.[29]

The Selden-Ford patent suit had now entered its fourth year; its protagonists continued to slug away at each other like groggy prizefighters. Little did they know that another five years of withering litigation lay ahead of them. George Day, still at the helm of the Electric Vehicle Company, seemingly charmed everyone he met, including his adversary Henry Ford, who called Day "a gentleman for whom personally I have the greatest respect." In August 1906, Ford and Day encountered each other unexpectedly in a Detroit hotel lobby. Ford broke the ice, extended his hand, and asked, "How'd you like to look over our plant?"

"We'd be delighted," answered Day, and the bitter adversaries and their aides piled into a Ford auto and wheeled away for a tour of the factory.[30]

The Panic of 1907 staggered the American economy, although remarkably the automobile industry as a whole weathered the storm. The Pope Motor Car Company and the Electric Vehicle Company were not quite as fortunate. By now, gasoline taxis had proven easier to maintain than the electrics,

After Hiram Percy Maxim left Pope's employ, he entered into the manufacturing business briefly, producing this 1907 Lenox electric even though his early passion had been for gasoline automobiles. *(Courtesy John Lee and Percy Maxim Lee.)*

which had never solved the storage battery problem, and the internal combustion engine became the standard for taxicabs. Had the Whitney vision proved out, his combine could have offset a major operating loss from electric vehicles with royalties on gasoline vehicles. But Alexander Winton and his midwestern cronies had outfoxed Wall Street's Whitney and bargained down the per vehicle royalty to a tiny fraction of the original demand. As a result, income from the Selden patent was less than $1.9 million as late as 1907, and the Electric Vehicle Company's share of that was less than $700,000.

The Electric Vehicle Company's best year was 1906, when it made $217,000, but the weight of $20 million in watered stock pulled the company inexorably downward. Sensing vulnerability, existing licensees forced down the royalty rate from 1.25 percent to 0.8 percent, further sapping the company's strength.[31] Historian John Rae's epitaph for the Electric Vehicle Company calls it a "parasitical growth on the automobile industry, and its demise was regretted only by those unfortunate enough to hold its securities."[32]

In 1907, the Pope company published a 30-year retrospective of the building of its industrial empire, entitled *An Industrial Achievement,* fully illustrated and lavishly produced. Yet when its proud leaders turned to their bankers for credit to pay off $1.6 million in outstanding notes, the door to the vault slammed in their faces, which would have been an unthinkable event when Pope was at the apex of the bicycle industry. But now, a Darwinian shake-out was rocking the automobile industry. Only the strong would survive, and Wall Street was betting that Pope wouldn't be among them. A buyer's market prevailed, and shrewd bargainers circled the fallen carcasses.

Final Straw

The final straw was Pope's inability to pay a pitifully small, $4,306.30 debt to a Toledo firm, whose attorneys petitioned Pope's company into receivership. When creditors got wind of this, their claims snowballed and overwhelmed the company. A sign of the Colonel's declining health was that while in 1903 a court had appointed the domineering industrialist as receiver of the bankrupt American Bicycle Company, the bankruptcy court now designated Albert Linder Pope to dig the company's grave.[33]

History had repeated itself, a bitter legacy that Albert Pope had dedicated his career to reversing. In 1852, hopelessly overextended in real estate speculation, a dispirited Charles Pope had signed a document turning over all his assets to his creditors. He was never again the same. Now, fifty-five years later, the son who had set out to redeem the family name gave up control of all his corporate assets. The important distinction was that his earnings had already made the Colonel a wealthy man. Unlike his father, Albert's personal assets were sufficient to enable generations after him to live comfortably. But the quest to install the name Pope firmly at the apex of the industrial pyramid had failed. And, like his father in that respect, Albert Augustus Pope was a broken man.

Bottom feeders turned out in force when it came time to pick over the Pope assets. No longer would the Pope-Tribune offer a low-priced challenge to Henry Ford, as the auctioneer's gavel signaled a $57,000 sale in 1907. The Elyria steel plant went for a paltry $35,000 the same year. Toledo held out for two years before John North Willys bought it for $285,000, to become the new home of Willys Overland cars.[34] And Herbert H. Rice, a Pope employee since 1892, picked up the Waverley factory and would continue producing electric vehicles there until 1915, when he would join the Cadillac Motor Company, which he would eventually head as president.[35]

In his dotage, Colonel Pope gazes haughtily at the photographer. The man who popularized bicycles and motorized vehicles during his career here chooses a more primitive form of locomotion. (*Courtesy William Pope, Sr.*)

If it was any consolation to the Colonel, the Electric Vehicle Company fared no better. When it finally collapsed in 1907, it claimed only $3.6 million in debts against $17 million in assets, which would have been respectable had not $14 million of it represented intangibles: goodwill, patents, and licenses. Of this, the book value of the Selden patent itself was $11.5 million. But the cash cupboard was virtually bare, containing only $12,000.[36]

The Panic of 1907 marked a fundamental winnowing of the automobile industry, which had grown from an output of $16 million worth of vehicles in 1903 to $89 million four years later. Gone were the Electric Vehicle Company and the Pope Manufacturing Company. Gone was the promise of that sultry July night in a glittering hotel ballroom in 1903. The magazine *Horseless Age*, which had so effusively welcomed Pope into the industry only a decade earlier, now wrote a vitriolic epitaph over the grave of the Electric Vehicle Company, entitled "The Trail of the Serpent."[37]

Hartford had lost its title, briefly held, of automobile capital of the world.

Instead, such cities as Syracuse and Tarrytown in New York and Toledo and Cleveland in Ohio came to the fore, with Detroit close behind.[38] When the dust had settled, the mantle of industry had moved sharply westward, and the Northeast lost, once and forever, the chance to become home to Motown. "When consolidation came, its operating (though not its financial) headquarters were to be in Michigan."[39]

Unlike Pope, the dashing Whitney was spared the ignominy of receivership, even though his company wasn't. In early 1904, he had attended a performance of *Parsifal* at the Metropolitan Opera after telling his secretary that he felt unwell. He collapsed in his seat and was rushed to the hospital; his badly inflamed appendix led to peritonitis, blood poisoning, and death. So totemic a figure was he in the financial industry that the stock exchanges hushed up his mid-afternoon death until the stock market had closed at 5 P.M., to avoid a market tumble. The New York state legislature, by rising vote, adjourned upon hearing the news.[40]

With bankruptcy, Colonel Pope retired to the circle of his family and the sympathetic embrace of his grandchildren in family gatherings in Boston and Cohasset. His final quest, to make the name Pope as well known in the twentieth century as it had been in the nineteenth, had failed. And to top it off, he would live to see Henry Ford introduce the Model T.[41]

Notes

1. "Colonel Albert Pope Dies of Pneumonia," *Hartford Courant*, August 11, 1909, p. 1.

2. Dean, Clarence, "Pope-Hartford Started Auspiciously in Auto Field," *Hartford Courant*, p. 1.

3. *Hartford Globe*, April 26, 1903, p. 24.

4. Rae, John, *The American Automobile Industry: The First Forty Years*, p. 16; Epperson, Bruce, "A Model of Technological Dissonance," p. 24.

5. Burpee, C.W., *History of Hartford County, Connecticut, 1633–1928*, p. 527.

6. "Was Leader in Good Roads Movement," *Boston Globe*, August 11, 1909.

7. Goddard, Stephen B., *Getting There: The Epic Struggle Between Road and Rail in the American Century*, p. 159.

8. Oppel, Frank, *Motoring in America*, p. 88.

9. Ibid., pp. 83, 89.

10. Ibid., p. 93.

11. Flink, James J., *The Automobile Age*, p. 9.

12. Corrigan, David, "Corporate Genealogies."

13. Rae, p. 62.

14. Dean, "Pope-Hartford," p. 1.

15. William Pope, Sr., interview September 9, 1999.

16. Rae, p. 28.

17. Maxim, Hiram Percy, *Horseless Carriage Days*, p. 528.

18. Flink, p. 32; Bentley, John, *Great American Automobiles*, p. 136.

19. McCraw, Jim, "Ghosts of Detroit's Past in Ford's Old Buildings," *New York Times,* October 15, 1999, p. F1.

20. Nevins, Allan, *Ford: The Times, the Man, the Company,* p. 200.

21. Ibid., p. 221.

22. Rae, p. 28.

23. Flink, p. 33.

24. Georgano, G.N., ed., *The Complete Encyclopedia of Motorcars, 1885–1968.*

25. Flink, p. 29.

26. Tebbel, John et al, *The Magazine in America, 1741–1990,* p. 87.

27. Grant, Ellsworth, *The Colt Armory,* p. 72.

28. Interview with Percy Lee, September 29, 1999.

29. Lee, Percy Maxim and John Glessner, *Family Reunion,* p. 185.

30. Nevins, p. 322.

31. Nevins, p. 321.

32. Rae, p. 311.

33. "Was Leader in Good Roads Movement," p. 1.

34. Rae, p. 27.

35. Rae, *The First Forty Years,* p. 62; Rae, *The American Automobile Industry,* p. 27.

36. Rae, *The American Automobile Industry,* pp. 309–310; Greenleaf, William, *Monopoly on Wheels: Henry Ford and the Seldon Patent Suit,* p. 185.

37. Greenleaf, p. 185.

38. Oppel, p. 94.

39. Durant, William, *Dream Maker,* p. 122.

40. Hirsh, Mark D., *William C. Whitney: Modern Warwick,* p. 599.

41. Rae, *The American Automobile Industry,* chapter 5.

CHAPTER 12

PARTING

The career of Colonel Pope was a career of ceaseless energy, a progressive demonstration of almost unerring foresight, keen judgment and an executive ability that built up and welded together into a compact, frictionless system, five great manufacturing plants whose product more than anything else will contribute to his fame long years after his death.

Hartford Times

NEAR THE END of Jerusalem Road in the seaside town of Cohasset—fifteen miles southeast of Boston as the crow flies—sits a high promontory with a panoramic view of the Atlantic Ocean. Albert Pope had emulated so many men of his generation by building his grand manse on the highest hill around. Set on fifty acres of land, which sloped gradually to the shore line through massive growths of rhododendron, chrysanthemums, and orchids, with views clear across to Boston's North Shore, the stone house was called Lyndemere in honor of his wife's birth name, Linder. It contained dozens of rooms and three guest cottages, which later Pope generations would call "trophy rooms" after the dozens of awards their progenitor had won in motor tours and bicycle competitions and displayed for guests to admire.[1]

Lyndemere was the ultimate symbol of Colonel Pope's success and the embodiment of an "edifice complex," which commonly afflicted the well-to-do of his day, particularly the self-made, as Pope liked to pretend he was. There, he sat with S. S. McClure in his darkest hour, sending him away smiling with a cash infusion to keep his magazine afloat. There, he entertained next-door neighbor Henry Payne Whitney, whose friendship would introduce him to Henry's brother, William Collins Whitney. There, Abby would gather with her children, home from school and work for rousing weekends of sailing, surf, and sun. There, the Colonel's guests, enjoying the idyllic setting, would frequently overstay their welcome, stirring the ire of their hostess. There, Albert watched his children swim their first strokes and learn to sail,

Wicker furniture, a crystal chandelier and a grand piano grace the living room of Pope's Cohasset estate, Lyndemere, overlooking the Atlantic Ocean. *(Courtesy William Pope, Sr.)*

a passion that won the heart of his firstborn son, Albert, and took the life of his third son, Charles, in a sailing accident.

Lifestyles of the rich and famous, then and now, fascinate readers, so it's no wonder that newspapers and fashionable magazines ran photographic spreads that featured the imposing, ivy-covered, wood porte cochere at Lyndemere's front entrance. One can imagine the great and near-great alighting from carriages to spend the weekend with New England's leading industrialist. Displayed for the voyeuristic public were a profusion of crimson ramblers, trumpet flowers, and woodbine hugging the house's foundation and the family's conservatories and palm house. Readers would learn that the same man who had become a symbol of industrial might was passionate about cultivating orchids and tending his grape arbors. The publications might invite their readers inside the house to view the Victorian wicker furniture, oak clawfoot tables, oriental rugs, rolltop desk, and grand piano.

A large living room punctuated one end of the rectangular house, and a den sat at the other. In between, dinner guests overlooked the Atlantic Ocean;

From the Cohasset shoreline, Lyndemere and its guest cottages rise grandly from the gardens, flower beds and greenhouses below. *(Courtesy William Pope, Sr.)*

the windows were thrown open to the salt air, while they ate fresh lobster on fine china. Near the tennis courts sat a smaller building housing a billiard room, bowling alley, lounging room, and a gymnasium plus a bath and two bedrooms. The number of rooms in the Pope house is lost in the mists of history, but it clearly was in the dozens; the estate superintendent's house alone held nineteen rooms. Stables held horses sufficient for the large family and its guests while full-blooded Jersey cows grazed beside the sea.[2]

No other residence the Colonel built—not the Commonwealth Avenue townhouse near the Harvard Club nor the elegant Capitol Avenue penthouse in Hartford—more aptly described the man than Lyndemere. So it seemed fitting that his last days on earth would be spent propped up in bed, watching the billowing sails of August, boats heeled over in a stiff breeze, as he slowly succumbed to the wasting illness that had been consuming him for nearly a decade. Although he was likely past caring by now, the U.S. Court of Appeals ruled that the Selden patent was legitimate, thereby validating the now-defunct Electric Vehicle Company and enhancing the worth of his son Albert's Columbia company, which had inherited the patent.[3]

It wasn't the usual joyous summer gathering of family this August, 1909, as carriages delivered the Colonel's sisters Leonora, Augusta, and Emily to Lyndemere's imposing front entrance. Monday, August 9, Dr. Oliver Howe, the family's physician, told Abby solemnly that the end was near. She telegrammed and phoned those who were not present, while Albert Linder, the heir apparent, and Ralph, still in his twenties, sat by their father's side. Only two months before, Prince Albert had completed reorganizing the remains of the Electric Vehicle Company into the Columbia Motor Car Company, but the time for corporate chatter had passed, and the time for goodbyes had come.

Last Vigil

One by one, aunts and siblings began to arrive. As the Colonel began his slide toward death, he may not even have heard the heavy wooden door open as family members entered the downstairs foyer, with its massive stone fireplace and oak inglenook, and ascended the meandering turned staircase, the women's long skirts whooshing along its risers. Margaret, now Mrs. Freeman Hinckley, arrived from Boston shortly after the Colonel breathed his last Monday at 5:45 P.M. as the summer sun sank lower in the western sky. Meanwhile, Harold Pope, superintendent of the Toledo factory, was rushing eastward by train.

Pneumonia, complicated by arteriosclerosis, Dr. Howe would write on the death certificate. Pneumonia was the verdict of the *Boston Post* and the *Boston Globe*, although the *Post* would hint at a deeper cause in a glancing reference to "the breaking down of his nervous system" and note that he had been confined to bed since the previous May. Only the Hartford newspapers gave "locomotor ataxia" as the cause of death, although neither the newspapers nor his own doctors understood what that signified. Locomotor ataxia was an umbrella term used to label a constellation of symptoms that were then a puzzlement to the medical community.

In more recent years, the symptoms typifying locomotor ataxia have been identified as the same as those attending the last stage of syphilis. They are linked to a weakening of the muscles of the lower body. Further complicating any postmortem diagnosis is the fact that Pope's son Ralph and Ralph's own son both suffered from Parkinson's disease, a malady that also weakens the muscles and reduces the worst-afflicted to a shuffling gait. The Colonel was a man who had traveled widely across the globe; his Civil War diary teems with romantic attachments; and he was believed to have been given to amorous extramarital liaisons from time to time. He may well have suffered from syphilis, since the disease was not uncommon at the time.

Pope's remains were taken to Boston for cremation and burial in the Forest Hills Cemetery in the Jamaica Plain neighborhood, the same cemetery that holds the remains of such prominent Bostonians as William Lloyd Garrison and Edward Everett Hale.

The Cohasset estate had become a haven for the family's five grown children and many grandchildren. Albert Pope Hinckley, the Colonel's grandson, recalls attending there the annual reunion of Pope's regiment, "for which he assumed the entire expense."[4] But Abby couldn't stand to return without the Colonel. She immediately placed the estate up for sale.

Mixed Record

The *Hartford Times*, in its tribute to the man who for years was that city's leading employer, wrote:

> The career of Colonel Pope was a career of ceaseless energy, a progressive demonstration of almost unerring foresight, keen judgment and an executive ability that built up and welded together into a compact, frictionless system, five great manufacturing plants whose product more than anything else will contribute to his fame long years after his death [Aug. 11, 1909].

Parsing the *Times* obituary is instructive. Pope undeniably brought to his career ceaseless energy and executive ability, although it was more suited to nineteenth- than twentieth-century industrial competition. He displayed far from "unerring foresight and keen judgment," and yet his career demonstrates abundantly how he melded his strengths and his failings into a coherent strategy that often prevailed against the odds.

During the 1880s, the Colonel had journeyed to Britain to inspect the safety bicycle which, by equalizing the size of its wheels, enabled others than the highly athletic to ride bicycles and thus widened the market exponentially for their sales. Upon his return, he told the press that America had nothing to learn from the British about building bicycles, but other manufacturers saw the future in the safeties immediately. While Pope had been asleep at the switch, once he realized his error, the formidable Colonel's manufacturing plant was able to gain on, reach, and surpass his competitors who had beaten him to the punch.

Pope must have realized in retrospect that his decision in 1899 to join forces with William C. Whitney, trading his patents, expertise, and production capacity for Whitney's access to money, was a mistake, as he watched the Electric Vehicle Company fold in 1907. Perhaps Pope saw his return to auto manufacturing in 1903 as a parallel to his decision to retool and gain on his safety bicycle competitors in the 1880s. Yet the world in which he was operating had changed beyond recognition, and this spelled the difference. And so, the *Times'* prophecy that Pope's fame would live on long after his death proved off the mark as well. As with many other pioneers, timing, circumstance, and a couple of crucial mistakes prevented Pope from becoming the household name that Henry Ford became.

Notes

1. Interviews with William Pope, Sr., on September 9, 1999, and with Tina Pope Rowley and Albert A. Pope II on May 8, 1999.

2. "A Seaside Home Beautiful with Flowers and Gardens," *Town and Country*, September 2, 1905, pp. 10–12.

3. Dean, Clarence, "Pope-Hartford Started Auspiciously in Auto Field," p. 1.

4. R.F.S., "The Great Bicycle Delirium," p. 102.

CHAPTER 13

LEAVING HIS MARK

Pope has good claims to be ranked close to Ford and [Frederick Winslow] Taylor as a pioneer in the development of mass production.[1]

The bicycle, which rose in somewhat the same way [as the automobile] had its fall because it could find no great place in the country's commercial life.[2]

W HAT ARE WE TO MAKE of the tumultuous life of Albert Augustus Pope, this roller coaster of unprecedented success and crushing failure? In terms of lasting impact on the lives of Americans, can his name be spoken in the same sentence as Thomas Edison or Henry Ford? The nature of societal progress is for each generation to stand on the shoulders of the one that preceded it. In this sense, the debt that the twentieth-century automobile industry owes to Colonel Pope is great. Historians list him in the first rank of contributors to modern industry based on his refinement of mass production and the use of interchangeable parts. Indeed, he was the first manufacturer to mass-produce automobiles.

Neither the American bicycle industry nor the automotive industry could have thrived without the creative championing—by Pope or someone like him—of a nationwide network of paved roads, a hitherto foreign concept. As an insightful judge of talent, Pope nurtured and developed a cadre of engineers and managers; they dispersed before and after Pope's death into many parts of the automobile industry. Many became leaders in the field. And, by fully grasping the American ethos of individuality, Pope helped change fundamentally the way people of his era dressed, moved from place to place, and looked at the world.

In his declining years, Pope spent more and more time in the restful atmosphere of his seaside estate, a straw hat his only concession to office dress. *(Courtesy William Pope.)*

Numbers Game

The words *Henry Ford* and *mass production* in 1999 turned up 908 matches on an Internet search engine. The words *Albert Pope* and *mass production* produced none. And yet industrial historians widely credit Colonel Pope with laying a foundation for mass automobile assembly and production that not only preceded Henry Ford but which some say led Ford to Hartford to study it. "The key to mass production wasn't—as many people then and now believe—the moving or continuous assembly line," writes one. "Rather it was the complete and consistent interchangeability of parts and the simplicity of attaching them to each other."[3] While Ford's assembly line would revolutionize the use of factory labor in ways that made headlines, the methods Pope evolved to ensure quality control through an unparalleled degree of testing would stamp an indelible mark on the development of the auto industry.

Pope had become sold on interchangeable parts as early as his 1878 trip to England to scout around for bicycles to import to America. But parts, to be interchangeable, must be machined to fine tolerances, so Pope invested heavily in a geographical area that was one of America's leading machine tool centers, having become so because of precision gun manufacturing. By the turn of the century, the bevel gears on his chainless bicycles were machined to 1/2000 inch, compared to the 1/64 inch that Henry Ford was able to attain for automobile parts as late as 1903. Each Pope bicycle was inspected more than 500 times by twenty-four separate inspectors.[4]

Specialization actually dated back to the writings of Adam Smith in the eighteenth century, and Frederick Winslow Taylor—the father of efficiency experts—had espoused division of labor in Pope's era, but it was Pope who put the theory to the test. Norcliffe writes that by 1894, each Columbia bicycle required 840 parts (more than 1,000 for the woman's bicycle). Among the specialized functions found at a Pope plant were forge buildings, test rooms, tool and assembly rooms, and areas for brazing, inspecting, buffing, polishing, nickel plating, and case hardening. Tubing and rubber works occupied entirely separate buildings.

Streamlining industrial production, however, made Pope as many enemies as friends; advocates for an increasingly vocal labor force contended that these efficiencies spelled layoffs for employees. Pope countered:

> Experience shows that the greater the number of inventions, the higher is the rate of wages and the larger the number of men employed. In the old countries of Europe, where there is little or no machinery, and where most of the work is done by hand, the condition of the working man is far worse than in the countries where there is modern machinery.[5]

Pope's argument tended to hold during the good times in which it was uttered. But by 1899, bicycle revenues had spiraled into free fall, and the Colonel had slashed prices; as they decreased by half, Colonel Pope reluctantly laid off employees.[6]

Ford, during his reported visits to Hartford, fed off Pope's experience in the same way Pope had learned from the Weed operation. It, in turn, had refined its techniques from Samuel Colt, who manufactured rifles in Hartford before the Civil War, and before him, Eli Whitney, who pioneered interchangeable parts in his cotton gin. This historical continuity gave rise to the term armory practice. Typical of the techniques that underwent refinement was drop forging, wherein a metal piece is cast and then milled; afterward, ever-smaller bits of excess metal are machined off the forging.[7]

Early on, Pope faced a choice: buy tubing, tires, and other components necessary for a finished bicycle from subcontractors or make them in-house. His decision to produce components in his own, specialized departments rather than buying them from subcontractors is known today as vertical integration, and Pope created, in the words of Norcliffe, "a fabrication and assembly facility that served as a prototype for the Fordist plant," referring to the Ford-set standards that would revolutionize the industry.[8]

Hollow tubing—so crucial to lightening bicycles—had been imported from Britain until 1892, when Pope added a seamless tubing factory, with a capacity of a million feet of tubing per year, to his Capitol Avenue bicycle plant. Hartford manufacturer John Gray had started importing rubber from Sumatra and making solid rubber tires in 1885; soon Pope bought out his Hartford Rubber Works, which gave the Pope enterprises in-house capacity to manufacture first solid, then cushion, and finally pneumatic tires.

Organizationally, Pope created holding companies as early as 1889, which gave him flexibility in managing his far-flung empire, while protecting his assets against risk as he started new ventures. Accordingly, Pope's main corporate and personal assets wouldn't be at risk should a new business fail.

Although used earlier in the decade by such burgeoning enterprises as John D. Rockefeller's Standard Oil Company, the need for holding companies signified a size and scope hitherto little known, at least before the advent of the railroad industry.

While Pope was an expert in standardization and interchangeability of parts, he may have missed a way to maximize their advantage. In a 1909 article that could have served as a sidebar to Pope's obituary the same year, *Scientific American* wrote that the success of such standardization lay in producing great numbers of one model and eliminating annual design changes "that necessitate the making of costly jigs, gauges and special machinery." Such an analysis would have been an anathema to Alfred P. Sloan and a later generation of General Motors designers, who built an industry on annual model changes that would mark one's personal chariot as the latest thing. But this was 1909, and the paradigm of a car in every garage had not yet taken hold. The magazine credited Henry Ford with becoming aware of the principle first, ahead of his competitors. "By the time they had come to understand it sufficiently, he was so far ahead in design and production engineering that most lacked the capital and talent to catch up."[9]

Business historians have viewed the turn of the twentieth century as far more than lifting the page of a calendar. Nineteenth-century industrialists, nurtured in the teachings of Adam Smith and his notion of an invisible hand that guides their actions, held a much more deterministic view of industrial progress than those of the scientific management era that succeeded them. They viewed the market "with Malthusian fatalism, seeing the market as a never ending cycle of mindless, grinding industrial competition that inevitably drove all firms—good, bad and indifferent—to destruction."[10] Monopolizing markets might hold back the floodgates, but the forces of nature would not be denied. Pope stands squarely within this tradition, so when he tried to play by twentieth-century rules, in which innovation, flexibility, and scientific management were paramount, it is not surprising that he soon found himself adrift.[11]

In John Rae's view, Colonel Pope died, "worn out by the struggle to preserve what was left of the great enterprise that he had founded. If he made mistakes, they were honest ones, and they do not begin to offset his achievements: first to manufacture motor vehicles in quantity, pioneer in making technical research a part of industry, and organizer of the Good Roads Movement."[12]

Automotive Diaspora

Perhaps chief among Pope's positive attributes was his eye for selecting the best and the brightest and giving them their head. Chief among them, of course, is George H. Day. Pope found him just after the 30-year-old had cut his eyeteeth on standardizing parts throughout Weed's sewing machine plant. Day understood the role of cutting-edge research and, though a college dropout himself, was instrumental in recruiting a cadre of college-trained engineers, a process in which, says Bruce Epperson, Colonel Pope was "a detached but appreciative observer."[13] Day had the good grace to recede to vice president in 1890, when Albert Pope decided he wanted to become chief executive of the Pope Manufacturing Company. And Day assumed the helm of the ill-fated Electric Vehicle Company in 1900, after Pope had lost the will to lead. Following Pope's death, Day went on to head the American League of Automobile Manufacturers. Accordingly, the legacy of Albert Augustus Pope to American industrial life is inextricably tied up with that of George Day.

Pope had the insight to name Hiram Percy Maxim, at age twenty-six, to head the new automotive division of the Pope Manufacturing Company in 1895, in spite of the lad's passionate commitment to the gasoline engine, which the Colonel felt was simply wrongheaded. The epilogue concluding this book will detail the contributions of other members of the Pope enterprise who survived him. Suffice it to say here that Pope gave their start to men such as Harold Hayden Eames and Herbert Rice, both of whom would later head major automobile manufacturers; Henry Souther, who would head the trade organization which standardized automobile production in America; and Milton Budlong and George Pope, both of whom would become presidents of influential industry organizations.

Indispensable Roads

No one individual can be given more credit in paving the way for a network of good roads, both locally and nationally, than Albert A. Pope. He, almost alone among automakers, had the vision and the resources to mount this crusade for more than a quarter century, although the cause did not bear fruit until after he was gone. It took seven years beyond his death for the federal government to legislate its first roads and not until 1921 did Congress decide to link up every county in America with paved roads.

Pope, the visionary, held a long view and understood that Rome wasn't built in a day. For hundreds of years, farmers had taken as a given that the spring freshets would put their roads out of commission for a few weeks each year and after heavy rains throughout the year. Such was the will of God. To tamper with nature by building roads with artificial surfaces was almost as foreign to them as the notion that they'd have to pay new taxes to construct them.

What Pope realized before nearly anyone else was that no lesson succeeds like an object lesson. By paving a strip of dirt along Columbus Avenue in Boston in the 1880s, he let people experience the feeling of riding on a road smooth as a tabletop. Once they had done so, Pope knew he'd be preaching to the choir. In a few years, his efforts turned nationwide, and he enlisted railroad executives to help him export object-lesson roads to the hinterlands. In the days before a strong federal government, legislative action to build roads focused on state capitals, so it was no surprise that by the early 1900s, most states were improving roads long before the federal government got into the act.

At the time of his death, Colonel Pope had been leading the Good Roads crusade for a full generation. However, so great was the progress, largely by states in creating highway departments and introducing paving techniques, that it must have been apparent to Colonel Pope on his deathbed that he had unleashed an irreversible force. In the history of American transportation, few challenge the view that the legitimate father of the Good Roads Movement is Albert A. Pope.[14]

Transitional Bicycle

The bicycle was a transitional vehicle, both industrially and socially. Had the bicycle never existed, the automobile industry would have taken much longer to get up to speed. Think of the components needed in auto manufacture that had been born in bicycle factories: pneumatic tires, hollow metal rims, variable speed gears, axle differentials, brakes, wheel bearings, spring suspension, steering mechanisms, refined ball bearings, and shaft drives. Consider such production innovations as electric welding, cold drawn steel, case hardening, and annealing. "Techniques that would become standard in metalworking industries were first developed in bicycle manufacture," says bicycle historian David Hounshell, and "these changes led almost inexorably to the introduction and soon the mass production and mass consumption of the American 'mother cow'—the automobile."[15]

Not only did the bicycle pave the way for auto production but it served as, what Glen Norcliffe calls, a "carrier wave" between industries of the nineteenth and twentieth centuries. It was not only an industry that spawned related innovations, such as the motorization of the bicycle but, moreover, it sparked the public imagination in such a way as to affect the way people dressed, acted, and looked at life.[16]

So, Pope's contribution to the times in which he lived were as much social as industrial. Remember that during the last quarter of the nineteenth century, when Pope did the bulk of his bicycle manufacturing, Americans had become dependent on the railroad for long-distance transportation. Yet monopoly control of many lines had often led railway leaders to become high-handed and their personnel surly. And, of course, a passenger was restricted by fixed track and schedules. Coming at the time it did, the bicycle suggested that one could go when and where one pleased, rather than being at the whim of an institutional force.

"In a social and economical as well as a technological sense," says Hounshell, "the bicycle was transitional because it brought Americans into contact with a personal mode of transportation."[17] Not only did the bicycle give a new command over time and space, but it let its rider control the throttle as well, introducing the concept of individualized speed and the aura of control over one's range of movement.

As the century wore on, the number of riders rose geometrically. By 1916, the competition had driven the price of a bicycle, $125 a generation earlier, down to a small fraction of that amount. Montgomery Ward's catalog advertised a price range of $13.65 to $28.80.[18]

For the Common Weal

While he was not the first to do so, Albert Pope's use of his fortune for the benefit of humanity was nonetheless impressive. He had long felt strongly that philanthropy was instinctual, not learned. Once while being interviewed, a reporter called to Pope's attention his belief that Andrew Carnegie had hoarded his wealth until age fifty before undergoing a massive change of heart, which led Carnegie to try to give most of his money away before he died. "I don't believe it," scoffed Colonel Pope vigorously.

> I don't believe he ever said it. ... If it is not there when he is young, it is not there when he is old. ... Why I can recall that when I was a little fellow a boy shared oranges with me. Years after he wrote me, asking a $5 bill to help a struggling church in which he was interested. I sent him fifty—not because it was for a church, but because I remembered the boy and his oranges. To do good—to do the most good, a man must begin when he is young.[19]

In spite of his vigorous propounding of his position, Pope couldn't come up with concrete examples of good works done in his youth. To better understand this apparent contradiction, bear in mind the far-reaching effect of Andrew Carnegie's 1889 Gospel of Wealth speech, in which he exhorted his fellow industrialists to give away their fortunes to good causes. Pope might have been simply copying Carnegie's appeal. Yet, if philanthropy were something in the genes, Pope knew he wouldn't have to share credit with Carnegie or anyone else for his good works.

To Pope, a helping hand was not merely the duty of the well-to-do but of everyone, no matter how modest their circumstances. "No man is so poor that he cannot do something," the Colonel told a reporter. "If he cannot do good in a large way, he can do it in a small way—he can make some one happy—can add to some one's well being. I believe it is born in a man."[20]

Huge income disparities in the Gilded Age often cloaked good deeds with noblesse oblige. Pope recounted to a news reporter one such incident:

> Why, only the other day, I saw two street urchins looking up at me while I was in my automobile. I got down and took the youngsters into a drug store and gave each a glass of soda. They didn't know enough to thank me but their eyes showed their gratitude. It was a little thing but they'll never forget it.[21]

Regardless of his patriarchal attitude, Pope took a backseat to no one in his charitable contributions, which were many and varied. His gift of seventy-four acres and $100,000 for a public park in Hartford has already been described, along with other amenities he created for his workers. In Boston, he gave the Pope Dispensary at New England Hospital to the city of Boston as a token of gratitude for the saving of his sister from death's door. The record is silent on which sister or from what she had suffered.

Perhaps Albert Pope's most poignant contribution was the Pope Memorial Church at Cohasset, a graceful stone structure near the ocean, given as a tribute to his son Charles, who died as a teenager in a sailing accident. The design of the monument reveals Pope's religious philosophy. Engraved in stone on its walls are the words "Love to God and love to man." The church was declared open to any person or group with a religious belief, irrespective of what it might be.[22]

While Pope served on the boards of the American Loan and Trust Company, Winthrop Bank, and a dozen other corporations, he also donated his time as a visitor at Wellesley College and Lawrence Scientific School at Harvard. He had a brief, two-year career as a member of the Newton, Massachusetts, city council and was a member of the Algonquin, Art, Country, Athletic, New York Athletic, and other clubs; he was a vice president of the Beacon Society.

Man of Many Words

Over the fireplace in J. P. Morgan's lavishly appointed Manhattan study hung a framed motto in Provençal: *Pense moult, parle peu, ecris rien*, which means "Think a lot, say little, write nothing." Pope, a contemporary of Morgan's, is commonly lumped in with the Gilded Age capitalists personified by Morgan. However, Morgan's watchwords for life bear almost no resemblance to the manner in which Colonel Pope conducted his life.

Ironically, while both Morgan and Pope have strong Hartford connections, they never lived in the city at the same time. Morgan was born in the heart of downtown, a stone's throw from the earliest settlement in the city two centuries earlier. His father, Junius S. Morgan, started the Morgan family in banking but lived most of his life in London. His grandfather founded the Aetna Fire Insurance Company, a derivative of which still exists in Hartford today. Pope didn't move to the city until Morgan had left to pursue his financial career in New York City. Four years after Pope's death in 1909, Morgan returned to the city of his birth one last time, to be buried in the city's picturesque and rolling Cedar Hill Cemetery.[23]

Morgan, notoriously inarticulate, was no doubt uncomfortable trying to express himself in words, yet he had an uncanny ability to express himself in actions in such a way that let him lead the finance and railroad industries. And to leverage his deals, which saved the railroad industry from internal collapse time and again, he certainly must have done a lot of thinking.

A motto for Pope's life, whether he would have accepted its mantle or not, might have been, "Think not enough, say much, and write more." For a lad who dropped out of high school at age fifteen and never again returned to the classroom, his speaking and writings were voluminous, usually articulate, and occasionally eloquent, a clear tribute to self-teaching. He never published a book but self-published many pamphlets and broadsides and was eagerly sought after for dozens of guest articles in magazines, most on the benefits of the Good Roads Movement. He introduced the concept of the use of the roads as a basic American right, a concept that resonates profoundly to the present day.

From his days as a clerk, prior to entering the Civil War, Pope was a prodigious reader. During the war, while his fellow soldiers longed for cigars and warm clothing from home, Pope's often-expressed hope was for more books—tomes on history, literature, and, perhaps most important, rhetoric. On this subject, he loved to engage in bull sessions, sometimes with those far more educated than he, to better frame and sharpen his arguments, looking toward some undefined future in which he sensed he would need to communicate and to persuade fellow human beings. Perhaps the wish was father of the thought. During his Civil War days, Pope went so far as to deliver religious sermons to his men and felt justifiably proud when he had communicated his message effectively.

In a day before television and motion pictures, oratory served to entertain as well as to enlighten, and Pope was a frequent after-dinner speaker, whether his subject was bicycles, the Good Roads Movement, or automobiles. Tall, with a commanding presence, the Colonel held his audiences easily. Particularly during his extended sabbatical from the automobile business from 1900 to 1903, he was on the stump continuously, preaching his gospel of good roads, which seems to have been as effective as his printed articles in helping change public opinion.

Pope seems, however, to have been more inclined toward action than thought. Had he been otherwise, he might have avoided the near-calamity of dismissing the potential of the safety bicycle and the actual disaster of being led down the primrose path by the silver-tongued patrician William Collins Whitney. Certainly his final venture, from 1903 through 1907, to try to recapture the glory of the Pope name against staggering odds, was led far more by Pope's heart than by his head.

Remembering the War

Albert Pope's fondness for his Civil War honorific, "Colonel," reflected not only hardheaded image building but a fondness and nostalgia for the three years of his life which had served as a kind of field college for the high school dropout. Each summer, as his grandson Albert Pope Hinckley recalls, he hosted a lavish reunion at his Cohasset estate for all the members of his regiment who he had commanded and served with during the conflict.[24]

At Antietam, the war veteran constructed a monument to his comrades in the 35th Massachusetts Regiment who lost their lives in Pope's first and bloodiest Civil War battle. The monument stands at the entrance to the Burnside Bridge, which served the fateful funnel of men into rebel gunsights, and is constructed of highly polished granite surmounted by three cannon balls.[25]

To Those Nearest and Dearest

Pope's material legacy to his family, friends, and charities is as revealing of the man as anything he accomplished or expressed during his lifetime. As one would expect, Pope left his household effects to Abby along with a trust fund for her and the children, described below. His most frequent gift was in the form of stock in the Pope Manufacturing Company, with which he remembered grandnieces and grandnephews. Rewarding sustained loyalty, he left stock as well to his gardener at Cohasset, his secretary and public relations chief, Robert Winkley, and the Reverend William Meserve, his long-time friend and treasured comrade during the Civil War.

Charitable bequests under the Colonel's will weighed heavily in favor of organizations devoted to underprivileged children, a concern of his during life as well. Pope left ten shares of company stock to each of fourteen institutions, including the Boston YMCA, the Boston Young Men's Christian Union, the New England Home for Little Wanderers, Associated Charities of Boston, the Howard Benevolent Society of Boston, Parker's Boston Helping Hand Mission, the Massachusetts Society for Prevention of Cruelty to Children, the Boston Institute Seashore Home, and the Fresh Air Fund. Pope also remembered the Boston Floating Hospital and the Library Fund of the Massachusetts Commandery of the Military Order Loyal Lions of the United States. Although he lacked formal education, the Colonel also gifted two educational institutions: Lincoln Memorial University of Cumberland, Tennessee, and Berea College in Kentucky, which is notable for charging no tuition to worthy students.

Pope left the bulk of his estate in trust to his sons Albert Linder and Harold, who also were named as trustees along with Abby, Robert L. Winkley, cousin D. W. Pope, and Hartford attorney Charles E. Gross. According to the terms of his trust, Abby would receive $12,000 a year, equivalent to more than $100,000 a year in millennial dollars. Although his youngest child, Ralph L. Pope, was then twenty-two, his father directed a guardian to manage his annual payments of $2,000, to be used for his support and education. Pope's sisters Augusta, Emily, and Adelaide would receive $2,500 a year, the survivors sharing each sister's share upon her death. Each of his children would be entitled to $3,000 a year, $4,000 after age twenty-one. Pope's grandchildren would receive $1,000 a year until age twenty-one and $2,000 thereafter.

Hartford as Motown?

It is fitting to consider, in a chapter devoted to the marks that Albert Augustus Pope wrote on his time, a legacy that he *nearly* left. For Hartford in 1899 was considered to be the automobile capital of the world, turning out at the time more than half of all motorized vehicles manufactured in the United States. Historians have attributed the fact that Hartford lost its edge to several factors:

• Pope's choice of an electric standard over gasoline power, not irrational at the time he made it, floundered in the face of newly abundant gasoline and intractable problems with the electric storage battery. Additionally, electric companies had little incentive to set up inexpensive charging facilities because, since they owned most of the electric trolleys that potential car purchasers were riding, subsidizing a rider's move from electric trolley to electric automobile seemed a zero-sum game.[26]

• His decision to make a relatively few cars for rich customers rather than many cars for the masses.

• His opting to manufacture an array of models rather than making one in volume, thereby cutting unit costs.

• The failure of electric power companies to foster a network of charging facilities, as oil companies did with gas stations, thus allowing electric autos to be useful for long-distance travel.

• Raw materials needed for auto manufacture, particularly steel, were more cheaply procured and shipped in the Midwest than the East.

• Pope's choice to ally with an opportunistic financial wheeler dealer, which diverted his attention from producing quality products to chasing manipulative, get-rich-quick schemes.

• The New England capital markets were awash with quality, relatively low-risk projects in which to invest during a period of unparalleled industrial expansion, while investors in the less well developed Midwest had fewer proposals from which to choose.[27]

An old adage holds that one can learn more from failure than success. While Albert Augustus Pope's life brought personal and professional success in countless ways, his failures have been studied in business schools for generations. Perhaps, then, the Colonel's shortcomings as well as his triumphs are the legacy to those who, coming after him, seek to avoid life's pitfalls.

Notes

1. Norcliffe, Glen, "Popeism and Fordism: Examining the Roots of Mass Production," p. 268.

2. Oppel, Frank, *Motoring in America*, p. 95.

3. Womack, J.P. et al., *The Machine that Changed the World: The Story of Lean Production*, p. 274.

4. Norcliffe, pp. 274–75.

5. Norcliffe, "Bridging the American System and Mass Production," p. 3.

6. Norcliffe, "Popeism and Fordism," p. 271.

7. Grant, Ellsworth, *The Colt Armory: A History of Colt's Manufacturing Company, Inc.*, p. 75; Hounshell, David A., *From the America System to Mass Production 1800–1932*, p. 194.

8. Norcliffe, "Bridging," p. 4.

9. Flink, James J., *The Automobile Age*, p. 71.

10. Epperson, Bruce, "A Model of Technological Dissonance: Production and Management in the American Bicycle Industry, 1880–1910," p. 23.

11. Ibid., p. 24.

12. Rae, John, *The American Automobile Industry: The First Forty Years*, p. 63.

13. Epperson, p. 3.

14. Goddard, Stephen B., *Getting There: The Epic Struggle Between Road and Rail in the American Century*, p. 44.

15. Hounshell, "The Bicycle and Technology in Late Nineteenth-Century America," p. 44; Colvin, Fred H., "Influence of the Bicycle," pp. 84–85.

16. Norcliffe, "Bridging," p. 2.
17. Hounshell, p. 175.
18. Brown, Carrie, *Pedal Power: The Bicycle in Industry and Society,* p. 17.
19. *Brooklyn* (N.Y.) *Citizen,* August 6, 1899, p. 1.
20. Ibid.
21. Ibid.
22. *Who's Who in New England,* p. 637.
23. Courtney, Steve, "Oh, Wealth," p. 6.
24. R.F.S., "The Great Bicycle Delirium," p. 102.
25. *Officers of the Army and Navy,* July 2, 1894.
26. Schiffer, Michael Brian, *Taking Charge,* p. 74.
27. Ibid., p. 166.

EPILOGUE

*The automobile industry in New England was thus like the
seed that was sown on stony ground. ... It grew rapidly
at first but lacked staying power.*

John Rae

TO SAY THAT AN ERA ENDED with the 1909 death of Albert Augustus Pope
would be inaccurate, for other nineteenth-century titans of industry
lived on. J. P. Morgan, six years older than the Colonel, nevertheless survived
him by four years. John D. Rockefeller, Pope's junior, imposed on himself a
strict regimen of exercise and diet designed to let him live to one hundred
and missed the mark only by two years when he succumbed in 1937.[1] Andrew
Carnegie, prematurely retired from business, oversaw his benefactions until
his death in 1919. Henry Ford was a generation younger than Pope and,
therefore, was one of the twentieth century's first industrialists.

Yet Pope's death did mark, perhaps, the beginning of the end of an era
of corporate moguls who ruled by genius or force of personality, heraldic
figures who seemed to bend history to their wills. The world was about to
grow more complex. Within a decade, the United States would become a
major player on the world economic as well as geopolitical stage, thanks to
its real, if limited, role in helping the Allies win the First World War. Technology and accelerating market competition would force manufacturing to
run efficiently, and a cadre of college-educated businesspeople would emerge,
preaching the gospel of scientific management. It was a language largely foreign to Colonel Pope, one that left him bewildered and perhaps frustrated
as well. In an industrial sense, then, perhaps his death was timely.

Pope was not a man easily forgotten, however. As one writer put it, he
"cut a great swath." When seized by the impulse to introduce some Boston
businessmen to his manufacturing operations, it was de rigeur for the Colonel
to buy up all the seats in several parlor cars, whose luxurious appointments
put airline first-class seats to shame. Clambering aboard, ahead of the guests,

would be white-coated caterers, there to prepare and dispense the finest in food and libation. The Colonel would pass through the cars, his arms outstretched while he told jokes and anecdotes that would have his guests slapping their thighs. Yet if Albert Pope could give as well as get in the cutthroat competition of the age, he was also a man who remembered the gardener in his will, who built a church out of grief for the memory of his son, who erected a memorial at Antietam to his fallen Civil War comrades, and who performed, with some regularity, favors great and small for his workers.[2]

In spite of the popularity of the automobile as a fad in the first decade of the new century, critics ridiculed the first roads paved to accommodate them as "peacock alleys for the rich." Automobiling, at the Colonel's death, was still more of a sport than a means of conveyance. Henry Ford's Model T, introduced in 1908, heralded changing times. The financial markets, which had figuratively held their sides laughing at the notion of financing motor vehicles, were now rethinking their skepticism. By 1916, the year William Durant's General Motors declared its first stock dividend—the largest until then in the history of the New York Stock Exchange—"an early skepticism had turned to voguish enthusiasm."[3]

Indeed, it was the money men who would drive the growth of the automobile industry in the years ahead. Henry Ford, who had favored government ownership of roads, thought auto company shareholders should be limited to company employees. But even this giant of auto production changed his mind and agreed to allow the public to invest in car manufacturing when he realized how much money would be needed to dominate his industry. In fact, given the escalating public interest during the 1910s, he had little choice: either let the capital markets in or be dwarfed by competitors.[4]

Disconsolate Henry Ford

Pope died only six weeks prior to a court decision in the Selden patent case. When the news came in September 1909, after six years of trial testimony and thousands upon thousands of pages of transcript, the court ruled for Selden and against Ford. "Goliath Slays David," the newspapers might have screamed. No one had dreamed that Ford would have the staying power to endure such an expensive, enervating round of litigation, going up against the collective power of dozens of auto manufacturers and Wall Street money besides. He was deeply in debt to lawyers and creditors and drained physically, emotionally, and financially. "Ford was disconsolate," one biographer recalls, and he gave serious thought to selling out to the industry's rising star, William Crapo Durant.

A cartoonist's dream, the roly-poly, cigar-smoking Durant had been a smoke shop clerk and a salesman of city water, and he had made enough money making carriages to retire at age forty. Just as J. P. Morgan wasn't a railroad man but owned several as sidelines, so too William Durant wasn't an auto manufacturer in the sense of Albert Pope or Henry Ford; he was a deal maker and a builder of businesses. It was natural for such a speculator in the second decade of the century to be intrigued by the motor industry, and Durant settled on a company started by a Polish mechanic named David Buick. He next would have gobbled up Henry Ford, had his financial backers not nixed the deal, feeling Durant was already in too much debt.[5]

What, then, was Henry Ford to do? If he folded his cards, he'd have to endure the galling experience of sending checks to the Selden combine each time he sold a Model T. No, he had only one choice he could stomach and that was to fight on, however overextended he might be. So Ford moved to appeal the court's decision, brought in a brain trust with more borrowed money, and spent two years of further litigation in the federal court of appeals. And one day in 1911, the "Extra, Extra, Read All about It" hawkers told how Ford had busted both the Selden patent and the ALAM.[6] The circuit court of appeals had held that the gasoline automobile's basic technology was a "social invention," meaning its creator must make it available to all producers.[7] Further, it held that Ford's four-cycle engine was essentially different from Selden's two-cycle one.[8]

In reality, the victory was mainly symbolic, for the Selden patent, issued in 1895, expired on November 5, 1912, scarcely a year later. After that, it was open season. But Henry Ford had gained more public relations benefit from his David against Goliath fight in the years leading up to the final decision than he would from the patent protection in its last year.

"Moral Victory Is Mine"

George Selden would live on to 1917. In his dotage, despite his monumental court defeat, he would insist, "Nevertheless, the moral victory is mine."[9] In spite of the resonance of the name Selden in automotive history, only one vehicle bearing the Selden name was ever made, the prototype that the court insisted be constructed to show that the Selden patent would prove out. Built by Henry Cave, one of Pope's engineers, it was shipped years later to the Henry Ford Museum in Dearborn, Michigan, where it resides today. A model is displayed in Hartford at the site of the Capitol Avenue plant.

Albert Linder Pope, while undoubtedly chagrined at having to turn out the lights at the Pope factory in 1914, knew he had plenty of company in the industry. In the final liquidation of the Pope enterprises, the local firm of Pratt & Whitney bought the Capitol Avenue factory to exploit the growing

Lawyer and inventor George Selden, at the wheel of the vehicle constructed during his trial against Henry Ford, to demonstrate that his 1877 concept for a gasoline-powered automobile actually worked. His co-rider is unidentified. *(Courtesy National Automotive History Collection, Detroit Public Library.)*

market for yet another travel mode, aircraft. Westfield Manufacturing Company paid a half-million dollars for the Westfield plant. The proceeds allowed Prince Albert to hold his head reasonably high. In spite of the devastating industry shake-out, he had proved able to pay off creditors ninety-two cents on the dollar.

By 1915, the Stevens-Duryea Company had thrown in the towel. So stressful had competition become that Frank Duryea suffered what his generation called a "nervous breakdown" and was forced to abandon an active role in his company the year Pope died. The Stanley Steamer Company managed to stay afloat, but when F. E. Stanley died in 1918, ironically in an automobile accident, his brother lost interest in making automobiles. Likewise, the death of Locomobile's Samuel T. Davis in 1915 hastened its demise.

Electric vehicles might well have attracted a great following had it not

Albert Linder Pope, rumored to be a playboy who cared more about yachting than manufacturing, supports that theory as he parties aboard the yacht *Columbia* around the time of World War I. In fact, however, "Prince Albert" made important contributions to the family's enterprise. *(Courtesy John Lee and Percy Maxim Lee.)*

been for the phenomenal growth of the gasoline auto industry. Michael Brian Schiffer, in his book *Taking Charge*, makes the argument that gender as much as any other factor doomed the electric car, which was vastly more popular with women than the noisy, greasy (Schiffer would say more masculine) gasoline auto. Yet at the turn of the century, men earned the paychecks in most families and, as a result, had a greater say in choosing the family chariot.[10]

While steam-powered vehicles have been relegated to museums, environmental pollution proved a deus ex machina in the 1980s and 1990s; electric cars may enjoy a second wind. With state governments such as California mandating pollution reductions, the Big Three automakers, along with foreign manufacturers, have taken a second look at electric vehicles. Amazingly, the three primary storage battery systems in use—lead-acid, nickel-iron, and nickel-cadmium—all were in use before 1910, in spite of the across-the-board advances technology has wrought on American life. For passenger use, cars incorporating electric motors coupled to back-up gasoline- or ethanol-powered engines may offer the greatest promise, and both Toyota and Honda have brought such hybrids to market. General Motors, Daimler-Chrysler, Ford, and Nissan are marketing electric vehicles and a half dozen new manufacturers are offering vans and motorcycles powered by electricity, sometimes combined with solar power.[11] Writes John Rae:

> The automobile industry in New England was thus like the seed that was sown on stony ground. ... it grew rapidly at first but lacked staying power. It certainly did not attract anything like the quality of leadership that congregated

about Detroit. Maxim, Knox, J. F. Duryea and the Stanley brothers were all primarily technical men, not vitally concerned with the business end of auto manufacturing. The only New England producers who can be compared with the Detroiters were Albert A. Pope and Samuel T. Davis.[12]

Columbia bicycles have lived on, in a fashion, as of the writing of this book. In 1913, all Pope bicycle operations were consolidated at the Westfield, Massachusetts, plant, which had been sold to the Westfield Manufacturing Company. During this time, Columbia motorcycles were produced in this plant. The Colonel would have been pleased to know that, in 1923, the company changed its name to the Columbia Manufacturing Company, which it maintained for the rest of the century. During a bicycle boom in the early 1970s, sales reached 15 million worldwide. Yet as the 1990s began, sales began to plummet, an eerie parallel to Pope's fortunes exactly a hundred years earlier, and in 1991, the company filed for bankruptcy protection although it continues to exist. Its only line of bicycles, however, is a classic 1941 Columbia model, sold to bicycle enthusiasts.[13]

Talent Pool Unleashed

One of Albert Pope's most remarkable gifts to American industry was the diaspora of automotive talent that he contributed to the world. A few, such as George Day and cousin George Pope, were the Colonel's contemporaries; most, however, would live the bulk of their lives in the twentieth century and would shape the automotive world for decades beyond his death.

George Day, of course, had been present at the creation; he was on hand when Pope first walked his ungainly high-wheeler through the front doors of the Weed Sewing Machine Company amid the stares of plant workers. By the turn of the century, after helping Pope build Hartford into a forerunner of Silicon Valley through his contributions to bicycle manufacturing, Day was engaged in the third major industry of his career. Pope and he had been together for a full generation when the Colonel split from the Electric Vehicle Company, of which Day had become president, to pursue other interests. George Day would go on to head ALAM during the first part of its litigation over the Selden patent, only to die prematurely in 1907 at age fifty-six. Upon his death, his chief adversary, Henry Ford, called Day "a gentleman of whom personally I have the greatest respect."[14]

It is difficult to study the life of the Pope manufacturing enterprises without gaining a profound respect for both the competence and decency of George Day. In spite of the cutthroat competition in which he had to engage, Day was genuinely sensitive to the feelings of others, including supplicants who arrived at his door to sell him new products. "If Mr. Day did not buy their inventions," one writer notes, "he always dismissed them so courteously that they were invariably glad they had called on him, and were sure that they had at last met a man of sympathy and a gentleman."[15]

Pope's cousin George Pope and his wife, Annie Atwood Rich, had one child. George, who died in 1918, lived to see his daughter marry Charles Howard Gillette, who devised the "blue book," the industry's bible for rating automobile prices in the marketplace.[16] George himself would serve five terms as president of the National Association of Manufacturers and also served as treasurer of the National Automobile Chamber of Commerce.

After the Electric Vehicle Company folded, Harold Hayden Eames, who had managed Pope's important bicycle tube division, left Hartford and became general manager of Studebaker.[17] Henry Souther, who served ALAM as a consulting engineer and who worked with bicycles and automobiles for Pope for many years, became head of the Standards Committee of the Society of Automotive Engineers. While this seems at first glance to be a prosaic contribution, it was a hugely important one. "The lack of intercompany standardization was responsible for nine-tenths of the production troubles and most of the needless expense entailed in the manufacturing of motorcars," according to auto historian James Flink.[18] Souther would later head the Standard Roller Bearing Manufacturing Company.

Milton Budlong, who had worked in George Day's shadow for many years, came into his own, following the demise of the Electric Vehicle Company, by becoming president of the National Association of Automobile Manufacturers. Herbert Rice assumed the helm at Cadillac, and Herbert Alden, Hiram Maxim's long-time assistant, developed a successful consulting engineering practice. D. J. Post, company officer and the Colonel's "traveling man," became a vice president at Veeder Manufacturing Company of Hartford, manufacturer of meters; and company secretary Arthur Pattison joined Edward C. Burt and Company, a New York footwear manufacturer, as a vice president. Hermann Cuntz, who first recognized the significance of the Selden patent, lived into mid-century and wrote about the early days of motoring in retrospective newspaper articles. Henry Cave, who built the only Selden motorcar in 1906, lived a long life as well, cataloging industry developments over the years as an amateur historian.

Maxim's Fertile Future

Perhaps most interesting was the career of Hiram Percy Maxim, the wunderkind who graduated MIT at age seventeen and came to Pope in his midtwenties with already nearly a decade of engineering experience under his belt. Maxim's later career demonstrates that he was, first and foremost, an inventor. After leaving the Pope enterprises and the Electric Vehicle Company to build his own electric-powered vehicles, he experimented with gliders in 1909 before incorporating the Maxim Silencer Company, which manufactured one of the most misunderstood inventions of the twentieth century.

The silencer grew out of Hiram's efforts to improve the gasoline automobile, which in the early years of the century made a fearful racket. In his autobiography, *Horseless Carriage Days,* Maxim gave an insight into the inventive mind:

> One morning after my bath, I noticed in the bath tub the miniature whirl pool that forms over the drain hole when the plug is pulled and the water starts to run out. There was the familiar little hole down in the center of the whirl and it started me thinking that here was an exactly similar case to my powder gas and bullet problem. Here was water in a bath tub, the drain plug being pulled out, and yet the water was able to run out, but slowly because it was whirling. Why should not the powder gases act the same way as the water if they were whirled? ... Immediately I made a little "whirling tube" which would catch the powder gases as they burst from the muzzle of one of my rifles and whirl it around vigorously. In the center I provided a hole for the bullet to pass through but considerably larger than the bullet so it would not touch. The gases had no escape except through this central hole. Being central they could not possibly get out until they had slowed down. This of course meant that they must come out gradually and in consequence, noiselessly. ... This was the birth of the Maxim Silencer.[19]

The public and the press mistakenly assumed that the silencer would be a tool for evil and that criminals would attach it to their pistols. In actuality, it could be used only on a sealed breech rifle, and it never found wide demand. It proved to be fodder for demagogues and in many states and countries was prohibited. Eventually, it was discontinued because of the large demand for industrial silencers, which were utilized for gas and diesel engines, air compressors, and to suppress industrial noise.[20] More widely significant was the adaptation of the silencing principle to auto mufflers, safety valves, air compressors, and blowers. And in 1931, Maxim unveiled a room silencer, which eliminated what a later generation would call "white noise," as well as ventilating the room and filtering the air.

Maxim made other signal contributions in distinct areas; he collected a total of forty-nine patents during his lifetime.[21] He founded the Radio Relay League in 1914 and the International Radio Union in 1925; he developed an interest in movie making and founded the Amateur Cinema League in 1926. He was also a force behind the development of Hartford's Brainard Field in 1922. In 1921, the multifaceted Maxim wrote the scenario for a motion picture called *The Virgin Paradise,* which was produced the same year and starred Pearl White. He also was the author of three books, including *Horseless Carriage Days* and a memoir of his eccentric father entitled *Genius in the*

Family. Following Percy's death in 1936, his son, Hiram Hamilton Maxim, became president of his company, finally selling it to the Emhart Company in 1955.[22]

Pope's Line Lives On

Surviving at his death were six of the Colonel's siblings, some of whom would live many years after him. The Reverend Louis Pope, the beneficiary of his brother's tuition payments during divinity school, tended a rural congregation in Massachusetts. His illustrious sisters, Emily and Augusta, continued their medical practices well into the 1920s, by which time a female in medicine was only slightly less amazing than when they had completed their medical training in the 1870s. Leavitt Pope, grandson of the Colonel's adopted son, Harry, recalls visiting the "twin aunties" at their home on Newbury Street in Boston; they practiced medicine and drove around the city in their roadster into their eighties.[23] Adelaide Leonora, a retired schoolteacher, lived with the twin aunts in the home the Colonel had bought them, not far from his Commonwealth Avenue townhouse. Arthur, after inheriting the presidency of the Colonel's shoe-findings business in Boston, joined his brother's enterprises in Hartford and served on the board of directors of the Pope Manufacturing Company.

Abby returned to live in Boston, shutting away the seaside memories forever, and she devoted herself to her children and growing numbers of grandchildren until her death in 1921. The Harvard Club, which had built a four-story stone townhouse adjacent to the Pope homestead in 1913, bought the gracious Pope building from the estate and created an annex.

In May 1999, the author accompanied the Colonel's only namesake, Albert Augustus Pope II, and his sister, Tina Pope Rowley, on a nostalgic trip to Cohasset to visit the Colonel's summer compound. Stopping for directions, we asked a postman, who had been on the neighborhood beat for three decades, for directions to the old Pope estate. He told us he had no idea; he had never heard of Colonel Pope.

We eventually stumbled upon the compound and ran into Denise Dimaggio, an expectant woman who was moving out of one of ten condominiums into which the mansion had been converted. Her walls were covered with photos of the "Yankee Clipper," Joe DiMaggio, who her husband adores but to whom he is not related. She graciously showed us around, pointing out the seven garages and three guest cottages and the stained-glass and leaded windows into which family crests and aphorisms had been set, the kind of simple moral teachings which Colonel Pope often worked into his speeches. Close by the compound is the Pope Memorial Church, the Colonel's tribute to his son Charles. The church has now been purchased by a Greek congregation, which continues to use it as a house of worship. It overlooks marshes leading to the ocean and, hard by, are railroad tracks which may be the terminus of the line which carried the Popes regularly from Boston to Cohasset.

Prince Albert at the Helm

Albert Linder Pope continued to lead the Pope Manufacturing Company until it went into receivership for a final time in 1912, and he continued to live with his wife, Amy, and two children, William and Frances, in a fashionable section of West Hartford. Among other eastern firms that lost their fight to survive were the Locomobile Company of Bridgeport, Connecticut; Stevens-Duryea of East Springfield, Massachusetts; Knox in Springfield; Rockwell in Bristol, Connecticut; and Compound in Middletown, Connecticut. Stanley Steamer of Waltham, Massachusetts, lasted into the 1920s.[24]

Whatever judgment history may render as to his competence and dedication to the task, it would be demonstrably unfair to ascribe the death of the Pope auto manufacturing business to Albert Linder's management alone. As described above, the industry had experienced a giant shudder in 1907 and was shaking out all but a few stalwarts, which would eventually carve up the auto pie into a few giant companies.

While some in the Pope family believe the Colonel was basically displeased with how Albert Linder had acquitted himself as the son and heir, the *Boston Globe* obituary published the day after Pope's death relates a story that appears to run counter to that theory. Colonel Pope was having breakfast in a Manhattan hotel with Charles Schwab, then president of Carnegie Steel and soon to be the first president of U.S. Steel. He asked Schwab, "Can you find me a man capable of taking charge of a manufacturing plant at $25,000 a year?" An enterprising reporter heard the question and went to the Colonel to confirm the story. He asked if the Colonel would really give that salary and what kind of man he wanted. Pope said, "Yes, I will pay that salary and I want a man who will make good, who can create business, some one who can prove his fitness." He illustrated the point by relating the story of his son, who some years before was working for him at $1,500 a year but wanted something better. "Go take that store on Columbus Ave. and see what you can do." The son made good and got the $25,000, Pope told the reporter.

The story has the ring of the kind of anecdote that the Pope publicity machine used to turn out with great regularity, to prove whatever point the Colonel was striving to make at the moment. It seems unlikely that he'd relate this tale, whether real or apocryphal, if he harbored strong feelings that his son was inadequate.

After two years in receivership, the tatters of the Pope production capacity were reorganized as the Columbia Motor Car Company of Hartford, with capitalization of $2 million. For what it was worth by then, the Selden patent went with the deal. Whitney's associate Anthony Brady decided to back Benjamin Briscoe in his attempt to duplicate William C. Durant's feat in creating General Motors. Briscoe's venture was called the U.S. Motor Company, and Prince Albert agreed to join forces. But when the U.S. Motor Company went into receivership in 1912, Columbia Motor Car Company disappeared for good.[25]

Of Pope's three remaining children, Harold continued to run the Elyria plant in Ohio and later became vice president of the Curtis-Wright Aeronautical Company. Along the way, he moved to Rochester to pursue his twin passions of yachting and collecting Rolls Royces.[26] Margaret Pope married Freeman Hinckley, settled in Hingham, Massachusetts, and raised three children, one named after Albert Pope. Ralph, the baby of the family, had a successful career in the shoe and leather business, served as one of the Colonel's executors for two decades, and finally went into finance as a partner in Hornblower Weeks in Manhattan. But Ralph may have gained as much notice from his attachment to another historical figure as he did from his own accomplishments.

Favor for JFK

Whatever Albert Pope's perceived disgrace because of his father's misfortunes had been forgotten by the 1930s, when Ralph Pope became head of the Harvard nominating committee for the Spee Club, a major entree to which was alumni ties. Ralph was a contemporary of Joseph P. Kennedy, Jr. In later years, Ralph recalled,

> I had been on two or three different committees with Joe, Jr. That's how I got to know the father and Jack. Joe was a very attractive fellow. He said all the right things when he wanted and he got along very well in our class at Harvard. ... He was a real politician from way back. ... I think some of the things that he was saying were somebody else's ideas that I didn't think too sensible. Jack never gave you that feeling. By the time you could say something, he had a question or remark about it, which went right to the heart. You never had to fool around or wonder, "What the hell does he mean?" There was no question about it. ... I know when he came to our club in the fall of 1937 ... people said, "Why the hell did you pick Kennedy?"

Ralph was ashamed of such anti–Catholic prejudice "in a simple thing like a club at Harvard" and became determined to take Kennedy: "Just for that reason—that we needed somebody with some sense in the place. We were a bunch of lightweights."

"Ralph Pope did it," a classmate named Rousmaniere confirmed. "Ralph Pope came to us and said, 'OK, if you guys want this three man deal, we want it too. We'll take you all.'" Jack had made it, the first Kennedy ever to break in to the inner sanctum of Boston's WASP world, symbolized by the Spee Club, which at the time included such notables as Blair Clark and Cleveland Amory, both of whom served as editors on the *Harvard Crimson*.

The story underscores the independent Pope streak that resonates through the family—from the Colonel's jumping political party lines as a Republican mugwump to support Democrat Grover Cleveland for president, to his mother's "radical streak" and his twin sisters swimming against the tide to become physicians in the 1870s.

"Never again, as long as he lived," writes Nigel Hamilton, author of *JFK: Restless Youth,* "could anyone look down on Jack Kennedy."[27]

During World War II, Ralph joined JFK in becoming a PT boat commander. In his widow's house in Massachusetts hangs a photo of him with Senator John Kennedy when Ralph testified before a Senate hearing. Ralph kept in touch after Kennedy's presidential election and visited the White House.

As for the Hartford community that Pope built into a major manufacturing center, becoming its largest employer, there is not much there to commemorate the Colonel. While Mark Twain and Harriet Beecher Stowe have historical centers to which people flock from across America, the only community tribute to Colonel Pope is a 15-foot sculpted granite obelisk in Pope Park erected in 1913 "by friends" of the Colonel, including his lawyer, Charles Gross, and architect George Keller. At its top, Pope's profile looks out from a tarnished bronze medallion across his beloved park.[28] A fountain, once offering refreshment for passersby, is now inoperative and clogged with weeds and cigarette wrappers. It is inscribed: "To commemorate the industrial activities and public benefactions from 1880 to 1905 of Albert A. Pope all of which greatly advanced the prosperity of Hartford."

Notes

1. Chernow, Ron, *Titan*, p. 674.
2. "Colonel Albert Pope Dies of Pneumonia," *Hartford Courant*, August 11, 1909, p. 1.
3. Chernow, *The House of Morgan: An American Dynasty and the Rise of Modern Finance*, p. 222.
4. Ibid.
5. Collier, Peter and David Horowitz, *The Fords: An American Epic*, p. 57.
6. Maxim, Hiram Percy, *Horseless Carriage Days*, pp. 164–173.
7. Collier and Horowitz, p. 58.
8. Flink, James J., *The Automobile Age*, p. 54–55.
9. Purdy, Ken, *1904 Handbook of Gasoline Automobiles*, p. 11.

10. Schiffer, Michael Brian, *Taking Charge,* p. 169.

11. Ibid., p. 182.

12. Rae, John, *The American Automobile Industry: The First Forty Years,* p. 63.

13. Interview with Andrea Grimaldi, Columbia Manufacturing Company, October 28, 1999, and material from Columbia company pamphlets.

14. Grant, Ellsworth, *The Colt Armory,* p. 81.

15. Greenleaf, William, *Monopoly on Wheels: Henry Ford and the Selden Patent Suit,* p. 60.

16. Gay, John Curry, "1912 Pope-Hartford Model 28 6-Cylinder Roadster," pp. 11–12.

17. Epperson, Bruce, "A Model of Technological Dissonance," p. 77.

18. Flink, James J., *The Automobile Age,* p. 71.

19. Lee, Percy Maxim and John Glessner, *Family Reunion,* p. 208.

20. Burpee, C.W., *History of Hartford County, Connecticut, 1633–1928,* p. 99.

21. Schumacher, Alice Clink, *Hiram Percy Maxim,* p. 47.

22. Lee and Glessner, p. 210.

23. Interview with Leavitt Pope, October 11, 1999.

24. Dean, Clarence, "Pope-Hartford Started Auspiciously in Auto Field," *The Hartford Courant,* August 24, 1958, p. 1.

25. Rae, James, *The American Automobile Industry,* p. 48.

26. Interview with Albert A. Pope II, May 8, 1999.

27. Hamilton, Nigel, *JFK: Restless Youth,* pp. 207–10.

28. Agreement by Hartford Board of Trade, March 1, 1912, in George Keller Collection, Harriet Beecher Stowe Center, Hartford, CT.

THE FORD ENIGMA

*R*eports of meetings between Henry Ford and Colonel Pope are, like fireflies on a summer night, as elusive as they are abundant. Several books, newspaper articles, and magazine pieces, as recent as 1996, place Ford in Hartford during the 1890s as a bicycle mechanic employed in the Pope companies or for a competitor, as a young engineer seeking information on mass production techniques adopted by Pope and others, and as a fledgling automaker, seeking advice from New England's largest industrialist. Yet at the end of the night, after searching every nook and cranny, the jar remains empty of fireflies.

Albert A. Pope II says he recalls reading of his ancestor's link to the father of the Model T in the Colonel's unpublished autobiography, which he says was either misplaced, loaned and not returned, or destroyed some years ago. Albert says that what he saw was an onionskin copy, particularly notable in that it contained strikeouts and interlineations, allowing the reader to witness the Colonel's thought process. While various family members recall hearing of the work, Albert is the only family member who says he has read it.

Family lore has it, Albert says, that Ford came to Hartford on more than one occasion and apparently met with Pope, who was impressed with Ford's plans and determination. Years later, Pope argued unsuccessfully that the Association of Licensed Automobile Manufacturers (ALAM) admit Ford into its ranks rather than snub him, a rejection which ended up in the eight-year lawsuit over the Selden patent.

Proof that Pope had counseled or financed the young Ford during his formative years would clearly rate more than a footnote in industrial history. The historian seeks documentary sources for confirmation, but no major Ford biography mentions such a link. Allan Nevins's magisterial *Ford: The Times, the Man, the Company* has numerous references to Colonel Pope and his contributions to the industry but none to a meeting between the automakers. Nevins's work is so detailed that one thinks he would have mentioned such a connection had he known of one. The databases of the Henry Ford

Museum in Dearborn, Michigan, and the National Automotive History Collection at the Detroit Public Library have no documentary record of any Ford-Pope connection.

One next turns to primary sources, which might include diaries Ford and Pope kept or correspondence between them, and again the bucket comes up empty. Is all this not sufficient proof that the men never met? One must, it seems to me, place such a possible relationship in context. In 1896, when Henry Ford began tinkering with automobiles, he was a 33-year-old engineer for Detroit Edison, one of Thomas Edison's earliest electric companies. Pope was already producing automobiles, although not yet for sale, and was the largest industrialist in New England.

The ambitious, avaricious, or sycophantic alike continually sought out Pope for advice, contributions, or employment. His experiences with S.S. McClure and Hiram Percy Maxim demonstrate that the Colonel had a soft spot for young men of promise. He kept correspondence files, only some of which survive; as well as more complete files of news clippings. No mention of Henry Ford appears therein. However, if one of the nation's leading manufacturers had been visited by an unknown but ambitious young man—one in a long stream of such supplicants—how likely would it have been for Pope to have recorded the event?

Ford, however, would certainly have realized he was visiting a man of great importance, so doesn't it seem unusual that he would not have recorded the meeting? One must realize that, until 1903, Ford ran his auto operations out of his head and his hip pocket. He maintained no diary or notebooks and only set down his thoughts in detail in mid-life.

David Lewis, a University of Michigan historian and probably the leading Ford scholar, says he does not find the parties' failure to make notes of such a meeting to constitute proof that it never happened. In those days, he points out, Ford had no secretary and was not given to voluminous correspondence. But why would he not have recorded the connection in his written reminiscences many years later?

"We have too little information about Henry Ford," says Lewis, his biographer. "In the years before 1903, when he went into business manufacturing cars, we have only one or two family letters."[1] It is well known that later, when Ford set down his life story, he sought—perhaps even more than most memoirists—to create an idealized portrait of himself for posterity. And, Lewis says, Ford was not the sort of industrialist who went out of his way to give credit to others for their ideas.

What, then, accounts for the persistence of the rumors of Ford's connection to Hartford and to Pope? The answer illuminates the science of historical fact gathering. On May 12, 1996, *New York Times* reporter Rita Reif wrote an article on bicycles in which she quoted Pryor Dodge as saying,

"Henry Ford worked as a bicycle mechanic in Hartford in the 1890s." Dodge, a Manhattan writer, wrote a book entitled *The Bicycle*, which was published the same year. When contacted, Dodge said that he gleaned the information from a speech given by Albert Pope II at a bicycle history conference in Buffalo earlier in the decade. Pope told me that his information came from his recollections gleaned from the Colonel's autobiography, a work only Albert recalls seeing. So do all roads lead back to Albert the younger? Not really, for such reports appeared in magazine articles years earlier, although their sources are unattributed and their authors dead or unavailable.

Regardless, is the more telling connection between Pope and Ford a letter or personal meeting or is it the inclusion in Ford's production line and its product techniques and parts which were drawn from technologies evolved by the Pope Manufacturing Company? David Lewis says it is undeniable that during the last years of the nineteenth century, Ford drew upon Pope's achievements in developing bicycle wheels, gears, axles, and tires to evolve his own production of automobiles, echoing the material on this point in Chapter 13 on Pope's legacy. But one wouldn't be likely to learn of that from Ford's own lips or pen.

Consider also that industrialists of the time, including Pope himself, routinely purloined the ideas of others in the development of technologies that were evolving with dizzying speed. Their patent lawyers worked overtime to both prosecute violations of their patents and to defend against claims that they had stepped over what often were subtle lines between invention and theft. In such a climate, communications between industralists over comparative technology were probably best not committed to paper.

The one documented link between Henry Ford and the Pope industrial family was the fondness Ford developed for George Day during the Selden trial. Lengthy litigation, as the author knows from experience, develops relationships that might seem strange to one not intimately involved in the case. It is difficult during an adversarial matter that drags on for many months for opposing parties and their attorneys not to share a few light moments or to inquire about each other's families or interests. The knowledge gained may not soften the resolve of each party to prevail in the dispute, but it creates a subtext of family, vacation reminiscences, and even political views that allows parties on opposite sides to humanize themselves to each other.

By 1906, the Selden trial had been going for three years; five more years would pass before a final appeals court decision. During a break in the proceedings, Ford suggested to Day, then president of ALAM, that he might like a tour of Ford's plant on the outskirts of Detroit. Day immediately accepted the offer, and the two adversaries, together with aides, piled into a Ford roadster and wheeled away with Henry Ford driving. A year later, after the genial Day died of a heart attack at age fifty-six, Ford expressed his condolences, calling his adversary "a gentleman of whom personally I had the greatest respect." Of course, Colonel Pope was in the waning days of his final industrial challenge by that time and no longer was Day's intimate or employer.

So the myth persists. History, after all, offers only what *is known* about what happened. As such, it is far from an accurate compilation of what actually *did occur*. How many greats and near-greats throughout the centuries have had encounters, the reporting of which didn't survive, but which may have contributed to changing the way we live? This is only part of the mystery of history.

Notes

1. Telephone interview with Professor David Lewis, October 4, 1999.

POPE MANUFACTURING COMPANY CORPORATE GENEALOGY

Courtesy David Carrigan,
Curator Museum of Connecticut History,
Hartford Connecticut

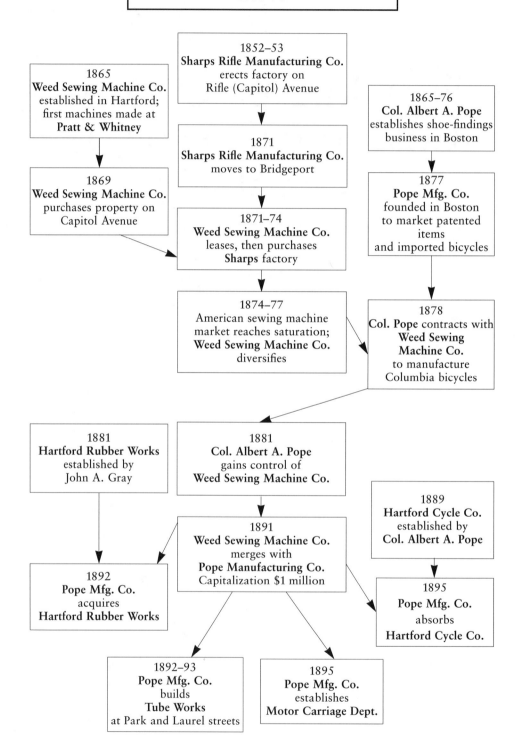

**POPE MANUFACTURING COMPANY
CORPORATE GENEALOGY
1865–95**

1852–53
Sharps Rifle Manufacturing Co.
erects factory on
Rifle (Capitol) Avenue

1865
Weed Sewing Machine Co.
established in Hartford;
first machines made at
Pratt & Whitney

1865–76
Col. Albert A. Pope
establishes shoe-findings
business in Boston

1871
Sharps Rifle Manufacturing Co.
moves to Bridgeport

1869
Weed Sewing Machine Co.
purchases property on
Capitol Avenue

1877
Pope Mfg. Co.
founded in Boston
to market patented
items
and imported bicycles

1871–74
Weed Sewing Machine Co.
leases, then purchases
Sharps factory

1874–77
American sewing machine
market reaches saturation;
Weed Sewing Machine Co.
diversifies

1878
Col. Pope contracts with
**Weed Sewing
Machine Co.**
to manufacture
Columbia bicycles

1881
Hartford Rubber Works
established by
John A. Gray

1881
Col. Albert A. Pope
gains control of
Weed Sewing Machine Co.

1889
Hartford Cycle Co.
established by
Col. Albert A. Pope

1892
Pope Mfg. Co.
acquires
Hartford Rubber Works

1891
Weed Sewing Machine Co.
merges with
Pope Manufacturing Co.
Capitalization $1 million

1895
Pope Mfg. Co.
absorbs
Hartford Cycle Co.

1892–93
Pope Mfg. Co.
builds
Tube Works
at Park and Laurel streets

1895
Pope Mfg. Co.
establishes
Motor Carriage Dept.

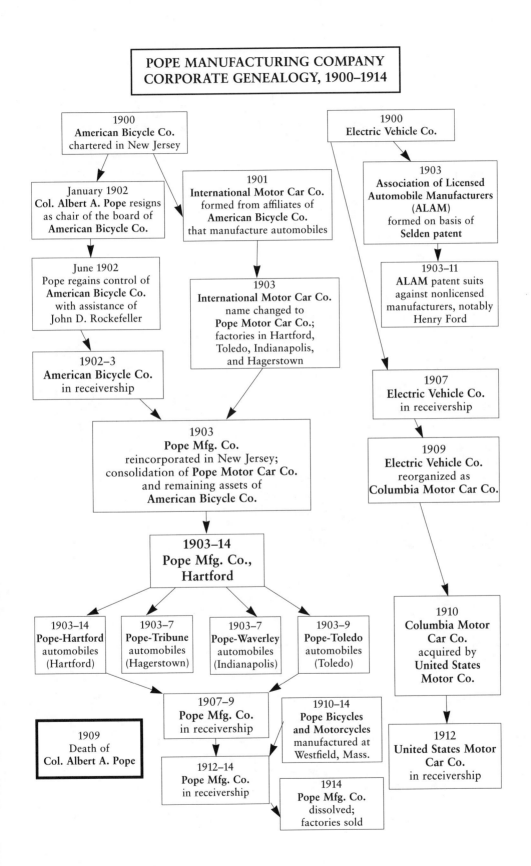

POPE MANUFACTURING COMPANY
CORPORATE GENEALOGY, 1900–1914

1900
American Bicycle Co.
chartered in New Jersey

1900
Electric Vehicle Co.

January 1902
Col. Albert A. Pope resigns
as chair of the board of
American Bicycle Co.

1901
International Motor Car Co.
formed from affiliates of
American Bicycle Co.
that manufacture automobiles

1903
**Association of Licensed
Automobile Manufacturers
(ALAM)**
formed on basis of
Selden patent

June 1902
Pope regains control of
American Bicycle Co.
with assistance of
John D. Rockefeller

1903
International Motor Car Co.
name changed to
Pope Motor Car Co.;
factories in Hartford,
Toledo, Indianapolis,
and Hagerstown

1903–11
ALAM patent suits
against nonlicensed
manufacturers, notably
Henry Ford

1902–3
American Bicycle Co.
in receivership

1907
Electric Vehicle Co.
in receivership

1903
Pope Mfg. Co.
reincorporated in New Jersey;
consolidation of **Pope Motor Car Co.**
and remaining assets of
American Bicycle Co.

1909
Electric Vehicle Co.
reorganized as
Columbia Motor Car Co.

**1903–14
Pope Mfg. Co.,
Hartford**

1903–14
Pope-Hartford
automobiles
(Hartford)

1903–7
Pope-Tribune
automobiles
(Hagerstown)

1903–7
Pope-Waverley
automobiles
(Indianapolis)

1903–9
Pope-Toledo
automobiles
(Toledo)

1910
**Columbia Motor
Car Co.**
acquired by
**United States
Motor Co.**

1909
Death of
Col. Albert A. Pope

1907–9
Pope Mfg. Co.
in receivership

1910–14
**Pope Bicycles
and Motorcycles**
manufactured at
Westfield, Mass.

1912–14
Pope Mfg. Co.
in receivership

1914
Pope Mfg. Co.
dissolved;
factories sold

1912
**United States Motor
Car Co.**
in receivership

POPE MANUFACTURING COMPANY CORPORATE GENEALOGY, 1895–1900

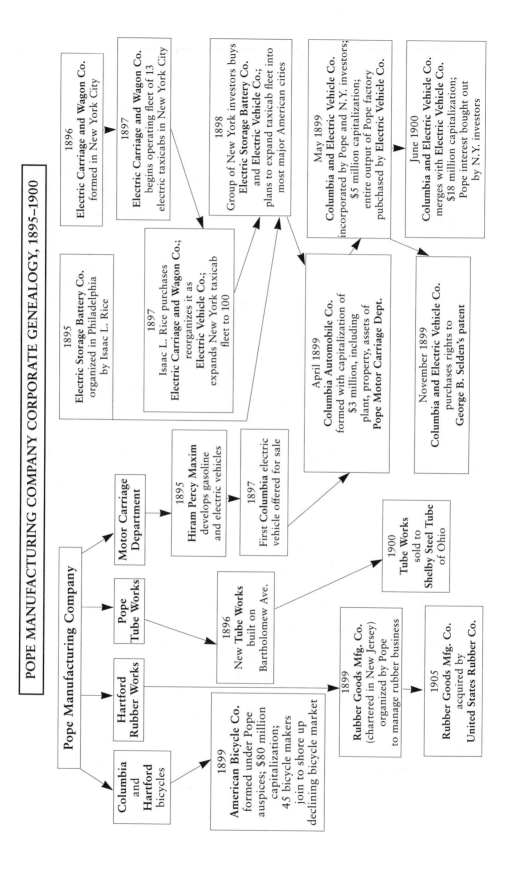

BIBLIOGRAPHY

Books and Publications

Adams, G. Donald, *Collecting and Restoring Antique Bicycles,* 2d ed. (New York: Quality Books, 1996).

Alexopoulos, John, *The Nineteenth-Century Parks of Hartford: A Legacy to the Nation* (Hartford, CT: Hartford Architecture Conservancy, 1983).

American Cyclist, April 15, 1894.

American Heritage, August 1973.

American Heritage, "Postscripts to History," December 1975.

The American Wheelman, 49, November 1896, p. 14.

Angelucci, Enzo, and Alberto Bellucci, *The Automobile from Steam to Gasoline* (New York: McGraw Hill, 1974).

Automobile Quarterly, *General Motors: The First 75 Years* (New York: Crown, 1983).

Batchelor, Ray, *Henry Ford: Mass Production, Modernism and Design* (New York: Manchester University Press, 1994).

Bentley, John, *Great American Automobiles* (New York: Prentice-Hall, 1957).

Bicycling World, May 1880.

Bird, Anthony, *The Motor Car: 1765–1914* (London: B.T. Batsford, 1960).

Boston of Today: A Glance at Its History and Characteristics (Boston: Columbia, 1892).

Brown, Carrie, *Pedal Power: The Bicycle in Industry and Society* (Windsor, VT: American Precision Museum, 1997).

Burpee, C.W., *History of Hartford County, Connecticut, 1633–1928* (Chicago: S.J. Clarke, 1928).

Cady, Edwin H., *Stephen Crane* (Boston: Twayne, 1980).

Catton, Bruce, *This Hallowed Ground* (New York: Doubleday, 1956).

Cave, Henry, "Chronological Hartford Auto Happenings," February 1947, unpublished.

Chandler, Alfred Dupont, and Stephen Salsbury, *Pierre S. DuPont and the Making of the Modern Corporation*(New York: Harper & Row, 1971).

____, *The Visible Hand: The Managerial Revolution in American Business* (Cambridge: Belknap, 1977).

Chernow, Ron, *The House of Morgan: An American Dynasty and the Rise of Modern Finance* (New York: Atlantic Monthly Press, 1990).

____, *Titan* (New York: Random House, 1998).

Clark, Victor S., *History of Manufactures in the United States: 1607–1860* (Washington, DC: Carnegie Institution of Washington, 1916).

Collier, Peter and David Horowitz, *The Fords: An American Epic* (New York: Summit, 1987).

"Col. A.A. Pope Dies at Summer Home," *Boston Post,* August 10, 1909.

"Col. Albert A. Pope: Was Leader in Good Roads Movement; His Benefactions Numerous," *Boston Globe,* August 11, 1909.

"Colonel Albert A. Pope: A Victim of Pneumonia," *Hartford Daily Times,* August 11, 1909.

"Colonel Albert Pope Dies of Pneumonia," *Hartford Courant,* August 11, 1909.

"Columbia Chronology," at Columbiamgfinc.com/historydoc.htm.

Columbia Encyclopedia, 5th ed. (New York: Columbia University Press, 1993).

Colvin, Fred H., "Influence of the Bicycle upon Machine Tools," in *60 Years with Men and Machines* (New York: McGraw Hill, 1947).

Committee of the Regimental Association, *History of the Thirty-Fifth Regiment Massachusetts Volunteers, 1862–65* (Boston: Mills, Knight, 1884).

Connecticut State Register and Manual (Hartford: Secretary of the State, 1991).

"Correspondence of the Hartford Cycle Co., 1890–95," Connecticut State Library Archives, Hartford.

Corrigan, David, "Series of Corporate Genealogies of Pope Enterprises," Connecticut State Library, Hartford.

Courtney, Steve, "Oh, Wealth," *Northeast Magazine* of the *Hartford Courant,* June 18, 1995.

Cuntz, Hermann, "Hartford: The Birthplace of Automobile Industry," *Hartford Times,* September 16, 1947.

____, "Story of the Selden Case and Hartford," partial manuscript dated August, 1940, in Henry Cave Collection, National Automotive History Collection, Detroit Public Library.

Davis, Kenneth C., *Don't Know Much about the Civil War* (New York: Avon, 1996).

Dean, Clarence, "Pope-Hartford Started Auspiciously in Auto Field," *Hartford Courant,* August 24, 1958.

Dearing, Charles L., *American Highway Policy* (Washington, DC: Brookings Institution, 1941).

Denison, Merrill, *The Power To Go: The Story of the Automotive Industry* (New York: Doubleday, 1956).

DePew, Chauncey M., ed., *One Hundred Years of American Commerce* (New York: D.O. Hanes, 1895).

DiGregorio, William A., *The Complete Book of U.S. Presidents* (New York: Wings, 1984).

Dos Passos, John, *U.S.A.: The Big Money.*

Drachman, Virginia G., *Hospital with a Heart: Women Doctors and the Paradox of Separatism at the New England Hospital, 1862–69* (Ithaca, NY: Cornell University Press, 1984).

Dunham, Norman Leslie, "The Bicycle Era," (in partial satisfaction for a Ph.D., Harvard University, 1957).

Durant, William, *Dream Maker* (Boston: Little, Brown, 1979).

Epperson, Bruce, "A Model of Technological Dissonance: Production and Management in the American Bicycle Industry, 1880–1910," paper prepared for the annual meeting of the Society for the History of Technology in Pasadena, CA., October 1997.

Finch, Christopher, *Highways to Heaven: The AUTObiography of America* (New York: HarperCollins, 1991).

Fitzpatrick, Jim, "Pope's Military Bicycles," *Journal of American History* 34 (April 1999).

Flink, James J., *America Adopts the Automobile, 1895–1910* (Cambridge, MA: MIT Press, 1970).

____, *The Automobile Age* (Cambridge, MA: MIT Press, 1988).

Foote, Shelby, *The Civil War,* vol. 50 (New York: Random House, 1958).

Gay, John Curry, "1912 Pope-Hartford Model 28 6-cylinder Roadster," self-published, 1992, contained in archives of the late Frances Walker of Cornish Flat, New Hampshire (Col. Pope's grandaughter).

Gelderman, Carol, *Henry Ford: The Wayward Capitalist* (New York: Dial Press, 1981).

Georgano, G.N., ed., *The Complete Encyclopedia of Motorcars, 1885–1968* (New York: E.P. Dutton, 1968).

Goddard, Stephen B., *Getting There: The Epic Struggle between Road and Rail in the American Century* (New York: Basic, 1994).

Good Roads Magazine, "Obituary," September 1909.

Good Roads Magazine, "Transportation," April 1904.

Grant, Ellsworth, *The Colt Armory: A History of Colt's Manufacturing Company, Inc.* (Lincoln, RI: Mowbray, 1982).

____, *The Miracle of Connecticut* (Hartford, CT: Connecticut Historical Society and Fenwick Productions, 1992).

____, *Yankee Dreamers and Doers* (Chester, CT: Pequot Press, 1978).

Greenleaf, William, *Monopoly on Wheels: Henry Ford and the Selden Patent Suit* (Detroit: Wayne State University Press, 1961).

Hamilton, Nigel, *JFK: Restless Youth* (New York: Random House, 1992).

Harrod, Steven, "Death Wish: The Good Roads Trains Impact on American Transportation Policy," paper submitted in partial fulfillment of master's degree, Massachusetts Institute of Technology, 1992.

Hartford Land Records, Office of Town Clerk, City Hall, Hartford, CT.

"Hartford Was Cradle," by Hermann Cuntz, *Hartford Times,* September 16, 1947, p. 1.

Henry, Carl, "Buckingham Square," unpublished paper contained in archives of the Hartford Collection Wing, Hartford Public Library, Hartford.

Herlihy, David V., "The Bicycle Story," *American Heritage of Invention & Technology* (Spring 1992).

Hirsh, Mark D., *William C. Whitney: Modern Warwick* (New York: Dodd, Mead, 1948).

Hoehne, M., "Hoehne Pages," *hoehne.aol.com*

Holloran, Peter C., *Boston's Wayward Children: Social Services for Homeless Children, 1830–1930,* (Teaneck, NJ: Fairleigh-Dickinson University Press, 1990).

Hounshell, David A., *From the American System to Mass Production 1800–1932* (Baltimore: Johns Hopkins University Press, 1984).

____, "The Bicycle and Technology in Late Nineteenth Century America," Tekniska Museet Symposia 2 (1980).

Jackson, Kenneth, *Crabgrass Frontier: The Suburbanization of the United States* (New York: Oxford University Press, 1983).

Jardim, A., *The First Henry Ford: A Study in Personality and Business Leadership* (Cambridge: Massachusetts Institute of Technology, 1970).

Kahn, E.J., Jr., *Jock: The Life and Times of John Hay Whitney* (Garden City, NY: Doubleday, 1981).

Kanigel, Robert, *The One Best Way* (New York: Viking, 1997).

Kelly, Fred C., "The Great Bicycle Craze," *American Heritage* (December 1956).

Kennedy, E.D., *The Automobile Industry: The Coming of Age of Capitalism's Favorite Child* (New York: Reynal & Hitchcock, 1941).

Kinder, Gary, *Ship of Gold in the Deep Blue Sea* (New York: Atlantic Monthly Press, 1998).

Lacey, Robert, *Ford: The Men and the Machine* (Boston: Little, Brown, 1986).

Lauber, John, *Inventions of Mark Twain* (New York: Hill & Wang, 1990).

Lee, Percy Maxim and John Glessner, *Family Reunion: An Incomplete Account of the Maxim-Lee Family History* (privately printed, 1971), archived in Hartford Collection Wing, Hartford Public Library, Hartford.

Lewis, D.L., *The Public Image of Henry Ford: An American Folk Hero and His Company* (Detroit: Wayne State University Press, 1976).

Lewis, Tom, *Divided Highways: Building the Interstate Highways, Transforming American Life* (New York: Viking, 1997).

Lupiano, Vincent dePaul and Ken W. Sayers, *It Was a Very Good Year: A Cultural History of the United States* (Holbrook, MA: Bob Adams, 1994).

Lyon, Peter, *Success Story: The Life and Times of S.S. McClure* (New York: Charles Scribner's Sons, 1963).

McCallum, Iain, *Blood Brothers: Hiram & Hudson Maxim, Pioneers of Modern Warfare* (London: Chatham, 1999).

McClure, S.S., *My Autobiography* (New York: Frederick A. Stokes, 1963).

McCraw, Jim, "Ghosts of Detroit's Past in Ford's Old Buildings," *New York Times*, October 15, 1999.

McShane, Clay, *The Automobile: A Chronology of Its Antecedents, Development, and Impact* (Westport, CT: Greenwood, 1997).

Mandel, Leon, *American Cars* (New York: Stewart, Tabori & Chang, 1982).

Martin, Albro, *Railroads Triumphant* (New York: Oxford University Press, 1992).

Massachusetts of Today: A Memorial of the State Issued for the World's Columbian Exposition at Chicago (Boston: Columbia, 1892).

Maxim, Hiram Percy, "Electric Vehicles and Their Relation to Central Stations," *Horseless Age* (March 1899).

____, *Horseless Carriage Days* (New York: Harper & Brothers, 1937).

____, Scrapbook, 1893–95, Connecticut State Library, Hartford.

____, Workbook, vol. 1 (August 8, 1896–January 13, 1897).

Morison, Samuel Eliot, *One Boy's Boston* (Boston: Northeastern University Press, 1983).

Musselman, M.M., *Get a Horse! The Story of the Automobile in America* (Philadelphia: J.B. Lippincott, 1950).

Nevins, Allan, *Ford: The Times, the Man, the Company* (New York: Charles Scribner's Sons, 1954).

New Encyclopaedia Britannica (Chicago: Encyclopaedia Britannica, Inc., 1978).

Norcliffe, Glen, "Bridging the American System and Mass Production: Albert Pope's System of Bicycle Manufacture," in *Tools & Technology*, newsletter of the American Precision Museum in Windsor, VT.

____, "Popeism and Fordism: Examining the Roots of Mass Production," *Regional Studies* 31, no. 3 (1997).

Officers of the Army and Navy, (Philadelphia: L.R. Hamersby & Co., 1893).

Oppel, Frank, ed., *Motoring in America: The Early Years* (Secaucus, NJ: Castle, 1989).

Perry, David B., *Bike Cult: The Ultimate Guide to Human-Powered Vehicles* (New York: Four Walls Eight Windows, 1995).

Peterson, Joyce Shaw, *American Auto Workers 1900–1933* (Albany: State University of New York Press, 1987).

Pope, Colonel Albert A., "Automobiles and Good Roads," *Munsey's Magazine* 22 (May 1903).

____, "Journal of the Southern Campaign, War of the Rebellion, August 27, 1862–June 9, 1865" (self-published, n.d.), in archives of Albert A. Pope II, New York, NY.

____, "Transportation," *Good Roads Magazine*, April 1904.

Pope, Charles Henry, *A History of the Dorchester Pope Family, 1634–1888* (Boston: self-published, 1888), in archives of Albert A. Pope II, New York, NY.

Pope Manufacturing Company, "An Industrial Achievement, 1877–1907" (self-published, 1907), archived in Hartford Collection Wing, Hartford Public Library, Hartford.

"Pope Manufacturing Company Correspondence, 1890–94," Connecticut State Library, Hartford.

Potter, Isaac B., "History of the Movement," *Good Roads Magazine*, May 1903.

Purdy, Ken, *1904 Handbook of Gasoline Automobiles* (New York: Chelsea House, 1969).

Rae, John, *The American Automobile Industry* (New York: Twayne, 1984).

____, *The American Automobile Industry: The First Forty Years* (Philadelphia: Chilton, 1959).

____, *The American Automobile Industry: The First Forty Years* (Chicago: University of Chicago Press, 1965).

Railroad Gazette, article November 8, 1901, pp. 769–70.

Representative Men of Massachusetts, 1890–1900 (Everett, MA: Massachusetts Publishing, 1893).

R.F.S., "The Great Bicycle Delirium," *American Heritage*, June 1975.

Rybczynski, Witold, *A Clearing in the Distance: Frederick Law Olmsted and America in the Nineteenth Century* (New York: Scribner, 1999).

St. Botolph, June 3, 1993

Schlessinger, Arthur M., *The Almanac of American History* (New York: Barnes & Noble Books, 1993).

Schumacher, Alice Clink, *Hiram Percy Maxim* (Cortez, CA: Electric Radio Press, 1998).

Sclereth, Thomas, *Victorian America: Transformations in Everyday Life* (New York: HarperPerennial, 1991).

Scott, Roy V., *Railroad Development Programs in the Twentieth Century* (Ames: Iowa State University, 1985).

Simonds, William Adams, *Henry Ford: His Life, His Work, His Genius* (Indianapolis: Bobbs-Merrill, 1943).

____, *Henry Ford: Motor Genius* (New York: Doubleday, Doran, 1929).

Smith, Page, *America Enters the World: A People's History of the Progressive Era and World War I* (New York: McGraw-Hill, 1985).

Smith, Philip Hillyer, *Wheels Within Wheels: A Short History of American Motor Car Manufacturing* (New York: Funk & Wagnalls, 1968).

Smith, Robert A., *A Social History of the Bicycle: Its Early Life and Times in America* (New York: American Heritage, 1972).

Stallman, R.W. et al., eds., *Stephen Crane: A Biography* (New York: George Brazilier, 1968).

___, *Stephen Crane: Letters* (New York: New York University Press, 1960).

Stockinger, Herbert B., "The Bicycle Railroad," *American Heritage Invention and Technology*, Spring 1992.

Strouse, Jean, *Morgan, American Financier* (New York: Random House, 1999).

Tebbel, John, et al., *The Magazine in America: 1741–1990* (New York: Oxford University Press, 1991).

U.S. Department of Transportation, *America's Highways 1776–1976: A History of the Federal Aid Program* (Washington, DC: U.S. Government Printing Office, 1976).

Weisberger, Bernard A., *The Dream Maker: William C. Durant, Founder of General Motors* (Boston: Little, Brown, 1979).

Who's Who in New England, 1949.

Williamson, Harold F., et al., *The American Petroleum Industry, 1899–1959: The Age of Energy* (Evanston, IL: Northwestern University Press, 1963).

Womack, J.P. et al., *The Machine that Changed the World: The Story of Lean Production* (New York: Harper's, 1990).

Yergin, Daniel, *The Prize: The Epic Quest for Oil, Money and Power* (New York: Touchstone, 1991).

Zinn, Howard, *A People's History of the United States* (New York: HarperPerennial, 1990).

Interviews

Bohlen, Elizabeth—9/6/99

Casey, Robert—10/1/99

Corrigan, David—numerous dates

Fuerst, Linda—2/7/99

Hannan, Katherine—6/2/99

Hays, Susan—9/6/99

Herlihy, David—7/20/99

Lee, Percy Maxim—9/29/99

Lewis, David—10/4/99

Lum, Beth—2/7/99

Patrick, Mark—various dates

Pope, Albert A. II—numerous dates

Pope, Leavitt—10/11/99

Pope, Thelma Morales—5/8/99

Pope, Victoria—10/8/99

Pope, William, Jr.—9/15/98 and brief phone interviews

Pope, William, Sr.—numerous dates

Rowley, Tina Pope—5/8/99

Scharcsburg, Richard—10/1/99

Walker, Frances—2/7/99

Wise, Margaret—9/6/99

INDEX

Model T (Ford product) 193, 221
Model 30 Relay Century Columbia 99
Modern Age 81
Montgomery-Ward 213
Montpelier Manufacturing Co. 69
Morgan, John Pierpont 4, 214, 220, 222
Morgan, Junius S. 215
Morison, Samuel Eliot 117
Morris, Henry 133, 151
Motor Age magazine 14, 195
Motor magazine 14, 195
Motor World magazine 14, 195
Motorcycle magazine 14
motorized vehicles 3
Mount Holly & Smithville Bicycle Railroad 98
muckraking journalism 148
Mugwumps 184
Munich Exposition 132

Naismith, James 94
Napoleonic roads 115
National Association of Automobile Manufacturers 226
National Association of Manufacturers 226
National Automobile Chamber of Commerce 226
National Cyclists' Union (Britain) 119
National Good Roads Convention 173
National Grange of the Patrons of Husbandry 167
National League (baseball) 68
National League of American Wheelmen 76
Neale, Rachel 25
Needham, MA 84
Neponset River 23
Nevins, Allan 112, 171
New England Female Medical College (Boston) 31

New England Home for Little Wanderers 8, 217
New England Hospital for Women and Children 31, 61, 62
New England Hospital Medical Society 62
New Jersey Agricultural College 122
New Jersey Road Improvement Association 120
New York Athletic Club 214
New York Central Railroad 104, 132
New York, New Haven and Hartford Railroad 11, 108, 146, 152
New York Record 110
New York Stock Exchange 221
New York Sun 131
New York World 133
Newton, MA 22, 63, 84, 214
Newton Theological Seminary 60
Nightingale, Florence 49
Nissan automobiles 224
Nook Farm, Hartford 9
Norcliffe, Glen 208, 209, 212
Norris, Frank 183
North Carolina General Assembly 116
Notes on Nursing 49

Oakley, Annie 75
The Octopus 183
Offenbach, Jacques 66
Office of Road Inquiry 117, 120, 171
Olds, Ramson Eli 134
Olds Motor Works 140, 161
Olmsted, Frederick Law 107
Opel automobiles 126
orphan trains 58, 72
Otis, Elisha 67, 188
Outing 81
Overman, Albert 87
Overman Company 86, 87

Packard, J.W. 140

Packard Motor Company 161
Page, Logan 120
Panama Canal 27
Paris Exposition 125, 133
Parker, the Rev. Theodore 34
Parker's Boston Helping Hand Mission 217
Parkman, Francis 29
Patent Office (U.S.) 8
patents 14–15
Pattison, Arthur 226
Peerless Company 186
Pennsylvania Avenue (Washington, D.C.) 116
Pennsylvania Steel Company 99
Petersburg, VA 51
Peugeot, Armand 14, 15, 126, 145
Philadelphia, PA 66
Phillips, John 79
Phillips Andover Academy 110
Pickering and Davis 73
Pierce, S.S. Company 22
Pierce family of Massachusetts 20
Pittman, Will R. 71
Plymouth, England 23
Plymouth, MA 23
Pontchartrain Hotel (Detroit) 166–67
Pond, Charles M. 108
Pope, Abby 3, 12, 64
Pope, Adelaide Leonora 29, 61, 204, 217, 228
Pope, Albert II 228
Pope, Albert Linder 64, 110–12, 149, 183, 190, 191, 197, 204, 217, 222, 224, 229
Pope, Alexander 24
Pope, Andrew J. 27
Pope, Arthur Wallace 29, 65
Pope, Augusta 28, 61, 204, 217, 228
Pope, Charles 20, 27, 29–31, 59, 61, 148, 197
Pope Charles Allen 29, 61
Pope, Charles Linder 64
Pope, D.W. 217
Pope, Edward 65, 71, 111